MANAGING RISKS AND DECISIONS IN MAJOR PROJECTS

MANAGING RISKS AND DECISIONS IN MAJOR PROJECTS

John C. Chicken
J.C. Consultancy Ltd, Godalming, Surrey, UK

CHAPMAN & HALL
University and Professional Division
London · Glasgow · Weinheim · New York · Tokyo · Melbourne · Madras

Published by Chapman & Hall, 2–6 Boundary Row, London SE1 8HN, UK

Chapman & Hall, 2–6 Boundary Row, London SE1 8HN, UK

Blackie Academic & Professional, Wester Cleddens Road, Bishopbriggs, Glasgow G64 2NZ, UK

Chapman & Hall GmbH, Pappelallee 3, 69469 Weinheim, Germany

Chapman & Hall Inc., One Penn Plaza, 41st Floor, New York, NY 10119, USA

Chapman & Hall Japan, Thomson Publishing Japan, Hirakawacho Nemoto Building, 6F, 1-7-11 Hirakawa-cho, Chiyoda-ku, Tokyo 102, Japan

Chapman & Hall Australia, Thomas Nelson Australia, 102 Dodds Street, South Melbourne, Victoria 3205, Australia

Chapman & Hall India, R. Seshadri, 32 Second Main Road, CIT East, Madras 600 035, India

First edition 1994

Typeset in 10/12½pt Times by Gray Publishing, Tunbridge Wells, Kent

Printed in England by Clays Ltd, St Ives plc

ISBN 0 412 58730 0

A catalogue record for this book is available from the British Library

Library of Congress Catalog Card Number 93-74214

∞ Printed on permanent acid-free paper, manufactured in accordance with ANSI/NISO Z 39.48-1992 and ANSI/NISO Z 39.48-1984 (Permanence of Paper).

CONTENTS

PREFACE

The aim of this book is to present a critical comparison of the ways major project decision options can be assessed and the optimum decision identified. The optimum decision is one that is most acceptable in technical, economic and socio-political terms. An analysis is presented of the decision-making processes and the contribution various techniques can make to the assessment of decision options. Although attention is given to the technical, economic and socio-political factors associated with decision making, special attention is given to assessing the acceptability from the financial perspective. A critical analysis of the theoretical foundation of the assessment techniques is provided. The magnitude of risk associated with various types of project is examined and how acceptability can be determined when the project is novel and there are few or no data available on which to base the assessment. The efficacy of the various methods of assessment is compared with that of the Risk Ranking Technique. The reason for using the Risk Ranking Technique as the basis for comparison is that it encapsulates all the features essential for a comprehensive assessment of all the factors associated with a complex project.

In the book, first the process of decision making is described, then the methods that financial institutions such as banks and insurance companies use to assess the acceptability of financial risks they are exposed to are examined. This is followed by assessment of the problems of evaluating technical, economic and socio-political aspects of risk and the theoretical justification of the procedures. The possible alternative assessment techniques are then discussed. The efficacy of these alternatives is compared by testing them against major decisions. This is followed by a comparison of the Risk Ranking Technique with the specific methods used by banks and insurance companies to assess the acceptability of risk. Finally an optimum method for assessing decision options is postulated and justified.

The main conclusions from the study are:

1. For an assessment of decision options to be valid it must be based on comprehensive assessment of the technical, economic and socio-political factors involved.
2. The assessment of acceptability must be transparent to the proposer and the lay public.
3. The assessment process must have a logically defensible structure.
4. With the Risk Ranking Technique and the other techniques considered their efficacy as aids to decision making is enhanced if the criteria they use are tailored to suit particular families of decisions they are applied to.
5. For assessment of some decisions the acceptability criteria used by financial institutions can, with advantage, be incorporated in the ranking technique.

It is hoped that the book will be of use to decision makers, proximate decision makers and people studying management, banking and insurance at the graduate and postgraduate levels.

I would like to thank my friends at Lloyds Bank, National Westminster Bank, Swiss Bank Corporation, Swiss Reinsurance Company, the Bank of England, City University and Mike Hayns of AEA Technology, Alan Jessop of Durham University and Martin Binks of Nottingham University, for their very perceptive and constructive discussions on decision making and risk assessment.

JOHN C. CHICKEN
Godalming, Surrey

ACKNOWLEDGEMENTS

In the preparation of this book information from many sources has been drawn upon and permission to use the following material is gratefully acknowledged.

Permission has been granted by the Bank of England to include extracts of BSD/1990/3 *Notice to Institutions: Implementation in the United Kingdom of the Solvency Ratio Directive,* authorized under the Banking Act 1987, in Appendix 1. Pergamon Press has given permission to reproduce Figures 4.1 and 4.2 from *The Risk Ranking Technique in Decision Making* by J. C. Chicken and M. R. Hayns (1989). The Civil Aviation Authority has granted permission to reproduce Figure 5.1, taken from *Joint Airworthiness Requirements 25.1309,* published in JAR 25 for the Airworthiness Steering Committee by the Civil Aviation Authority, Cheltenham, UK (1986). The Swiss Bank has given permission to publish material from *Economic and Financial Prospects,* Supplement, Vol. 1 (1988) which appears in Appendix 2 while The World Bank has given permission for the use of an extract from *Guidelines to Use of Consultants by World Bank Borrowers and by The World Bank as Executing Agency,* first published 1981, 9th printing 1988, by The World Bank, Washington, USA, pp. 13–20, which appears in Appendix 7. Finally Lloyds Bank has granted permission to include in the text details of their risk assessment procedures as set out in *External Debt Assessment,* written by C. Johnson and published by Lloyds Bank, London, UK (1985).

1 INTRODUCTION

Nothing is more difficult, and therefore more precious, than being able to decide.

Napoleon I, *Maxims* (1804–15)

❑ SUMMARY

The concept of comprehensive risk assessment for decision making is introduced. Comprehensive risk assessment takes account of all the technical, economic and socio-political factors involved. The method is illustrated using the case of the Channel crossing decision. The logic for the layout of the book is described.

AIM

It is hoped that the analysis presented in this book will show top decision makers and their advisors, whether they are in government, financial institutions or industry, how the range of factors that have to be considered in evaluating the acceptability of decision options can be assessed in a reliable and consistent way. Besides examining the implications of technical, economic and socio-political factors attention is given to the problems that arise from regulatory requirements and lack of relevant quantitative data.

The specific aims are to present an examination of the problems involved in making decisions about the acceptability of complex major projects, and from a critical assessment of the efficacy of the various assessment techniques postulate the optimum procedure. In order to illustrate the range of factors that have to be considered in decision making attention is given to the Comprehensive Risk Ranking Technique, which although originally developed as an aid to assessing the acceptability of the risks associated with potentially hazardous installations can be used for assessment of the acceptability of major projects (Chicken, 1986; Chicken and Hayns, 1987b). The reason for introducing the Risk Ranking Technique is that it draws attention to the range of factors that must be considered in any major decision-making process and how the significance of the various factors can be integrated. The method therefore serves as a sound base against which to compare other aids to decision making.

RISK RANKING

The Risk Ranking Technique was designed to present the decision maker with a comprehensive non-dimensional assessment of the technical, economic and socio-political factors associated with a decision, in a manner that does not conflict with the best traditions of statistical analysis. In some ways the design of the technique was influenced by systems thinking. The extent of the influence is that the ranking technique aims to unify the effects of various factors into a coherent whole (Checkland, 1988). The technique has also been influenced by Lindley's approach to scoring, uncertainty and blending numerate ideas with less formal approaches (Lindley, 1985). Hogarth's view that many of the existing aids to decision making lack the flexibility necessary to capture the essence of the problems inherent in major decisions provided the encouragement to develop the risk ranking method of assessing decision options (Hogarth, 1988).

Important considerations in developing the Risk Ranking Technique were to provide decision makers with a coherent, transparent and defensible way of arriving at decisions, which could be used to justify decisions to the lay public. The specification of a coherent and transparent assessment implies that the method must be simple, logical and uncomplicated. These practical requirements mean that use of elegant statistical methods has to be kept to a minimum. The importance attached to being able to justify complex decisions to the lay public is recognition of the fact that often every aspect of decision making related to major projects, and to expenditure of public funds, has to be defended in public against searching examination by official organizations and by the media. Unless the basis for a decision can be explained and defended in clear terms, easily understood by the general public, there is a distinct possibility that the arguments will be misunderstood and perhaps even unintentionally will generate opposition. The need for comprehensive justification of decisions is illustrated by: the range of topics examined in Public Inquiries such as the Sizewell 'B' Public Inquiry (Layfield, 1987); the way in which international companies such as Ford and Nissan decide where to build their plants; the way international financial institutions such as banks assess the creditworthiness of countries; why the Bank of Industry, Credit and Commerce was allowed to continue operating until it failed in such a spectacular way; and why money from the Mirror Group pension fund was allowed to evaporate. Such decision making has to take account of a combination, but not always the same combination, of many factors. The specific combinations of factors and the criteria used for assessing acceptability are often not clearly stated in advance, nor is any indication given of the weight attributed to each factor in arriving at an overall view about acceptability. The ranking technique is seen as one way of overcoming these problems by providing a consistent way of assessing each factor as well as a predictable way of weighting and combining each factor to give a consistent overall assessment.

To illustrate the nature of the factors that have to be considered in decision making, and to structure the analysis in later chapters of the problems of assessing decision options, first the form of the Risk Ranking Technique is explained and then an example of its application given.

Essentially, the technique consists of an assessment of the significance of all the factors associated with the acceptability of the risks inherent in each option that has to be considered. In this book the term risk is used to denote the measure of uncertainty about acceptability associated with any estimate of the significance of a factor. For assessment purposes the factors are considered under three broad headings: technical, economic and socio-political. These three groups of factors are intended to cover every aspect of acceptability and taken together they provide a realistic basis for ranking the overall acceptability of a proposal. One possible composition of the factors is shown in Table 1.1. To rate the acceptability of each group of factors they are scored against specific criteria on a numerical scale. The higher the score the lower the factor's acceptability, the overall ranking of the acceptability of a project being calculated by integrating the scores of the individual factors. The integrated score determines which of four ranks of acceptability the proposal as a whole belongs to. How the overall risk ranks are defined and the ranks related to the ranking scores of the individual factors is shown in Table 1.2. The scoring scheme is designed so that overall ranking will be dominated by the factors with the highest score. The higher the score the less acceptable are the factors.

Ranks 2 and 3 are both rankings of proposals that can be made universally acceptable by modifying the proposal. The changes required to make a Rank 2 proposal acceptable are much more extensive than those required to make a Rank 3 proposal acceptable.

To some extent the success of the ranking technique depends on having available a relevant reliable analysis of each factor. Ideally the analysis should be quantitative with the degree of uncertainty clearly defined. But the technique is also useful when, as is often the case in decision making, there is little or no reliable data available as in such cases the technique provides a logical structure to the assessment.

APPLICATION OF RISK RANKING

Application of the ranking technique requires, like any comprehensive assessment

Table 1.1 Composition of main groups of ranking factors

Factor	Nature of risk	Possible composition of factors
Technical	Plant would not perform as required	Plant performance Plant reliability Harm to the public
Economic	Less that optimum benefit from financial commitment	Supply and demand Magnitude of possible financial loss Payoff Index of harm/benefit Cost–benefit analysis Through-life cost
Socio-political	Not politically acceptable	Public acceptability Results of public inquiries Political climate Views on current quality of life

Table 1.2 Construction of risk ranks

Risk rank	Acceptability	Possibile action to make ranking more acceptable	Score for any factor in this rank	Total score range
1	Unlikely	Unlikely any possible	14	16–42
2	Only if risk can be reduced	Greater investment or organizational and major technical changes	5	7–15
3	Subject to certain action	Organizational changes or minor technical changes	2	4–6
4	Without restriction	None required	1	3

of decision options, six basic steps. The steps are:

1. define decision;
2. specify the criteria that have to be used to judge the acceptability of the parameters associated with each factor;
3. identify the options available;
4. identify the data available about each factor associated with each option;
5. with the data available assess the ranking justified for each option;
6. using the rankings obtained determine which decision option is the most comprehensively acceptable.

In reality, each step involves a considerable amount of analysis, but before delving into the detail of the technique a simple illustration of the application of the technique is given.

ASSESSMENT OF THE CHANNEL TUNNEL DECISION

The illustration chosen is a *post hoc* examination of the decision to build the Channel Tunnel and the evidence that is used is mainly that given in the official case presented to Parliament. The official case provided the basic data on which the decision to build the Channel Tunnel was made. It is stressed that the criteria used in this illustration to assess acceptability are very general and in the later chapters the problems of refining and developing criteria for specific decisions are discussed in detail. The fact that the cost of the tunnel was much higher than estimated shows something of the magnitude of the real uncertainty associated with the data on which such decisions have to be based.

In arriving at the decision to build a channel tunnel the government had five options to consider. These were known as: Eurobridge, Euroroute, Channel Tunnel, Channel Expressway and No Fixed Link. Their essential features are summarized in Table 1.3. As with any application of the ranking technique, criteria have to be postulated for assessing the ranking of the acceptability of the risk associated with the technical, economic and socio-political factors of each option.

Table 1.3 Summary of the essential features of Channel crossing proposals

Proposal (Proposers)	Essential construction features	Technical problems
Eurobridge (Laing, Brown and Root, and ICI)	Suspension bridge of seven 5 km spans plus 6 m diameter rail tunnel. Traffic lanes enclosed in a Superferrolo tube. The suspension cables 1.4 m diameter Parafil	Suspension tower to withstand impact of a 250,000 ton ship. Oscillation of spans. Ventilation of traffic tube. Explosions on the bridge. Driver fatigue. Life of components
Euroroute (Trafalgar House, British Steel and banks)	For road transport two bridges from each coast to artificial islands. Islands linked by tunnel on the sea bed. Also a rail tunnel on sea bed coast to coast	Ventilation of the tunnels. Earth movement. Resisitance of the 34 protective caisons to damage by shipping. Explosions in the tunnel. Life of components
Channel Tunnel (five UK and three French construction companies and banks)	A three-tunnel system, two railway and one service tunnels. Terminals for loading and unloading road vehicles on and off trains	Ventilation. Earth movements. Life of components. Explosions in the tunnels
Channel Expressway (British Ferries)	A twin-tunnel system, each tunnel taking both road and rail traffic. Would be the largest drive through tunnel in the world	Ventilation. Earth movement. Life components. Driver fatigue
No Fixed Link option	Revision of ferry regulatory requirements	Redevelopment of ports and congestion in ports and sea lanes

Simple subjective qualitative criteria were adopted; these criteria are summarized in Table 1.4. It is stressed that the criteria are for demonstration only and in a real case more quantitative criteria may be used. Quantification does not imply absolute precision. Some uncertainty is associated with all predictions. In Chapters 4 and 11 the problem of how the significance of uncertainty can be assessed and allowed for is discussed. The problem of developing general and special criteria for judging the acceptability of each factor is returned to in Chapters 11 and 12.

One reason for using simplified criteria was that in the evidence, presented to Parliament, no attempt was made to quantify the probability associated with the various predictions. The evidence used did not draw attention to such facts as the real experience with the material proposed for the suspension-bridge cables was only about one-seventh of the life proposed for the material and no justification was given for the acceptability of the explosion risk in long tunnels. Nor for every option was there discussion of the possible variation in construction costs. In this

Table 1.4 Ranking criteria assumed for illustration

Factor	Ranking score	Criteria
Technical	1	No technical problems
	2	Minor changes required to overcome technical problems
	5	Major changes required to overcome technical problems
	14	Technical problems unlikely to be solved
Economic	1	Capital required easily raised. Return on investment above average
	2	Capital can be raised. Return on investment at least average
	5	Capital can only be raised with difficulty. Return lower than average
	14	Negative return on investment. Unlikely capital can be raised
Socio-political	1	Acceptability by the public
	2	Minor objections by the public
	5	To satisfy objections by the public major changes have to be made
	14	Unacceptable to the public

context it is important to remember that there can be considerable variations in the factors peculiar to novel construction projects. For example, quite unrelated projects like the Sydney Opera House and Concorde escalated to about ten times the original estimate (Hall, 1980). The Thames Barrier was initially estimated to cost £23 million whereas the actual cost was £461 million (HMSO, 1985b).

The ranking scores considered to be justified for each factor of each of the options described in the Channel Fixed Link proposal (HMSO, 1985a) are shown in Table 1.5. By integrating the scores for each factor, an overall ranking for each option is attained, the results being shown in Table 1.6. The conclusion that the ranking exercise appears to endorse is that, on the basis of the evidence used, overall the Channel Tunnel was the most acceptable option.

In other words, the Government's decision to approve the building of the Channel Tunnel was justified. However, in 1989 it appeared that the Channel Tunnel would cost 40% more than the original estimate, so perhaps the favourable view taken of the contingency allowance in the original figures was not warranted (HMSO, 1985b; Feltham, 1989).

Ranking has been used in various ways including assessing the acceptability of

Table 1.5 Justification of the Channel crossing options' ranking scores

Proposal	Technical	Economic	Socio-political
Eurobridge	Limited life data about some materials it was proposed to use: Score 5	Cost estimate £5.9 bn; possible variation not discussed. Return 21–22%: Score 2	No structured survey of opinion made. No serious objection reported: Score 1
Euroroute	Although not all technical issues examined, technical justification adequate: Score 2	Estimated costs might reach £10.7 bn. Return 17%: Score 5	No structured survey of opinion made. No serious objection reported: Score 1
Channel Tunnel	Although not all technical issues examined, technical justification adequate: Score 2	Maximum debt allowing for contingency estimated to be £4.75 bn. Return 19%: Score 1	No structured survey of opinion made. No serious objection reported: Score 1
Channel Expressway	Although not all technical issues examined, technical justification adequate: Score 2	Cost estimated to be £2.5 bn. No discussion of possible variation. Return 27%: Score 2	No structured survey of opinion made. No serious objection reported: Score 1
No Fixed Link	Requirement not known. No designs presented: Score 5	No costs given but financial risks assumed to be similar to present pattern: Score 2	Present crossing service considered inadequate: Score 2

potentially hazardous plant project options and policy options (Chicken and Hayns, 1989). Prior to the use of Comprehensive Risk Ranking acceptability of hazards had tended to be judged just on technical issues. Although the Commission of the European Community (CEC) has encouraged the development of comprehensive assessment of the acceptability of proposals involving potentially major hazards, such methods have not yet been adopted as a mandatory part of the regulatory procedure. However, at a CEC seminar in Nice in September 1988 the representative of the Netherlands Ministry of Housing, Physical Planning and Environment announced that the Dutch government was considering adopting, as part of its regulatory procedure, a comprehensive form of ranking the acceptability of risks that takes into account technical, economic and socio-political factors. The approach is similar in concept to the procedure just described, but details of the procedure have not yet been made public.

Table 1.6 Overall ranking of the acceptability of Channel crossing proposals

Proposal	Total score	Rank
Eurobridge	8	2
Euroroute	8	2
Channel Tunnel	4	3
Channel Expressway	5	2
No Fixed Link option	9	2

THE RANGE OF ARGUMENTS IN THE FOLLOWING CHAPTERS

As the aim of this book is to critically examine the problems of decision making associated with determining the acceptability of complex major projects first the general nature of the decision-making process is examined then a comparison is made with the techniques used by financial institutions. Banks are of special interest, as in many ways they are at the heart of the commercial world. One recent incentive banks have had to improve the way they assess creditworthiness on the macro scale has been the international debt rescheduling problems that have increased dramatically since 1979. It has been suggested by Channon (1988) that the primary cause of the need to reschedule debt interest payments and debt repayment was the disturbance to the balance of world capital flows caused by changes in the price of oil in 1974. Another incentive banks have had for improving their assessment of creditworthiness has been the bad debt provision they have had to make during the 1990–92 recession.

One possible way, examined in this book, of avoiding this problem in the future is by improved assessment of the magnitude and implications of the risks before they are accepted. In the process of developing a justification for an improved method of assessing the acceptability of risks the methods used by various banks to assess risks inherent in the loans they consider making are discussed. Particular attention is given to the procedures the Swiss Bank Corporation developed for assessing the creditworthiness of countries, as this is quite a comprehensive form of assessment. They introduced their method in the early 1980s and over the years they have refined it to take account of experience. Their technique incorporates an assessment of the country's domestic economy, external economy, debt, the political risk involved and the per capita growth in the gross domestic product. The criteria the Swiss Bank Corporation use for judging acceptability have some synergy with the criteria, described above, for ranking of the Channel crossing options. In the examination of the decision-making process attention is also given to the procedures used in the insurance industry and to the regulatory processes used by government bodies.

Following examination of the decision-making process and the assessment of the techniques used by financial institutions an assessment is presented of the theoretical considerations of evaluating the technical, economic and socio-political aspects of the acceptability of risks in general and for the Risk Ranking Technique in particular. Then the various alternative methods of assessing decision options are reviewed and compared with the Risk Ranking Technique and the methods used by financial institutions. Appendices describe: rules for deriving data from expert opinion, analysis of costs and benefits, the capability of Bayesian and fuzzy analysis and multivariate analysis. Finally, the optimum method of assessing decision options is postulated.

The rest of this book is arranged to present the analysis of decision making in ten steps, each one of which is dealt with in a separate chapter. The steps are:

1. examination of the decision-making process;
2. description of the approach of financial institutions to the assessment of risks;
3. assessment of the theoretical considerations underlying the Ranking Technique of the form described;
4. evaluation of the problems of assessing the technical aspects of risk;
5. evaluation of the problems of assessing the economic aspects of the risk;
6. evaluation of the problems of assessing the socio-political aspects of the risk;
7. review of possible alternatives to the Ranking Technique and the banks' approach to assessing risk;
8. comparison of efficacy of alternatives;
9. comparison of the efficacy of the Comprehensive Risk Ranking Technique with the Swiss Bank Corporation's Country Risk Assessment approach, the methods used by some British banks and also the insurance industry;
10. postulation of the optimum method of assessing decision options.

Finally, from the assessment of aids to decision making, a number of general conclusions are drawn about their potential capability.

2 THE PROCESS OF DECISION MAKING

❑ SUMMARY

The nature of the process of decision making associated with major projects is described. The characteristics are examined using a hypothetical example of a major development proposal for a Third World country and a formalized picture of the factors involved and the way they interact is developed.

THE NATURE OF MAJOR DECISIONS

It is easy to understand how anyone outside the decision-making process may have the impression that major decisions are just the product of a single event, the single meeting being perhaps a dramatic meeting between all the interested parties or else an instruction handed down from some person with the status of a deity. Of course, a moment's reflection will show the decision-making process is generally quite protracted. For example, there was discussion about a channel tunnel at the time of the Napoleonic Wars (1799–1815). The discussions that led to the decision to build a channel tunnel, which it is hoped will be completed in 1994 or soon after, started in 1979 (HMSO, 1982). The aircraft industry provides many examples of the time it takes to move from design concept to an aeroplane entering service. The specification that led to the development of the English Electric Lightning supersonic fighter was issued by the Ministry of Supply in 1947. Prototypes of the aircraft flew during the 1950s and the aircraft finally entered squadron service in 1960 (Philpott, 1984). Another example is the Harrier Jump Jet aircraft which were flying operationally in both the Falklands and Kuwait Wars. The first experiments to test the feasibility of a vertical take off fixed-wing aircraft, as opposed to rotating-wing aircraft such as autogyros or helicopters, were made in 1953 at Rolls Royce Flight Development Centre at Hucknall in Nottinghamshire on a flying test rig known as the Flying Bedstead (Donne, 1981). These experiments led to the development of the Harrier aircraft which first flew in 1960 and entered squadron service a few years later. Such examples show how the gestation time of a major project may be spread over several years and involve several parties.

Although this book is primarily concerned with major or end decisions it must be recognized that in general the end decision is the product of a whole series of subsidiary decisions and the interaction of many interested parties. Regardless of the size of the project involved each of these subsidiary decisions will involve assessment of a similar pattern of considerations, so in several ways the discussion of the decision-making process that follows is equally applicable to both small and large projects. To structure this discussion of the decision-making process, with the aid of a hypothetical case, the various parties that typically make up the decision-making set are identified, then the way the various parties interact in the decision-making process is examined. In examining the way the parties interact attention is given to the way the interaction changes at the various stages of the project and the way the type of information on which decisions are based develops.

A HYPOTHETICAL EXAMPLE OF DECISION MAKING

For the first part of the discussion a hypothetical project in a Third World country is considered. The project is to build a railway system connecting a potential inland industrial area and a good agricultural area with a port. A map of the area is shown in Figure 2.1, which gives the most important details about the country. The government of the country in question is stable and very concerned to improve the standard of living of the people and to do this by commercial exploitation of the country's natural resources. There is a somewhat unstable aggressive country to the north, but this is not considered an immediate threat.

An international development agency made an assessment of the economic potential of the country and recommended that the iron and bauxite ore in the east should be mined and refined locally and metal-using industries should be established around the refineries so that transport costs would be saved. The possibility of becoming a supplier of finished and part-finished components for the German and Japanese car industries was being explored. It was recognized that the success of such a project depended on the supply of skilled labour. To solve this problem special training courses would be organized to develop an adequate pool of labour by the time the plants are ready. The development agency also recommended that the fertile land south of the proposed industrial area should be developed as an area for intensive farming, the intention being that some of the land would be devoted to production of food for local consumption. It was anticipated that consumption of food per head would increase as greater income per head allows the standard of living of the country to improve. The rest of the land would be devoted to intensive production of high quality fruit and vegetables for export. To transport the industrial and agricultural products to market a railway was considered a requirement, to link industrial and agricultural centres with the port, new town and airport.

The government of the country accepted the need for, and the concept of, the railway and they decided to have a design assessment made so that the cost implications of the project could be evaluated. The issues the design assessment was meant to deal with are listed in Table 2.1. Essentially, the object of a design assessment is to determine whether or not the proposed project is a practical proposition. The output of the design assessment should be a specification for the detailed design of the project. Although the example chosen is one with a high

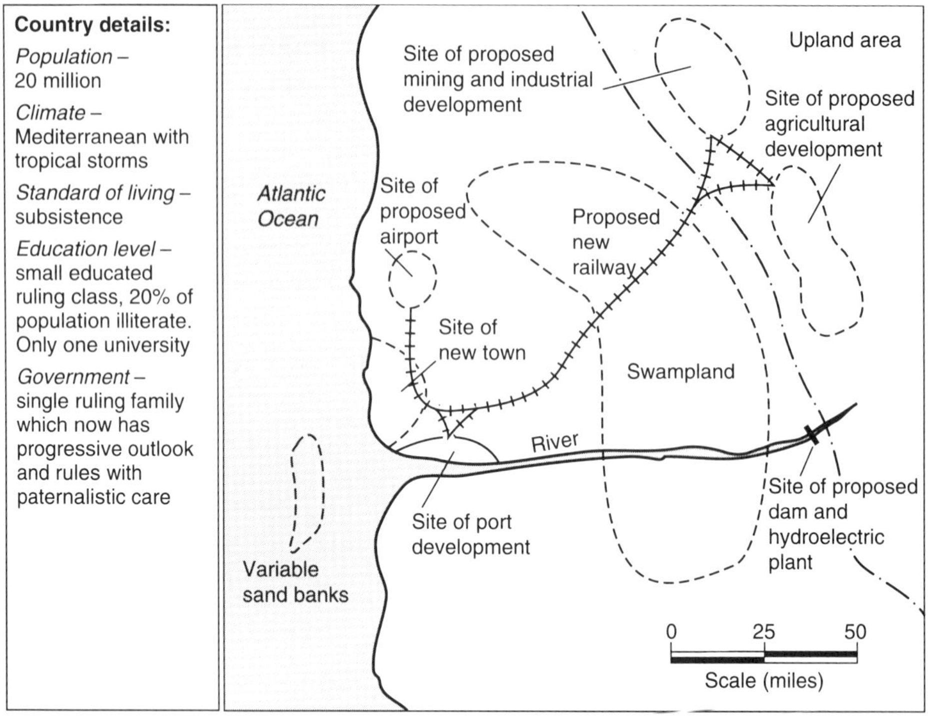
Country details:
Population – 20 million
Climate – Mediterranean with tropical storms
Standard of living – subsistence
Education level – small educated ruling class, 20% of population illiterate. Only one university
Government – single ruling family which now has progressive outlook and rules with paternalistic care
Site of proposed mining and industrial development
Upland area
Site of proposed agricultural development
Atlantic Ocean
Site of proposed airport
Proposed new railway
Site of new town
Swampland
River
Site of proposed dam and hydroelectric plant
Site of port development
Variable sand banks
0
25
50
Scale (miles)

Figure 2.1 Map of hypothetical development area.

engineering content, analogous questions have to be studied in projects involving non-traded goods or services. At the end of the design assessment stage, a decision has to be taken as to whether or not to proceed to the detailed design stage. Often the detailed design involves organizations that will eventually undertake at least part of the construction and supply of equipment.

In a project of the type described in the example, with completion of the detailed design, tenders for construction and supply of equipment will be called for. When the tenders have been received the decision has to be made about which tender to accept. Although the lowest tender should be accepted, the definition of 'lowest tender' needs some qualification. It should be the lowest tender from a financially sound company that has competence and experience in the subject of the tender. If the tender involves well-proven technology, like that mentioned in the example about which there is a wealth of experience around the world, it should be possible to select a sound company that has competence and experience. However, some projects involve novel technology about which there is little or no experience and some may even require the technology to be developed. In such cases the degree of uncertainty about the outcome must be considerable. The development of the Lightning supersonic fighter and the Harrier Jump Jet, which were mentioned earlier, indicates something of the time that may be involved in developing a new technology. The considerable length of time needed to develop new technology is not peculiar to the aircraft industry. In many other areas,

Table 2.1 Design assessment issues

Issue	Composition of the issue
Is the route optimum	Are all likely users connected? Would a better route be around the swamp area?
Growth of traffic	Would a railway be required for the construction of industrial areas or development of agricultural areas? To what extent does development of the railway depend on development of port, new town, airport, industrial and agricultural centres?
Competition	To what extent would development of an improved road or development of a canal system eliminate the need for a rail system?
Engineering problems	Will it be possible to make a reliable crossing of the swamp land? Will there be an adequate electric power supply for electrically powered trains? How much and what design of rolling stock will be required?
Supply problems	Where will supply of equipment and constructors be sought from?
Operational problems	With an inadequate supply of local labour where will adequate operating teams be obtained from? Will foreign contract operators be used?
Timescale	When will project start and when will it have to be finished by?
Cost	What will the total cost of the project be including stations, signal equipment and access roads and how will the necessary funds be raised?
Infrastructure	Will services available include: telephone, fire, deep water port, cranes, radio and satellite communication? Also will there be adequate hospitals, hotels and housing?

technologies such as those involved in medical drugs, fusion reactors, autonomous robots, equipment for outer space and ceramic composites, may take many years to develop. Before deciding to accept a tender and to go ahead with a project many other issues, besides bid price and the competence of the tenderer, have to be resolved. For example the following questions have to be answered:

1. Can the project be funded in an acceptable way?
2. Is the tenderer likely to be reliable?
3. What provision is likely to be required for possible cost overruns?
4. Is the project likely to be completed on time?
5. Are the consequences of delays in completion likely to be acceptable?
6. If the project is funded by loans of some kind, is the project likely to yield a sufficient return to repay the loan?
7. Is the project socially and politically acceptable and does it satisfy all the requirements of regulatory authorities?

It now becomes clear that all those associated with the project, either directly or indirectly, have their own important decisions to make. If the project is to be funded by some financial institution the institution will need to be satisfied that the proposer and proposal are sound and that the proposer will be able to meet the interest and loan repayments. Regulatory bodies will need to be convinced that the proposal will satisfy their requirements. The proposer will want to be satisfied that the project will satisfy all his technical, economic and socio-political criteria. From this discussion of a hypothetical project a picture of the various parties that are likely to be involved in decision making related to major projects can be built up. Figure 2.2 gives an indication of the likely composition of a decision-making set of parties.

GENERAL NATURE OF DECISION MAKING

Having examined the decision-making processes involved in a hypothetical example, the general case of decision making can be examined. In Figure 2.3 the essential steps in the process of making a major decision are outlined and the basis for justifying the outcome of each step indicated. This very generalized picture of the decision-making process associated with major projects has to be refined to make a more comprehensive basis for the analysis presented in the chapters that follow. So each step in the process, as identified in Figure 2.3, is now described in more detail.

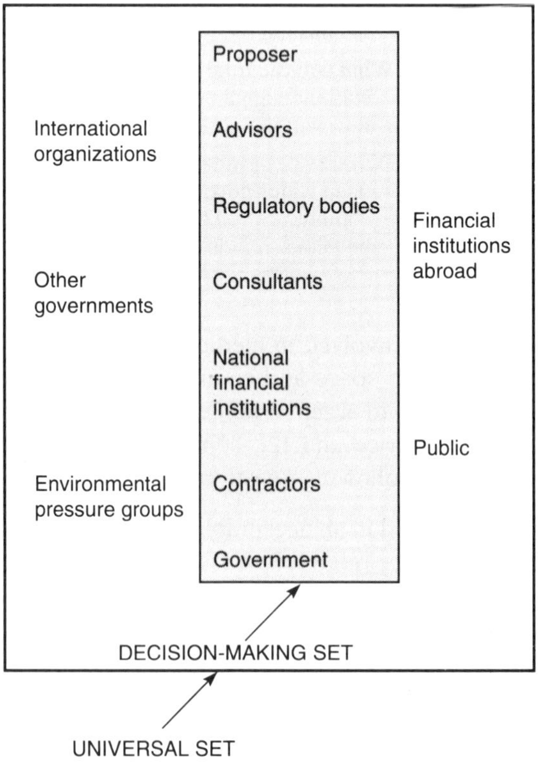
Proposer
International organizations
Advisors
Regulatory bodies
Financial institutions abroad
Other governments
Consultants
National financial institutions
Public
Environmental pressure groups
Contractors
Government
DECISION-MAKING SET
UNIVERSAL SET

Figure 2.2 Composition of the decision-making set.

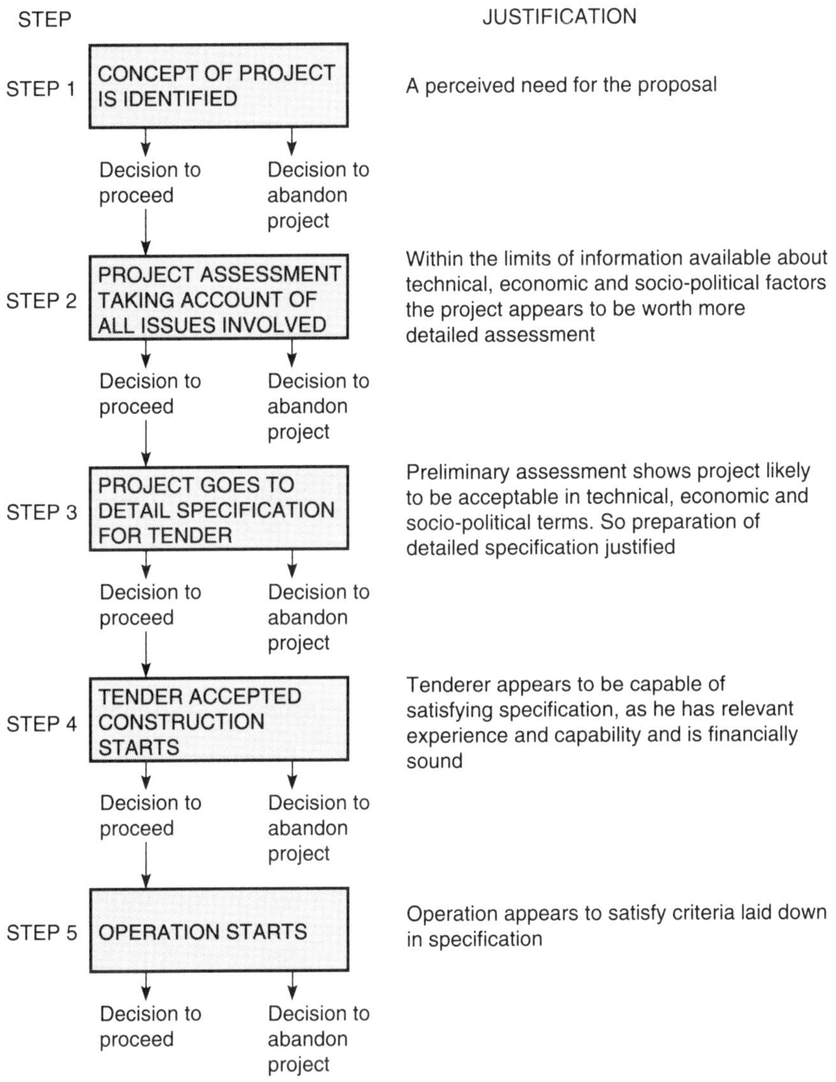
STEP
JUSTIFICATION
STEP 1
CONCEPT OF PROJECT IS IDENTIFIED
A perceived need for the proposal
Decision to proceed
Decision to abandon project
STEP 2
PROJECT ASSESSMENT TAKING ACCOUNT OF ALL ISSUES INVOLVED
Within the limits of information available about technical, economic and socio-political factors the project appears to be worth more detailed assessment
Decision to proceed
Decision to abandon project
STEP 3
PROJECT GOES TO DETAIL SPECIFICATION FOR TENDER
Preliminary assessment shows project likely to be acceptable in technical, economic and socio-political terms. So preparation of detailed specification justified
Decision to proceed
Decision to abandon project
STEP 4
TENDER ACCEPTED CONSTRUCTION STARTS
Tenderer appears to be capable of satisfying specification, as he has relevant experience and capability and is financially sound
Decision to proceed
Decision to abandon project
STEP 5
OPERATION STARTS
Operation appears to satisfy criteria laid down in specification
Decision to proceed
Decision to abandon project

Figure 2.3 Essential steps in the process of making a major decision.

Step 1

The conceptual need for a particular project can arise in several ways, but mainly as a result of an assessment of future requirements. The assessment of future needs may be made by a team within an organization or on the advice of external experts that have been consulted. Generally, the expenditure on identifying the conceptual need for a project is quite modest in comparison to the ultimate overall cost of a project. Typically a conceptual study will identify the technical solution required, the likely economic merit in solving the problem, and the likely acceptability of the project in socio-political terms. Assessment of the economic merit should include comparison of differences in the through-life benefit of the options considered.

Assessment of through-life benefit is discussed further in Chapter 6. If the project is likely to require external finance, that is finance by a financial institution rather than being funded by the proposing organization's own internal funds, then there will have to be preliminary discussion with a financial institution to determine whether or not they are likely to be willing to provide the necessary funds. At the end of the conceptual study step a decision will have to be made about proceeding to Step 2 and making a detailed assessment of the project. If the project moves to Step 2 then funding for that step will be required.

Step 2

Assuming the decision has been made to develop the project further then a detailed assessment will have to be made of all the technical, economic and socio-political factors involved. Because of the extensive detail produced by such an assessment, the process of making a decision to proceed to the specification for tender is more complicated. Although the detail may be extensive it may be qualitative and based on subjective knowledge; this will be particularly the case when the project is novel.

As the whole spectrum of major project decision making is being considered two main types of novelty have to be recognized:

1. the project is technically novel;
2. the project employs an established technology in a novel environment.

Technically novel projects could be a new design of aeroplane or a new design of nuclear reactor. Examples of an established technology in a novel environment are building a railway system or a hydroelectric power station in a Third World country. Although building an airport would normally be considered as being an established technology if the airport has to be built, in a permafrost area it would usually be considered as a novel project.

The reason for stressing the variability in the quality of the data that have to be used in the second step is to draw attention to the fact that during the second step the degree of uncertainty associated with each factor will begin to emerge. An understanding of the uncertainties associated with any proposal, no matter what its size, is essential if a decision maker is to make a defensible decision. A bank manager asked to make a loan to someone wanting to open a shop will be just as keen to assess the uncertainties involved as an underwriter will be in assessing the acceptability of the risks associated with an offshore oil rig.

Step 3

If the outcome of Step 2 is to proceed with the preparation of a proposal in sufficient detail for suppliers to tender for completing the project, then a tender specification has to be prepared. The concept of a tender specification does imply a process more associated with an engineering project in the private sector. But, the concept is not limited to engineering projects or the private sector; for social projects in the public sector the tender specification process can be equally efficacious.

The particular benefit of a tender specification is that it defines, or at least it should define, exactly what work the tenderer is required to do. In an ideal world, the tender specification should identify everything that has to be done and the contract that is subsequently placed should simply confirm that the work that has to be completed is the work identified in the contract specification. The enormous volume of contract litigation that takes place shows something of the extent of the differences that can exist between what was originally contracted for and what had to be done to complete a project.

The Channel Tunnel project is a good example of just how large the variations can be. The magnitude of the possible variation in cost underlines the importance of understanding at each stage of a project the magnitude of the uncertainties that may be associated with every aspect of a project. Before a tender specification is issued it is prudent to confirm that the project is acceptable to regulatory authorities and that adequate finance for the project is available. The process of obtaining regulatory authorities' confirmation that a project is likely to be acceptable could involve a public inquiry or similar approval procedure that may delay the start of a project by two or three years. The public inquiry that considered the acceptability of siting a pressurized water nuclear power reactor at Sizewell on the Suffolk coast in England took nearly three years (Layfield, 1981). The inquiry started in January 1983 and was complete in March 1985 but it was December 1986 before the report was presented to the Minister. The overall time taken to obtain a decision was even longer as the Central Electricity Generating Board first applied for approval for the siting in January 1981.

The project financers will need to be convinced that the project is viable, that the proposer is sound and has the experience and capability to drive the project to a successful conclusion. These caveats apply equally to all projects regardless of size. If it is decided that the project is to proceed to the next step, the last phase of Step 3 is to issue the tender specification to appropriately qualified tenderers.

Step 4

The first action in Step 4 is to decide if one of the tenders should be accepted. In the process of confirming if a particular tender is acceptable, it will also have to be confirmed that the tenderer has the appropriate experience, capability and adequate financial resources. If the project is being undertaken in the public sector the questions asked might be phrased slightly differently, but their intent would be the same. If the project has to be undertaken by a government department there would be concern to establish that the department involved had adequate resources in terms of manpower with the appropriate skills and financial resources to enable the project to be completed to the required timescale. Although the decision might be given to start a project it is possible that some change in the operating environment requires the project to be stopped. Among the possible reasons for stopping a project are: change in public acceptability, funds found to be inadequate, the project found to be technically unsound and change in demand.

Step 5

Assuming all the other steps area completed satisfactorily, a decision has to be taken to start operating the project. Even if operation of a project is started the project might have to be stopped if the environment it operates in changes.

CONCLUSIONS ABOUT PROJECT DECISION MAKING

From this examination of the steps in the decision-making process associated with determining the acceptability of a major project it is possible to detect characteristics common to the decision-making processes associated with all projects. The common characteristics are identified in Figure 2.4. From the figure it can be seen that the decision maker with comprehensive responsibility for determining the acceptability of a project will require detailed information about the acceptability of the technical, economic and socio-political aspects of a project. It also has to be recognized that, at each step in the decision process and in each part of the supporting assessment, there may have to be iterative development to take account of improvements in data that take place as the project proceeds and improvements in the understanding of requirements.

Ultimately, a project will not go ahead unless there is adequate funding, so in the next chapter an examination is made of the way financial institutions arrive at decisions about the acceptability of a project for funding. This is followed in later chapters by examination of the problems involved in assessing the acceptability of the technical, economic and socio-political aspects of a proposal.

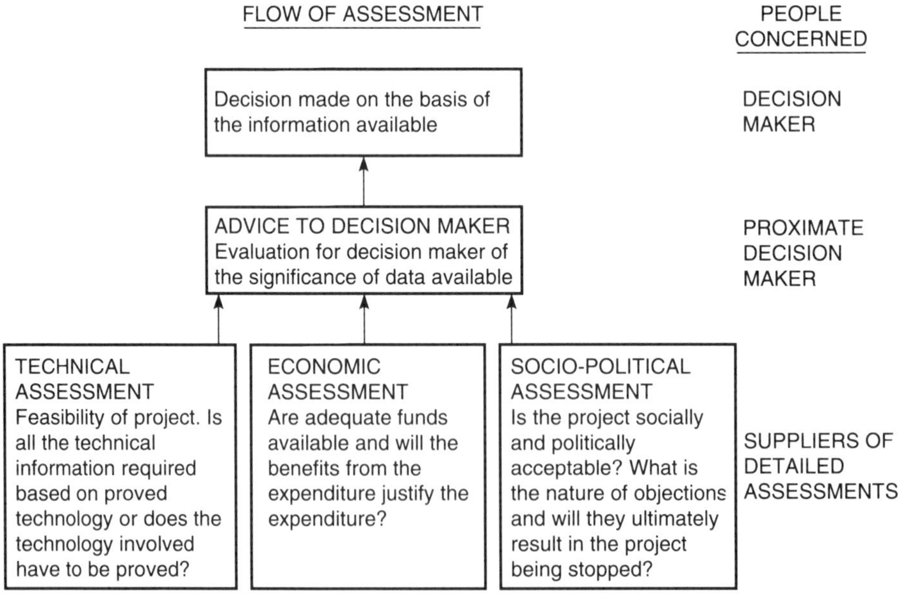
FLOW OF ASSESSMENT
PEOPLE CONCERNED
Decision made on the basis of the information available
DECISION MAKER
ADVICE TO DECISION MAKER
Evaluation for decision maker of the significance of data available
PROXIMATE DECISION MAKER
TECHNICAL ASSESSMENT
Feasibility of project. Is all the technical information required based on proved technology or does the technology involved have to be proved?
ECONOMIC ASSESSMENT
Are adequate funds available and will the benefits from the expenditure justify the expenditure?
SOCIO-POLITICAL ASSESSMENT
Is the project socially and politically acceptable? What is the nature of objections and will they ultimately result in the project being stopped?
SUPPLIERS OF DETAILED ASSESSMENTS

Figure 2.4 Common characteristics of project decision making.

3 APPROACH OF FINANCIAL INSTITUTIONS TO RISK ASSESSMENT

❑ SUMMARY

Attention is concentrated on identifying the range of techniques that banks use to assess the acceptability of the risks they consider undertaking. The methods examined cover the range from small loans up to major loans to foreign countries.

FINANCIAL INSTITUTIONS' VIEW OF RISK

In this chapter, the ways in which financial institutions assess the risks associated with their lending procedures they are exposed to are examined to determine what features their practices have in common with other aids to decision making. Banks' views on risk management were put into perspective by Aloys Schwietert, Vice President and Chief Economist of the Swiss Bank Corporation, when he introduced a paper on the Swiss Bank Corporation's approach to Country Risk Assessment. He then described the role of a banker in the following terms (Schwietert, 1988):

> The banker's job is to manage risk rather than merely avoid it. The recent stock market crash reminded the world at large that risk management is increasingly important in the area of international finance. One major aspect of risk management is the assessment of the risk: before you can try to manage your risks – by diversifying, hedging or at least bracing yourself for what lies ahead – you have to identify them and put them in perspective. This is true whether we're talking about conventional credit risks or the 'country' attached to loans to foreign borrowers.
>
> Not all banks are equally willing to take on risk exposure. There is a broad

> spectrum of lending policies ranging from extremely cautious to highly aggressive. Each bank follows its own course and develops its own parameters for the risk/reward targets governing its operations.
>
> At the same time, the banks draw on a long tradition of shared experience and professional procedures in developing the information base from which risk assessments can be derived. Country Risk Assessment is a case in point.

Schwietert also mentioned that the Country Risk Assessment procedure his bank used had proved to be a useful aid to monitoring the economic stability of developing nations and industrialized countries. He also recognized that the general subject of Country Risk Assessment is still evolving as a discipline. This leaves open the question of how the problem is dealt with by other corporations or government agencies.

Banks like other financial institutions are subject to both internal and external control over the amount of risk they can accept. The external controls are those imposed by government regulatory authorities and in the case of countries in the European Economic Community imposed by directives of the Council of the European Community. In the case of Britain the Bank of England is the regulatory authority and the body that advises British banks on the way European Economic Community directives must be implemented. The two directives that are particularly relevant to the amount of risk a financial institution can accept in general are the directives on: Credit Institutions' own Funds (Council of Economic Community, 1989) and a Solvency Ratio for Credit Institutions (Council of Economic Community, 1989). These directives were implemented by the Bank of England in two notices they issued to institutions authorized under the Banking Act 1987 (Bank of England, 1990a and b). One notice dealt with implementation in the United Kingdom of the directive on own funds of credit institutions and the other dealt with implementation in the United Kingdom of the solvency ratio directive.

The importance of these directives and the way they have been implemented is their implication for risk acceptance. Although the directive uses the term 'solvency' ratio the Bank of England in their notices prefer to use the term 'risk asset ratio', which makes the concern about risk clearer. The risk asset ratio is the ratio of a bank's capital to the risk-adjusted values of assets and off-balance sheet items. Both the directive and the Bank of England notice say the ratio should not be less than 8%. Various asset items included in the calculations are risk weighted according to type and location. Although the directive specifies risk weightings it also states that competent authorities may fix higher weightings. The Bank of England's risk weightings are given in Appendix 1. Perhaps the most important implication of the directives is that they represent an external influence on banks, which attempts to harmonize the magnitude of financial risk in their portfolio of risks in relation to their assets.

The internal controls banks use to manage their portfolios of risks take several forms, each bank tending to develop its own methods. There are, however, important common features. The precise criteria used are to a certain extent variable, the criteria being adjusted to reflect the current economic climate and developments in what are considered to be important parameters in assessing the acceptability of risk. For example, in Britain in the early 1990s, it is much more difficult for a company to borrow money from a bank than it was in the mid-1980s. Because the recession had resulted in banks having to make extensive provision for bad debts, they were more demanding about the quality of the loans they got involved in.

METHODS BANKS USE TO ASSESS RISK ACCEPTABILITY

The methods banks use to assess the acceptability of risks in the loans they make vary, not only between banks, but also according to the size of the loan. The assessment of a small business' application for a ten thousand pound loan is somewhat simpler than the assessment made of a country's application for a five hundred million pound loan. This does not mean that the more detailed assessment is necessarily more accurate. A fair judgement on the methods used would be that they give the experienced loans officer a qualitative indication of the magnitude of the risks associated with a particular loan.

At the heart of any decision about the acceptability of a loan will be an assessment of the five basic characteristics that determine the acceptability of a loan proposal. The characteristics are, in order of importance:

1. ability of borrower to repay;
2. willingness of lender to make loan;
3. wealth of borrower;
4. security against loan;
5. the economic environment.

The risk may be categorized on a seven-point scale of the type shown in Table 3.1. Every organization may have its own special classification system but the general concept is the same.

At the level of a personal loan a bank simply assesses a person's income, outgoings, employment record, age and marital record. For slightly larger loans their

Table 3.1 Generalized loan risk classification

Risk class	Risk code	Interest charged
1 Nominal or No risk	A+ to A–	Standard
2 Minimal risk	B+ to B–	Standard
3 Reasonable risk	C+ to C–	Standard + 10%
4 More than normal risk	C– to D+	Standard + 25%
5 Cash basis loan only	D	Standard + 40%
6 High risk	D– to F+	Standard + 50% to 100%
7 Unacceptable	F	No loan possible

account may be reviewed, a security or guarantee called for and a general check made on their creditworthiness. A small business seeking a loan would be expected to show three years' accounts to prove that it was trading profitably. In addition, a cash flow forecast certified by an accountant may be called for. In assessing a company's financial report the figures would be assessed under five main groups: activity ratios, selling expense ratios, leverage ratios, liquidity ratios and profitability ratios. The composition of these five groups is shown in Table 3.2. Just one year's figures can often give a misleading impression and a better feeling can be developed by looking at trends over three or more years. The acceptable ratios will not be the same for all industries; for example, the fluctuations in the fashion trade may be seasonal and in an engineering consultancy there may be a three year cycle.

Some analysts have recently been using fifteen cause and effect ratios. Some of these ratios are very similar to the financial statement ratios just mentioned. The fifteen ratios are shown in Table 3.3. Taken together, the ratios just described give a good indication of the past performance of a company, but it should be stressed that they only indicate the past performance. Because the ratios are calculated from financial statements they tend to be out of date and past performance is no measure of current or future performance. Dun and Bradstreet, the international business information company, claim one factor that gives quite a good indication of the viability of a company is the length of time they take to pay their bills. The gradual extension of the time taken to settle accounts may be taken as a sure sign that a company is heading for financial difficulties, perhaps even bankruptcy.

Another method that is claimed to be 90% accurate in predicting financial problems is the so-called Z-score model (Thornhill, 1990). The general form of the Z-score model is:

$$Z = 1.2x_1 + 1.4x_2 + 3.3x_3 + 0.6x_4 + x_5$$

where

$$x_1 = \frac{(\text{Current assets} - \text{Current liabilities})}{\text{Total assets}}$$

$$x_2 = \frac{\text{Retained earnings}}{\text{Total assets}}$$

$$x_3 = \frac{\text{Earnings before interest and taxes}}{\text{Total assets}}$$

$$x_4 = \frac{\text{Market value of preferred and common equity}}{\text{Total debits}}$$

$$x_5 = \frac{\text{Sales}}{\text{Total assets}}$$

A firm with a Z-score below 1.8 is considered to be heading for bankruptcy. While the method has much to commend it for assessing the financial status of a company that has been operating for some years, it does not help with assessing the financial stability of a new company. Nor does the method make any allowance

Table 3.2 Composition of financial report assessment ratio groups

Ratio group	Component ratios
Activity ratios	$\text{Inventory turnover} = \frac{\text{Sales}}{\text{Inventory}}$
	$\text{Fixed asset turnover} = \frac{\text{Sales}}{\text{Net fixed assets}}$
	$\text{Total asset turnover} = \frac{\text{Sales}}{\text{Total assets}}$
Cost structure ratios	$\text{Gross profit margin} = \frac{\text{Sales less cost of sales}}{\text{Sales}}$
	$\text{Selling expense ratio} = \frac{\text{Selling expense}}{\text{Sales}}$
	$\text{General cost ratio} = \frac{\text{General and admin. costs}}{\text{Sales}}$
	$\text{Depreciation plus Lease and Rental costs ratio} = \frac{\text{Depreciation plus Lease and Rental costs}}{\text{Sales}}$
Leverage ratios	$\text{Leverage ratio} = \frac{\text{Total debt}}{\text{Total assets}}$
	$\text{Fixed charge coverage ratio} = \frac{\text{Income available for meeting fixed charges}}{\text{Fixed charges}}$
	$\text{Before-tax income required for sinking final payment} = \frac{\text{Sinking final payment}}{1.0 - \text{Tax rate}}$
Liquidity ratios	$\text{Current ratio} = \frac{\text{Current assets}}{\text{Current liabilities}}$
	$\text{Working capital} = \text{Current assets} - \text{Current liabilities}$
	$\text{Quick ratio} = \frac{\text{Current assets} - \text{Inventories}}{\text{Current liabilities}}$
Profitability ratios	$\text{Profit margin on Gross revenue} = \frac{\text{Net income}}{\text{Gross revenue}}$
	$\text{Return on investment} = \frac{\text{Net income} + \text{Interest}}{\text{Total assets}}$
	$\text{Return on net worth} = \frac{\text{Net income}}{\text{Net worth}}$

Table 3.3 Cause and effect ratios

Ratio group	Component ratios
Causal ratios	Inventory turnover $= \dfrac{\text{Net sales}}{\text{Inventory}}$
	Profit objective $= \dfrac{\text{Net profits}}{\text{Net sales}}$
	Recurables analysis $= \dfrac{\text{Current accounts recurable}}{\text{Longest credit terms}}$
	Use of capital $= \dfrac{\text{Fixed assets}}{\text{Net worth}}$
	Trading ratio $= \dfrac{\text{Net sales}}{\text{Net worth}}$
	Evaluation of assets classification $= \dfrac{\text{Miscellaneous assets}}{\text{Net worth}}$
Effect ratios	Current ratio $= \dfrac{\text{Current assets}}{\text{Current liabilities}}$
	Current liability ratio $= \dfrac{\text{Current liabilities}}{\text{Net worth}}$
	Total liability ratio $= \dfrac{\text{Total liabilities}}{\text{Net worth}}$
	Inventory ratio $= \dfrac{\text{Inventory}}{\text{Working capital}}$
	Receivable ratio $= \dfrac{\text{Trade receivable}}{\text{Working capital}}$
	Long-term liabilities ratio $= \dfrac{\text{Long-term liabilities}}{\text{Working capital}}$
	Net profit ratio $= \dfrac{\text{Net profit}}{\text{Net worth}}$
	Net sales ratio 1 $= \dfrac{\text{Net sales}}{\text{Fixed assets}}$
	Net sales ratio 2 $= \dfrac{\text{Net sales}}{\text{Working capital}}$

for the general economic environment. It may be that different weighting factors can be accepted in a time of deep recession and that there could be some flexibility in the 1.8 score.

For a new company without any trading record a detailed business plan would be called for and the proprietor's experience, capability and background investigated. In both the case of a new small company and a trading small company a bank is likely to call for some kind of security or guarantee for any loan it makes. The security may be: deposit of shares, a life insurance policy or call on the proprietor's property. Also the bank will expect to be kept informed about the company's trading performance. The loan contract will generally be such that if the company starts to perform in an unsatisfactory way the bank may call in the loan. It is easy to envisage that in some cases calling in a loan may force a company into liquidation. The problem for a bank is that it may not be in close enough contact with a company to know exactly when it is approaching a crisis in its financial affairs. As already suggested, credit rating systems may not tell the whole story, as they may not be adjusted to the circumstances of the particular company or proposer.

With large companies, that is companies who employ more than 500 people or have a turnover of more than £20 million, the risk problems are more complex. In the case of lending to governments these problems are even larger. Large companies tend to have assets they can offer as security for loans. Governments justify their creditworthiness by being backed by the wealth of the nation. But as will be shown immediately below, confidence in the assets of a company may prove to be useless as may be the value of the security a government gives for a loan. The justification for this scepticism is well illustrated by the series of dramatic bankruptcies that took place in the early 1990s. Some were due to falling property values which resulted in a reduction of the value of property-based securities given for loans. An important consequence of the reduction in the value of securities deposited as guarantees for loans was that banks wanted to reduce the loan facility they provided so that the loan was more closely equated with the value of the security. Another cause was that due to the recession turnover fell and some companies were unable to keep up interest and loan repayments. In cases where debt rescheduling could not be arranged liquidation was often the result.

SWISS ASSESSMENT OF RISKS IN LENDING TO FOREIGN COUNTRIES

Sometimes people have a view that a country would not default on paying the interest on a loan or repaying a loan by the due date. Such a view is seriously wrong. As mentioned in Chapter 1, debt rescheduling has increased dramatically since 1979 and has seriously disturbed world capital flows. In the past, wars and revolutions have often given governments an excuse to completely default on loans.

To demonstrate how careful a bank has to be in determining the acceptability of making loans the Swiss Bank Corporation's Country Risk Assessment procedure will now be described. The specially interesting feature of this procedure is the extensive range of factors it takes into account. The list of factors identified is intended to include all those that influence a borrower's ability to repay a loan. These factors are relevant for large companies as well as countries. There are five main parts to the assessment of each country (Junge, 1988):

1. examine the history of the domestic economy and from this examination assess its outlook;
2. examine the history of the external economy and from this examination assess its outlook;

3. examine the history of the country's debt characteristics and from this examination assess the outlook for this debt;
4. assess the political risk, unemployment and per capita growth;
5. based on the data collected and the views formed arrive at a judgement about risk potential, from the bank's point of view, of the country being considered.

Each of the five parts covers several topics, each of which is an important indicator in its own right. The domestic economy part could equally well be described as the assessment of the performance indicators as they indicate the economic and structural strengths of a country. Under this heading are included:

1. % real gross national product (GDP) growth over 12 months adjusted for inflation;
2. investment ratio % investment/GDP;
3. investment efficiency, i.e.

   $$\frac{\text{\% GDP growth (3 year average)}}{\text{Investment ratio (item 2)}};$$
4. % inflation;
5. % growth in money supply;
6. % real domestic credit creation;
7. % fiscal balance/GDP.

The external economy part of the assessment deals with the influence of the world market conditions. Under this heading are included:

- competitiveness index
- trade balance
- exports
- imports
- current account balance
- exports/GDP
- export concentration
- imports from Switzerland

The last item is specific to the interests of a Swiss financial institution and could easily be changed to imports from the country considering financial involvement with the country being assessed.

Assessment of the debt characteristics of a country takes into account total external debt (public and private), internal reserves (excluding gold), external debt service, external debt/exports, external debt service/exports, interest-adjusted current account/interest payments, international reserves/imports.

Assessment of the political/social factors, which form the fourth group of factors, involves qualitative data to a much greater extent than with the other factors. Consequently judgements about the significance of the factors must, to a very large extent, be subjective. The way the assessment of political and social factors is made in the Swiss Bank Corporation's Country Risk Assessment is analogous to the way socio-political factors are assessed in the Risk Ranking Technique described in Chapter 1. In the Country Risk Assessment the evaluation of political/social factors takes account of:

1. the character of the political system and political institutions as well as of the governments' control mechanisms;
2. the social and political conflicts between different population groups, caused by economic, religious or ethnic factors, or by language differences;
3. the existence of alternative governments or opposition movements, evaluation of their goals and importance;
4. relations with neighbouring countries and trading partners;
5. the strategic importance of the country;
6. international integration of the country.

The political and social stability is rated on a scale of 1 to 10, with 1 being the low-risk end of the scale. The scores are divided into four categories (or ranks) as shown in Table 3.4. Western democracies typically justify a Rank 1.

An example of the application of the Country Risk Assessment procedure to a fictitious country and based on invented numbers is given in Appendix 2. The assessment demonstrates how the conclusions are based on the data from several years. The estimate for 1988 and the outlook are summarized in Table 3.5. Despite the explicit forecast horizon being limited to about one and a half years the Country Risk Assessment procedure does give an overall picture of a country's economic stability and by implication it gives an indication of creditworthiness of a country. The value of the indication of creditworthiness of a country is dependent on the quality of the data available and in this context the Bank recognizes the importance of the evidence collected by their own staff with experience of the country involved.

The Bank also recognizes that Country Risk Assessment can only be part of the management apparatus of risk management. The assessment techniques have their natural limitations as, to a certain extent, future events are always uncertain. A prudent bank's approach to managing the risks inherent in its loan portfolio will be to diversify its loan portfolio in such a way that the bank can deal with unlikely or unforeseen events. The logical structure of the Country Risk Assessment procedure can provide an insight into the relative merits of the various loan portfolio strategy options available.

The Swiss Bank keeps the efficacy of the assessment process under review and refine it iteratively as found necessary.

Table 3.4 Political and social stability categories (or ranks)

Category or rank	Risk assessment	Rating score
1	Practically nil/low	1–3
2	Acceptable	4–6
3	High	7–9
4	Clearly excessive	10

Table 3.5 Summary of Country Risk Assessment for a fictitious country

Group	Indicators	Estimate 1988	Outlook 1989
Domestic economy	Real GDP growth %	–3.2	1.5
	Investment GDP (international average 25%)	14.7	Improving
	Investment efficiency (critical level < 0.2)	–0.11	Unchanged
	Inflation %	18.2	Improving
	Money supply growth %	9.8	Unchanged
	Real domestic credit creation %	–9.4	Up
	Fiscal balance/GDP %	–1.7	Deteriorating
External economy	Competitiveness index (1980 = 100)	80	Improving
	Trade balance (goods)	–0.80	Improving
	Exports (goods and services)	9.1	Improving
	Imports (goods and services)	10.3	Up
	Current account balance	–0.9	Improving
	Exports/GDP %	23	Unchanged
	Export concentration	35	Unchanged
	Imports from Switzerland	105	Improving
Debt characteristics	Total external debt (public and private)	28	Deteriorating
	International reserves excluding gold	1	Improving
	External debt service	3.4	Deteriorating
	External debt/exports (critical level > 150%)	308	Improving
	External debt service/exports (critical level > 25%)	37.3	Improving
	Interest adjusted current account/interest payments	67	Improving
	International reserves/imports	1.2	Improving
Socio-political factors	Political risk (on a 10-point rating score)	6	Unchanged
	Recorded unemployment rate	13.5	Unchanged
	Per capita GDP growth	–5.5	–0.8

Over the years the number of parameters included in the Country Risk Assessment Process has been increased from 20 to 25. The assessment process is only applied to large countries, as the Bank's loans exposure with small countries is not considered to be a problem. The Bank considers that critically monitoring the economic characteristics of a country for several years gives them a good indication of the creditworthiness of that country.

When a risk assessment report is presented to the Executive Management it is accompanied by a two-page brief which draws attention to the findings of the assessment report and advises the executive on the creditworthiness of the country involved. (The structure of the executive brief is described in Appendix 3.)

More recently the Swiss Bank has developed a version of its country risk procedure to focus specifically on assessing the creditworthiness of industrial countries (Junge and Schieler, 1993). In this version 30 parameters are considered, grouped under five headings: fundamentals, external sector, public sector, business sector and political risk. The incentive for this development came from the recent worsening of the external indebtedness of formerly well-positioned countries.

An example of the procedure for assessment of creditworthiness of industrial countries is given in Appendix 2, from which the influence of the original country risk assessment methodology can be seen. The emphasis given to: invisible balance, public foreign debt and business sector parameters is important. Evaluation of political risk is included in both assessment procedures. The five parameters identified as representing the business sector include corporate profit growth, business failures and household financial liabilities/income.

When finance for a major project is considered the acceptability of the proposal is assessed by the Bank's project finance group. In such an assessment the creditworthiness of the sponsors of the project is assessed. The assessment would take into account the experience of the sponsors in handling similar projects. For an assessment of the acceptability of the technical issues involved the Bank tends to use consultants.

SWISS ASSESSMENT OF THE INVESTMENT RISK OF A COMPANY

Another assessment process that is relevant to the discussion in this chapter is the way the Swiss Bank Corporation assesses the performance of leading Swiss firms to determine the nature of the risks associated with investing in them. To assist investors in public companies the Bank publishes an annual review of about 50 parameters, which they consider to be the essential indicators of the performance of leading Swiss firms (Swiss Bank Corporation, 1991). In the review no single parameter is identified as giving an adequate indication of performance. Instead the significance of the data is ranked on a scale from A to C under three headings: historical performance, dividend policy and transparency. Other somewhat similar share or bond rating systems are Standard and Poor's and Moody's. Standard and Poor ratings range from AAA down to D (Thornhill, 1990). But they do not overtly allow for transparency in the same way that the Swiss Bank rating method does. Recent major company collapses show how important it is for analysts and investors to understand the transparency of the figures they are presented with. For example, reading the annual report of the Bank of Credit Commerce International from the year before they went bankrupt it would be impossible to detect that the company were moving rapidly towards bankruptcy.

COMPARISON OF THE SWISS BANK'S AND BRITISH BANKS' RISK ASSESSMENT PRACTICES

To investigate to what extent the Swiss Bank's practices have features similar to British banks' these are now compared with those of two British banks, Lloyds and National Westminster.

The procedures Lloyds Bank uses for assessing the risks involved in lending to foreign countries include assessment of the characteristics of the country involved. Also the Bank assesses any proposal against its exposure limit, which is the amount they are willing to lend to that country. The indicators the Bank uses are a combination of judgemental and statistical indicators. The judgemental indicators are more forward looking: these attempt to assess a country's performance in qualitative terms and to actually attach scores to the qualitative judgements so that they end up with an ordinal measure of performance. The statistical scoring system is based on statistics of the past five years. They do not attempt to draw up statistical indicators based on judgements about the future. Such an approach could develop into a guessing game, where those bankers who wish to justify lending money to a country will come up with an optimistic statistical score based on their glorious vision of the country's future as an exporter of tin, or whatever it might be. Equally pessimistic sceptical economists could give a low score.

The judgemental factors are listed in Table 3.6 together with their scoring structure. The statistical factors and their scoring structure are listed in Table 3.7. The score range allocated to each factor reflects the weighting each factor is considered to warrant. To arrive at an overall index number the statistical and judgemental ratings are summed, the totals multiplied together and the product divided by 100; the practical reason, given by the Bank, for multiplying the total figures together is to amplify differences in scores to facilitate comparison. For specific problems other factors like primary surplus and debt service may be studied.

As with the Swiss Bank Corporation the advice Lloyds Credit Department passes to the executive is a brief based on their ranking of the risk indicators considered to be associated with a particular proposal. Attention is drawn to the fact that Lloyds rank risk factors while the Swiss Bank Corporation simply assesses each factor in qualitative terms such as improving or deteriorating.

It should also be noted that for general credit assessment Lloyds Bank has considered using a variation developed from the Bank of England's scheme for weighting the significance of various types of assets (see Appendix 1). A simplified description of the scheme is given in Table 3.8 and consists of scoring assets for rewards and significant risks on a two-point system, 0 for bad or neutral rewards and risks, and 1 for good rewards or risks (Johnson, 1985).

In the second part of the table, the scores that it is considered certain activities justify are described. In the schedule, retail lending is given a reward score of 1 while wholesale activities are given a score of 0. In comparing government lending with private sector lending the reward is assumed to be higher for the private sector. Lending to governments is considered to be lower risk than lending to the private sector so it gets a higher ranking score. For both domestic and foreign lending there is no special reward, but generally banks regard the risk of domestic lending

Table 3.6 Lloyds Country Risk Analysis judgemental factors and scoring structure

	Country Risk Analysis		
A	*Domestic economic policy*	*Maximum*	
1	Coherence of policy	5	
2	Business climate	5	
3	Stability of policy	5	
4	Quality of bureaucracy	5	
			20
B	*External economic policy*		
1	Debt management	10	
2	Handling of liquidity crises	5	
3	Management of exchange rate	5	
4	Management of trade policy	5	
5	Investment policy	5	
			30
C	*Political characteristics*		
1	Durability	10	
2	Effectiveness	10	
3	International position	5	
			25
D	*Political stability*		
1	Risk of local war	10	
2	Risk of violent revolution	10	
3	Political social tensions	5	
			25
	Grand total – maximum		100

as less than that of foreign lending as they tend to know more about their home market than they do about foreign markets. Both wholesale and retail business can be associated with government, private domestic and foreign types of activity. This gives an eight by six matrix as shown in the bottom of Table 3.8. The matrix shows the most acceptable ranking is with domestic retail lending, whether to the public or the private sector. The lowest ranking of 1 goes to wholesale lending to foreigners, whether governments or private borrowers. Everything else gets a medium ranking of 2, but that is based on different combinations of activities.

The National Westminster has for many years used a method of scoring to rank the economic and socio-political factors that influence the acceptability of credit risks. The Bank's representatives abroad are considered important sources of information on which to base their ranking of risk associated with credit to foreign countries. In project financing the National Westminster has among other projects been involved in the arrangements for financing the Channel Tunnel project, which was outlined in Chapter 1. Other large projects the Bank has been involved in financing include the coking coal mines in Queensland, Australia, the Hemlo Gold Mine in Canada, Howden Wind Parks in the USA, Dowington Waste Water Treatment plant in the USA and the Forties, Balmoral and Alwyn North fields in the North Sea. In assessing the acceptability of a project, the Bank assesses the technical, economic and political risks.

Table 3.7 Lloyds' Country Risk Analysis statistical factors and scoring structure

1	GNP per capita (range US$0–10,000)	10 (1 point = $1000)
2	Real GDP, annual growth rate of the last five years (range 0–5%)	10 (1 point = 1/2%)
3	Gross domestic investment as % of GDP (range 10–30%)	10 (1 point = 2% over 10%)
4	Export growth in US$, annual average 1980–84 (range 0–20%)	10 (1 point = 2%)
5	Export variability score Measured by the coefficient of variation (CV) of exports of the last ten years (range 0.4–0.1)	10 (1 point = 0.03)
6	Inflation rate over the last five years (range 50–0%)	10 (1 point = 5%)
7	Debt service/foreign exchange receipts (range 50–0%)	10 (1 point = 5%)
8	Interest service/foreign exchange receipts (range 20–0%)	10 (1 point = 2%)
9	Debt/GNP (range 100–0%)	10 (1 point = 10%)
10	Debt/foreign exchange receipts (range 400–0%)	10 (1 point = 40%)
	Total	100

In assessing the technical acceptability, account is taken of the proposer's capability and experience in dealing successfully with projects of a similar nature. For assessing many projects the Bank has its own 'in-house' specialists in many fields, for example, in the oil, gas and mining industries. The Special Financial Services Group which includes project finance, financial engineering and syndication teams has 80 specialists. But for assessing projects outside the capability of the Bank's own experts the Bank employs independent outside consultants with the appropriate skills.

In assessing the economic risks the Bank pays attention, among other things, to: the possibility of cost overruns, adequacy of reserve, inflation influence on operating costs and market and price fluctuations.

In assessing political risks attention is given to both fiscal and non-fiscal risks.

It appears that the National Westminster methods bear at least a superficial resemblance to the methods used by the Swiss Bank Corporation and Lloyds.

CONCLUSIONS

The conclusions that this examination of financial institutions' risk assessment practices appears to justify are:

1. There are formal external regulatory controls on the amount of financial risk financial institutions can accept.

Table 3.8 Ranking system factors considered by Lloyds Bank

A risk–reward matrix

The scoring system used

Rewards:	0 bad or neutral, 1 good
Risks:	0 bad or neutral, 1 good

Scoring schedule of representative categories of activity

Activity	Reward	Risk
Wholesale (W)	0	0
Retail (R)	1	0
Government (G)	0	1
Private (P)	1	0
Domestic (D)	0	1
Foreign (F)	0	0

Matrix of scores

Loan	Activity characteristics		Reward	Scores risks	Total
R	G	D	1	2	3
R	P	D	2	1	3
R	G	F	1	1	2
R	P	F	2	0	2
W	G	D	0	2	2
W	P	D	1	1	2
W	G	F	0	1	1
W	P	F	1	0	1

2. Banks do not share a common set of quantitative criteria by which they judge acceptability of risks.
3. There is considerable variety in the methods banks use internally to assess the acceptability of risks. In all cases the executive making the decision about the acceptability of a loan is allowed a larger degree of personal judgement.
4. Banks concentrate on assessing the economic aspects of risk.
5. Although banks are involved in assessing the acceptability of the technical, economic and socio-political aspects of proposals they do not attempt to make a unified comprehensive assessment of the acceptability in terms of these three factors in the same way the Risk Ranking Technique does.
6. The diversity of risk factors that banks consider in assessing the acceptability of proposals gives a clear illustration of problems of finding a single indicator of the stability of the economic environment surrounding a proposal, which all decision makers should use.
7. The value of a decision based on a presentation that obscures the truth is of doubtful value. The importance of the information on which investment decisions are made being transparent is recognized in the Swiss Bank's method of rating for investment purposes the quality of a company's performance.

4 THEORETICAL CONSIDERATIONS

❑ SUMMARY

The concerns about the theoretical justifiability of the methods proposed for making a comprehensive assessment of the acceptability of the risks associated with a proposal are examined. Particular attention is given regarding how to allow for uncertainty in the data that have to be used.

THE NATURE OF THEORETICAL CONSIDERATIONS

In the discussion so far there has been no attempt to justify the decision processes in theoretical terms, as the presentation has been somewhat pragmatic and concentrated on the practical problems associated with assessing risk acceptability. In this chapter an attempt is made to redress the balance by critically examining the extent to which the construction of a decision-making system can be justified in theoretical terms. In this case the phrase 'theoretical terms' is intended to define a form of reasoning that has the same precision that arithmetic has for processes involving numbers, or that geometric analysis has for processes describing lines (Schmucker, 1984). This examination of the quality of the theoretical justification really acts as a prelude to the discussion in later chapters of the problems of making a detailed assessment of a proposal and the alternative methods that may be used.

The starting point for this examination is recognition of the fact that any comprehensive assessment of the decision options has to take account of the technical, economic and socio-political factors. The central concerns are: how to weight the significance of the factors and how to structure in a logically defensible way the analysis of a complex mixture of qualitative and quantitative data.

Essentially the aim of any method of assessing decision options is to help the decision maker determine which decision option is most likely to successfully satisfy requirements. In constructing the assessment of a particular decision option it is assumed that any factor related to the decision making can be categorized under one of three headings, which are: technical (T), economic (E) and socio-political (S). The acceptability of each factor is scored in some way against specified criteria, the overall acceptability being determined by integrating the scores of the factors T, E and S. The integrated scores determine how the acceptability of each option can be categorized. Knowledge of each factor is likely to be imperfect, so a degree of uncertainty must be attached to each score.

THE NATURE OF THEORETICAL CONCERNS

In Table 4.1 the nature of the theoretical concerns about seven aspects of the ranking process is identified. With aspect 1 the concern is whether or not T, E and S adequately describe all the topics that should be considered. This concern has its origins in the suspicion that T, E and S may not, due to limitations on the data available, give a comprehensive description of the options to be considered. The data that have to be used for decision making can never be perfect and completely comprehensive. In the real world, particularly when the proposal being considered is novel, there will be uncertainty about the evidence, a topic that is returned to later, in the discussion of aspect 7 in Table 4.1.

The adequacy of the comprehensive description of an option depends on the way T, E and S are defined. The definition of the factors will have to be adjusted to suit the characteristics of each family of decisions considered. With the T and E factors there can be a certain amount of confidence that they can be adequately described in quantitative terms. The quantification of the evidence may be soft, nevertheless the criteria for judging the acceptability of the factor can be expressed in hard or at least firm quantified terms. Then as understanding of the proposal develops the quality of the quantification of the evidence can be improved iteratively. With a novel project it may be that the decision has to be made on the basis of soft data and that it will only be when the project is underway that the required hard data will be generated. The data generated may show that the project is unlikely to be successful and should be abandoned. An unacceptable project is always a possible outcome. The very nature of the S factor makes it the most difficult to deal with in quantitative terms. The criticism that is made of decision-aiding approaches related to the S factor include (Merkhofer, 1987):

1. Ethical considerations may not be adequately allowed for.
2. There may be errors in the logic of the assessment due to the difficulty of defining the optimum decision.
3. The data that have to be used are incomplete.
4. There is bias in the analysis that has to be used due to bias of the analyst.
5. The decision-making environment has changed since the data were collected and analysed.
6. There is a difference between decisions that are forced and democratic decisions which are arrived at by discussion.

SCORING SCALES FOR ACCEPTABILITY

The criticisms identified above should be answered when the criteria for scoring the S factor are constructed. This means the scoring criteria for ranking the significance of the S factor tend only to be constant for a limited family of decisions at a particular time. Changes in the decision-making environment may change the criteria that are required. This limitation is similar to that proposed for the criteria for scoring the acceptability of T and E. In other words there will be no direct comparability of ranking between families of decisions using different ranking criteria.

Table 4.1 Summary of theoretical concerns about ranking procedures

Aspect No.	Aspect description	Theoretical concerns
1	Identification of factors T, E and S	Do these factors adequately represent all the issues that a decision maker should consider?
2	Identification of ranking steps and scores for each factor	How many ranks/steps should there be and how should the steps be defined? How should scores be related to ranks?
3	Identify criteria for scoring factors	On what features of the factors should the scoring criteria be based?
4	Identify weighting of significance of each factor	How should the significance of one factor compared to another be related?
5	Identify basis for combining factors	Should the overall significance of the factors be considered as being the sum or product of the factors or should they be combined in other ways?
6	Combine weighted scores to give overall weighting	Does the overall ranking adequately represent an assessment of the options before the decision maker or is there some bias in the overall ranking?
7	Influence that uncertainty about the data and methodology used can have on the ranking	As with any estimate there will be uncertainty about the significance of the numbers used. How the uncertainty should be treated needs justification. Can the consideration given to evaluating uncertainty be related to the size of the decision and the novelty of the decision?

But it does not reduce the comparability of ranking within a family of decisions in which each decision is based on exactly the same criteria.

Perhaps the most important feature that the criticisms draw attention to is the need for the analyst who is ranking the decision options to have an understanding of the ethical implications of the decision options.

The second aspect in Table 4.1 raises questions about how scoring scales should be related to the acceptability criteria. The central question is: how should the scoring scale for ranking acceptability be designed? It is considered the ranking steps should be sufficient to show something of the shades of acceptability in the decision options and not simply categorize the options as acceptable or not acceptable. Equally it is considered that there should not be so many steps in the ranking that the credibility of the data, on which the ranking would have to be based, would be stretched too far. It is suggested that four ranking steps would give an adequate description of the shades of acceptability of the various options open to the decision maker. An even number of steps is suggested to overcome the temptation for the analyst to use the neutral middle rank as being a safe, neutral, non-committal judgement. Some confidence in the acceptability of such a design is given by the fact that it is similar to the pattern of risk ranks Lord Ashby proposed in his definitive study of the acceptability of environmental risks (Ashby, 1978). In the scoring scale there should be sufficient difference between the steps in the scale to prevent an adverse ranking of one factor being masked. A scale such as 1, 2, 5, 14 would avoid an adverse score for one factor being masked. Further discussion of the theoretical considerations influencing the designs of ranking scales is given in Appendix 4.

CRITERIA FOR SCORING SCALES FOR ACCEPTABILITY

What has just been said about the design of the ranking scales underlines the importance of careful specification of the criteria for scoring. In Chapters 5, 6 and 7 the basis for scoring the acceptability of T, E and S factors is explored in some detail and at this point in the study it is only necessary to make some philosophic points about the nature of ideal scoring criteria. With each factor there is a tremendous range of topics to be considered. Simply defining criteria in natural language terms like: not acceptable, acceptable and very acceptable would give criteria that are too soft. Such natural language terms have to be supplemented by some quantitative statements that relate to technical and economic performance and to socio-political acceptability.

The criteria, identified in the later chapters, for T and E factors seem to adequately relate acceptability to quantitative evidence. This does not mean that the criteria cannot be improved. For example, the technical criteria could specifically relate the ranking score to the probability of a successful outcome. Similarly, the E factor criteria could be adjusted to include calculation of the rate of return on the total through-life investment that takes account of all the risks involved.

The problem of identifying suitable criteria for S factors is more open to criticism. Merkhofer has stated the position in the following terms:

> There exists no currently available decision-aiding approach for social risk decisions that is free from criticism. Furthermore, available approaches have different strengths and weaknesses. It is not possible, therefore, to identify any specific approach as in any absolute sense the 'best'.

Given that the decision maker has to make a decision he/she has to find some way of evaluating the significance of an S factor regardless of the possible criticism. A starting assumption for the criteria designer must be that everyone concerned or in any way associated with the proposal will be aware of the content of the proposal and the implications of the proposal in S factor terms. Also it is assumed that the decision making takes place in a democratic society, where everyone is free to express their opinion and attention is paid to the laws of the land. The details of the democratic processes vary from country to country. Examples of the variation in democratic processes are: frequent use of referenda in Switzerland and the frequent use of public inquiries in Britain. The possible uses of such processes have to be considered as ways of determining the acceptability of S factors in decisions. It would be misleading to suggest that acceptability in S factor terms could be judged precisely from the outcome of referenda or public inquiries. Such a view would completely ignore the continuous influence of pressure groups in a democratic society. The influence of pressure groups on policy development has been examined by Chicken (Chicken, 1975 and 1982), so all that need be said here is that there are factors whose impact has to be allowed for in determining the acceptability of an S factor.

Central to determination of public opinion about a proposal is the fact that the public must be informed about the nature of the proposal. In some countries the need for the public to be informed about some risks is entrenched in the law (Stallen and Coppack, 1987). For example, the European Commission has passed a Directive which states:

> Member states shall ensure that persons liable to be affected by a major accident originating in a notified industrial activity . . . are informed in an appropriate manner of the safety measures and of the correct behaviour to adopt in the event of an accident.

In a similar vein the US Congress enacted an emergency planning and community right to know Act. In general, the public have rights to object to applications for planning approval. The extent to which such rights are used varies from application to application and from country to country. From the above it is suggested that the criteria for ranking the significance of the S factor should be based on an assessment of the acceptability of the proposal to the public who will be at risk from implementation of the proposal. This leaves open the question of how the public's opinion is measured. In some cases sampling might be appropriate, and in other cases voting. (Criteria for ranking S factors are discussed in detail in Chapter 7.) With the S factor, more than with any other, the data on which the assessment are based are likely to change with time. Public opinion is fickle. Even a comprehensive assessment will only be valid for the time at which it is made; it will not indicate the changes in opinion that pressure group influence brings about in the future.

This survey of the form that criteria for ranking the acceptability of risk could take has shown they have to cover a very wide range of characteristics. The possibility of identifying criteria that would be satisfactory in all decision-making situations seems remote and not a goal worth pursuing. It appears more practical to identify the criteria for particular families of decisions. Such an approach would mean that it will only be possible to compare accurately the significance of decisions within a particular family of decisions. Comparison of the acceptability of risks between families of risks could be made, subject to some correlation factor being used to take account of the different principles on which the criteria were based. However, consistency in the logic of ranking decision options should improve the consistency of the quality of decision making. In Table 4.2 the general principles on which the criteria could be based are summarized.

WEIGHTING, COMBINING AND OVERALL RANKING FACTORS

The fourth, fifth and sixth theoretical aspects of the ranking risks are critical as they relate to how the significance of the three factors T, E and S are weighted and combined. Ideally the ranking would be applied only when the detailed assessment of T, E and S is complete. In practice the decision might have to be made before the detailed assessments are complete, but there may be opportunities for iteratively refining ranking as better information becomes available. There will always be a degree of uncertainty associated with the characteristics of each factor, but that is a slightly different problem and one that is returned to in discussion of aspect 7.

The design of the analytical process should be such that T, E and S factors are treated equally, thus avoiding the need to consider their being assessed in some

Table 4.2 Summary of the principles on which criteria for ranking risk should be based

Factor	Principles	Typical forms
Technical	Technical performance required, stated in quantitative terms. These requirements would include customer and statutory requirements	Technical evaluation of the operational life of the project. An assessment of the consequencces of the project failing to achieve its objective. An assessment of the capability of those who will implement proposals
Economic	For commercial projects acceptability should be expressed as a rate of return that takes into account the risks involved. For projects of a social welfare nature the benefit of the expenditure should be compared with the benefits of alternative expenditure	A quantitative assessment of the likely through-life investment required and the return on investment. The assessment would include a statement of the associated uncertainty
Socio-political	The criteria for assessing acceptability of socio-political factors should take account of the extent to which the exposed population understand the risk they are exposed to and the way in which they have been able to express their views about the acceptability of the risk	A survey of public opinion on the proposal, or the findings of a public inquiry into the proposal, or the result of a relevant referendum

preferred hierarchical order. It is implicit in such an approach that the relationship between the factors is assumed to be recursive, that is, there is no direct or indirect feedback between the factors. It is accepted that recursive relationships between the factors may be considered unrealistic and too rigid (Hilton, 1976). The recursive nature of the relationship assumed is justified by the fact that each decision factor considered is defined as being the end product of an iterative assessment process, in which the nature of each factor is explored and interactions between the factors and sub-factors are analysed in order to determine optimum relationships. In other words, before the ranking process starts the proposer will have determined what he/she considers to be the optimum relationship between the various factors related to the proposal.

Given that the ranking factors are specified as being independent and have to be assessed simultaneously the question that has to be answered is 'Should the factors be treated as having equal significance?'. To a certain extent the answer depends on the circumstances in which the decision has to be made. For example, in a state-controlled organization it is possible to envisage that the socio-political factor would predominate, as the Minister who is ultimately responsible for the organization may consider that the appropriateness of the decision to the current political climate is of overriding importance. In a similar way, in wartime the Prime Minister may consider technical developments that would improve the chances of winning the war many times more important than economic considerations. In free enterprise business situations there is some justification for assuming that the three factors are of equal weight. The justification for this view is that: unless the proposal is technically sound it will not be an acceptable business proposition; unless the proposal is economically sound it cannot be accepted; and if the proposal is not acceptable in socio-political terms it would not be worth pursuing. The way the scoring system is designed should ensure that if one factor is given an 'unlikely to be acceptable' score the total score of the proposal will be in the unlikely to be acceptable range. The conclusion that seems to be warranted is that for free enterprise business decisions allocating the three ranking factors equal weight is likely to be acceptable. However, for each application the appropriateness of the weighting scheme should be assessed.

Equal weighting of factors implies that they should be combined in an equal way. Adding the scores together to determine the overall ranking does not interfere with the concept of equality of each factor. If the factors' scores are combined by multiplying them together, certainly the numbers produced would be larger. For example, a simple 1, 2, 5, 14 scale would give total scores ranging from 1 to 2744 if the scores are multiplied as compared with 3 to 42 if they are added. Complicating the pattern of the rank scores does not appear to endow the ranking with any unique properties, but tends to destroy the simplicity of the scheme.

Accepting the justification for the weighting, and combination of the factors just given means the overall ranking score is a simple arithmetic operation. But simply performing the arithmetical operation does not answer the question of whether or not the ranking obtained gives the decision maker sufficient information about the merits of the various options. At least ranking gives a comparison of the options as measured by the values of T, E and S. The comparison is made in a logical and consistent way. One possible weakness of ranking is that it does not present any overt discussion of the strength of demand for the proposal. The adequacy of demand should in practice be tested in building up the assessment of E and to a lesser extent for assessment of the S factor. Calculating E requires that the rate of return on investment is determined. In order to calculate a rate of return the pattern of demand has to be determined, so the adequacy of the rate of return reflects the adequacy of the demand. S gives a measure of public support for or opposition to the proposal, which is not quite the same as measuring demand. However, support will suggest there is likely to be demand in economic terms. But the opposite is not necessarily true. Opposition may be local and not related to the main centre of demand. This draws attention to the importance of carefully assessing public opinion for determining the value of S. An example of understanding the importance of determining the relevance of measurements of public opinion is given by the opposition to the siting of the rail links and terminals for the Channel Tunnel. The opposition is mainly local and related to problems that can be overcome. Such opposition does not damage the usefulness of ranking but rather underlines the importance of a decision-making aid or procedure-making allowance for the impact of public opinion.

UNCERTAINTY OF ASSESSMENT

The concern about uncertainty mentioned in aspect 7 has implications for all aspects of assessing decision options. In the case of T factors for novel projects there will be considerable uncertainty about predictions of performance and reliability. Only when experience from the completed project is available will it be possible to validate the pre-decision predictions. In such cases T will have been calculated on the basis of advice from the best experts in the field. There is always an option of not making a decision because the evidence is inadequate. But if the chance of making progress is to be taken then the only course is to base the decision on expert opinion. The uncertainty in T will also generate uncertainty in E and S or, put another way, when there is a lack of good quantitative evidence on which to base the evaluation of T the uncertainty in estimating E and S will be proportionately larger. This is in slight conflict with the assumption made earlier, of the factors being recursive. It would be more precise to say that: by taking account of the uncertainty associated with T, E and S a degree of non-recursiveness is introduced into their characteristics. Certainly the ranking of options is only as good as the data on which it is based. Ordering the decision options available by ranking may not be the only way of presenting the options to the decision maker, but the method is honest, transparent and logical. For many decision-making situations the method should at least give a useful representation of the options available.

In applying ranking it is important to assess the significance of the uncertainties in the data that have to be used. This is perhaps no more than saying that, as with any piece of analysis, a sensitivity analysis should be performed to determine by how much assumptions must change to make a proposition unacceptable (Rosenhead, 1989). The data available for ranking will vary considerably from project to project, the accuracy being highest when the project is one of a series about which a comprehensive dossier of accurate information has been built up. At the other end of the scale when a project is novel and untested the uncertainty associated with the data will be considerable. The difficulties associated with a novel project must be tackled if progress is to be made. In the technical field some industries, like the aircraft and pharmaceutical industries, lay down detailed testing programmes that have to be followed to determine the acceptability of new products.

With a novel untested project, for which there are no quantitative data, assessment of acceptability has, at least initially, to be based on data derived from expert opinion. The uncertainties associated with such assessment are larger when opinions are collected in an unstructured way than when they are collected in a carefully designed way. In Appendix 6, some general rules are given that should be followed if uncertainty in deriving data from expert opinions is to be minimized.

It has been suggested (Chicken and Hayns, 1989) that, in complex cases where there are several options to consider and an identifiable degree of uncertainty, it may be helpful to display the options on a variation of Buckley's decision or pay off matrix (Buckley, 1986). Figure 4.1 shows this form of presentation for a case where there are four design options and four possible levels of investment – in other words a matrix of sixteen options. From the figure it can be seen that nine of the assumed options are acceptable with some adjustment and one of the four design options D_4 is acceptable without restriction even with the minimum investment level I_1. It is assumed that the rankings shown in the matrix are comprehensive rankings taking fully into account assessment of T, E and S. Figure 4.1 gives the impression that the rankings are absolute and devoid of error; such an impression is misleading. With each factor there will be an associated degree of uncertainty. Taken together these uncertainties will give a range of rankings. Figure 4.2 shows diagrammatically how the upper, mean and low levels of ranking, resulting from taking into account the uncertainty associated with the data that have to be used, can be displayed. In a real life case the proportion of uncertainty associated with each factor may be different. In the hypothetical example displayed at the upper end of the range of data assumed, six of the nine options are acceptable without restriction. At the bottom end of the range of uncertainty two options are unlikely to be acceptable and seven are only acceptable if they can be modified.

The matrix presentations shown in Figures 4.1 and 4.2 are little more than visual aids and do not contribute significantly to the theoretical analysis of the importance of uncertainty in the data. A slightly better way of assessing the sensitivity of the ranking is to examine the consequences of changes in the ranking scores of individual factors. For illustration, a base case is considered in which the T factor is scored 2, the E factor is scored 5 and the S factor is scored 2. Using the ranking scheme mentioned earlier, the score gives the base case a Rank 2, which is acceptable only if the risk can be reduced. If the ranking of the most adversely ranked factor is given a one-rank better ranking, the overall ranking would change from 2 to 3, thus rendering it acceptable, subject to some minor changes. If the ranking of the most adversely ranked factor is given a one-rank worse ranking, it would mean that the whole proposal would be ranked unlikely to be acceptable. As there is no middle or neutral, rank factors are ranked either with a tendency to be acceptable

Investment →
Level increasing

Design options ↑

	I_1	I_2	I_3	I_4
D_4	4	4	4	4
D_3	3	3	4	4
D_2	2	3	3	4
D_1	2	2	2	3

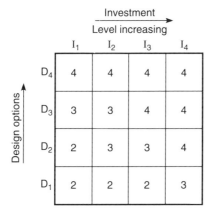

Note: Identification of risk rank:

Rank 1: unlikely to be acceptable
Rank 2: only acceptable if risk can be reduced
Rank 3: yes, subject to detailed adjustments of the proposal being made
Rank 4: acceptable without restriction

Figure 4.1 Matrix display of ranking results.

without restriction (Ranks 3 and 4) or with a tendency to be unlikely to be acceptable (Ranks 1 and 2). The implications of errors in data on ranking are summarized in Table 4.3. From the table it can be seen that an error of one rank may simply overemphasize the tendency of what would be the correct ranking. An error of two or more ranks distorts the overall ranking to the extent that it gives a very misleading indication of acceptability. The ranking concept assumes each rank represents a fairly wide range of data, the implication being that a one-rank error in the assessment of a factor is the most that has to be allowed for.

POSSIBLE APPLICATION OF FUZZY DATA ANALYSIS

Some claims have been made for the efficacy of fuzzy data analysis as a way of developing an understanding of the significance of uncertainty about conclusions that have to be based on data that is complex or ill-defined (Schmucker, 1984). Part of the attraction of fuzzy data analysis is that it offers a way of assessing mathematically a proposition expressed in natural language. When there is a considerable volume of data to be analysed use can be made of computer programs such as the fuzzy risk analysis (FRA) (Schmucker, 1984) or MAFDA (Abdul-Fattah, 1982). (A general description of the nature of fuzzy analysis is given in Appendix 5.)

The critical question is 'How then can the application of the process of fuzzy analysis improve the assessment of decision options in the ranking technique in situations when the assessment has to be based on qualitative data like expert opinion?'.

Essentially the definition of ranks codifies qualitative statements about acceptability. One application of fuzzy analysis could be assessment of the extent to

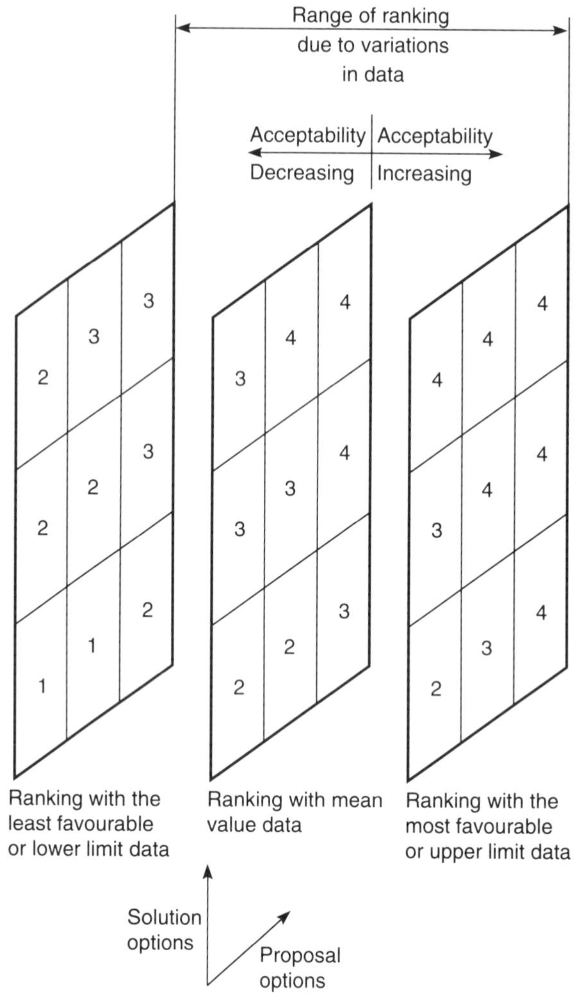
Range of ranking
due to variations
in data
Acceptability
Decreasing
Acceptability
Increasing
3
3
2
3
2
2
2
1
1
4
4
3
4
3
3
3
2
2
4
4
4
4
4
3
4
3
2
Ranking with the
least favourable
or lower limit data
Ranking with mean
value data
Ranking with the
most favourable
or upper limit data
Solution
options
Proposal
options

Note: Identification of risk rank:

Rank 1: unlikely to be acceptable
Rank 2: only acceptable if risk can be reduced
Rank 3: yes, subject to detailed adjustments of the proposal being made
Rank 4: acceptable without restriction

Figure 4.2 Ranking matrix limits.

which expert opinions really fit a particular rank. But it is not immediately clear what advantage fuzzy analysis would have over conventional statistical methods.

A very interesting relevant published demonstration of fuzzy set analysis is the study by Abdul-Fattah and Abulfaraj of the application of fuzzy decision analysis to the selection of sites for nuclear power plants (Abdul-Fattah, 1982). They considered seven main attributes of the possible sites, which were:

1. topography and oceanography;
2. geology, hydrology and seismology;

Table 4.3 Summary of implications of errors or uncertainty in ranking

	Original highest base ranking factor increasing acceptability			
Error in ranking	1	2	3	4
Highest ranked factor reduced by one rank	Not possible. Would stay Rank 1	Becomes unacceptable Rank 1	Becomes acceptable subject to major change Rank 2	Becomes acceptable subject to minor changes Rank 3
Highest ranked factor increased by one rank	Becomes acceptable subject to major changes Rank 2	Becomes acceptable subject to minor changes Rank 3	Becomes acceptable without restriction Rank 4	Not possible. Would stay Rank 4
Highest ranked factor reduced by two ranks	Not possible. Would stay Rank 1	Not possible. Could only become Rank 1	Becomes not acceptable Rank 1	Becomes acceptable with major changes Rank 2
Highest ranked factor increased by two ranks	Becomes acceptable with minor changes Rank 3	Becomes acceptable without restriction Rank 4	Not possible. Could only become Rank 4	Not possible. Could only become Rank 4
Highest ranked factor reduced by three ranks	Not possible. Would stay Rank 1	Not possible. Could only become Rank 1	Not possible. Could only become Rank 1	Becomes not acceptable. Would become Rank 1
Highest ranked factor increased by three ranks	Becomes acceptable Rank 4	Not possible. Could only become Rank 4	Not possible. Could only become Rank 4	Not possible. Would stay Rank 4

3. meteorology;
4. transportation;
5. population;
6. cooling water;
7. construction, services and domestic water.

In addition to the seven main attributes, 35 sub-attributes were considered. The significance of the attributes and sub-attributes were weighted, rated and ranked in terms of preferability. Then from the ranking of the attributes an overall ranking of preferability was deduced. The steps in the process are shown in Figure 4.3. The weighting scale used ranged from 0 to 1 and was related to a membership function (0.0, 0.0), which was the lowest weighting for an attribute considered very unimportant. At the other end of the scale (1.0, 0.0) was the highest rating for an attribute considered very important. The final ranking and degree of preference were calculated using a computer program (MAFDA). For the two sites it was shown that although one site was preferred the degree of preference over the other site was small, which may leave the decision maker with a problem. What the Abdul-Fattah and Abulfaraj study does show is that fuzzy analysis can be used to build up a ranking of acceptability from a qualitative description of its characteristics. This seems an effective use of fuzzy analysis as 42 attributes had to be considered, which makes the analysis required more complex than required for applications of the ranking technique.

Perhaps the most useful role for fuzzy analysis would be in the assessment of all the subsystems that have to be considered to establish the evidence on which the ranking can be based. Particularly suitable occasions are when ranking has to be built up using qualitative data that employs consistent natural language to describe the various characteristics that have to be assessed. Fuzzy analysis does not convert an assessment based on qualitative data into an assessment based on quantified

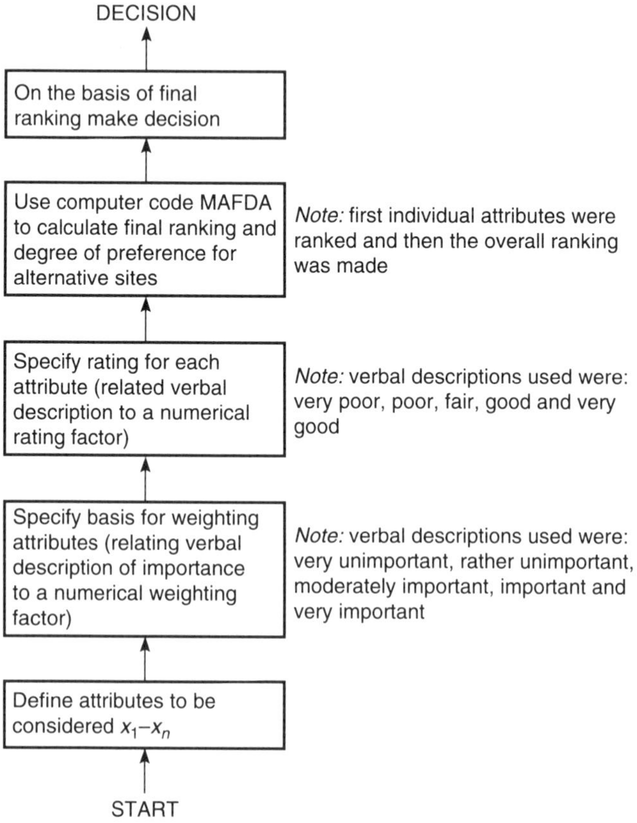
DECISION
On the basis of final ranking make decision
Use computer code MAFDA to calculate final ranking and degree of preference for alternative sites
Note: first individual attributes were ranked and then the overall ranking was made
Specify rating for each attribute (related verbal description to a numerical rating factor)
Note: verbal descriptions used were: very poor, poor, fair, good and very good
Specify basis for weighting attributes (relating verbal description of importance to a numerical weighting factor)
Note: verbal descriptions used were: very unimportant, rather unimportant, moderately important, important and very important
Define attributes to be considered x_1–x_n
START

Figure 4.3 Fuzzy analysis used for power plant site selection.

data; it merely assesses qualitative data in quantitative terms. It is this aspect of decision making that limits the help that some forms of numerical analysis can give. In decisions that have to be based on hard evidence, such as the acceptability of a medical drug or the design of an airliner, it is unlikely that fuzzy analysis of qualitative evidence would be considered acceptable by the relevant regulatory authorities. At the same time it has to be recognized that fuzzy analysis methods have been used for solving difficult control problems. When evaluation of evidence or ranking is required in stochastic terms then conventional statistical analyses are likely to be adequate. The justification for this somewhat arbitrary view is that the type of decision-making situation that the risk ranking is aimed at are those in which each step in the decision-making process has to be transparent and justifiable. This means that the process of building up the ranking must be simple and accurate and easily understood by the lay public. It does not mean that the analytical processes can be infantile, but rather that the rigour of the analysis is clear. It is in the detailed investigations necessary for determining what ranking score is justified that, as already mentioned, fuzzy analysis may be used to identify the most preferred data. Such calculations are not required to be submitted as part of the presentation of the ranking, but may be called in as evidence to substantiate the rank allocated.

CONCLUSIONS

From this examination of the theoretical considerations underlying the risk ranking seven conclusions appear to be justified. These provide a basis for assessing, in Chapters 8 and 9, the possible alternatives to the risk ranking. They are:

1. The design of the ranking scale appears to give an adequate distribution of the possible views on acceptability.
2. The method of weighting and combining the T, E and S factors seems acceptable and can be varied to match the requirements of special decision-making situations.
3. The criteria used for scoring the significance of the T, E and S factors can be adjusted to suit particular families of decision making.
4. The conclusions from ranking are not absolute. There is, by the very nature of the subject, a degree of uncertainty associated with each stage of the process.
5. In some cases the application of conventional statistical methods of analysis can give an understanding of the significance of the associated uncertainties.
6. A matrix form of presentation of the ranking of decision options can be used to give the decision maker a clear picture of the ranking of the options and of the influence of uncertainty in the data that have to be used.
7. The fuzzy data analysis methods can be used to assess factors described in qualitative terms. Such methods are most useful when the data are collected in a way that ensures a consistent pattern of words is used to describe the significance of each factor that has to be considered. Fuzzy analysis does not convert an assessment based on qualitative data into one based on quantified data; it merely assesses qualitative data in quantified terms.

5 PROBLEMS OF ASSESSING THE TECHNICAL ASPECTS OF RISK

❑ SUMMARY

The problems of assessing the technical aspects of a proposal are examined, particular attention being given to the problem of dealing with novel projects and the assessment of a proposer's capability and experience. Criteria for ranking the acceptability of the risks associated with technical factors are outlined.

THE NATURE OF TECHNICAL RISK FACTORS

The description given in Chapter 1 – of the way the acceptability of various proposals for a Channel crossing could be ranked – showed something of the nature of the technical problems that have to be considered in making decisions about major projects. Although the Channel tunnel is a major project that is technically quite complex, other projects may involve an even wider range of technical issues. Typical subjects of the type of decision making considered in this book would include a commitment to build a supersonic airliner, the building of an oil refinery, utilization of a process involving genetic engineering or computerization of welfare payments. In the discussion that follows attention is given to identifying how the acceptability of the technical features of projects can be assessed in a consistent and coherent way. Particular consideration is given to the problem of judging the acceptability of the technical risks associated with major novel projects.

ASSESSMENT OF TECHNICAL RISK FACTORS

In Chapter 3 it was shown how financial institutions rely on experts for assessing the technical aspects of proposals they are concerned with. In such assessments account is generally taken of the proposer's capability and experience in dealing with projects of a similar nature. There is no universally accepted way of making such judgements and often they are made on the basis of the opinion and experience of the executive responsible. With novel projects the best expert may be the proposer, but because he is so close to the project he may not be considered sufficiently impartial. The practice of consulting experts recognizes that with novel projects the evidence that has to be used may be largely qualitative and decisions may be intuitive. Finance for very novel projects may be difficult to obtain, simply because the magnitude of the technical aspects of the risks are unknown.

Technical factors may consist of a network of interacting components, the interactions possibly being non-linear or multi-directional, or even simply unpredictable. Analysis of such complex networks is difficult but not impossible. Techniques have been proposed for analysis of multivariable systems and these are discussed in Chapter 8 (Hilton, 1976). The problem is made more difficult with novel projects, particularly when the variables are only described in qualitative terms. When there is a complete lack of data the most that can be hoped for is the development of a vector giving an indication of the direction and significance of the factors and the magnitude of the uncertainty that can be associated with them. In contemplating modelling technical factors or any other factors it must be remembered, as French (1992) has so clearly stated, that if analysis is to help decision makers it must be understood by them.

When there are no hard quantitative data on which to base a decision recourse has to be made to the qualitative opinions of experts. This problem is not unique to technical factors; it also applies, perhaps with even more force, to economic and socio-political factors. So to set the scene for the discussion that follows in this and the next two chapters, the process of obtaining data from experts is considered. With hard quantitative data usually some indication can be obtained of the uncertainty associated with the data. With qualitative data obtained from experts, which may be no more than an informed guess, the uncertainty may be considerable. The errors will be greater if the opinions are collected in an unstructured way than if they are collected in a structured way. If several experts are consulted in a structured way it is at least possible to establish the distribution of their opinions. Some general rules that should be followed in deriving data from expert opinions are given in Appendix 6.

CONSULTING EXPERTS

Selecting experts is a problem in its own right. The procedures the World Bank suggests should be used are detailed in Appendix 7. Their procedures are particularly relevant to this study as they rank a consultant's suitability on the basis of three factors: a firm's general experience, their work plan and their key personnel. The importance of each of the three factors is weighted. Typical examples of the Bank's weighting are: a firm's experience is 0.15, the work plan in 0.33 and the typical weighting of key personnel is 0.5. This means that personnel are rated three and one-third times more important than a firm's experience. The validity of weighting is of course open for discussion, but the assessor must be prepared to justify the weightings adopted.

EVIDENCE REQUIRED TO JUSTIFY ACCEPTABILITY OF TECHNICAL FACTORS

Having set the scene for discussion about the problems of assessing technical factors, by describing the precautions that must be taken when consulting experts, the more general problems of assessing technical factors can be discussed. It has to be recognized that the understanding of the significance of a factor, no matter whether it is technical, economic or socio-political, may be quite different at the beginning of a project to the understanding of its significance at the end of the project. This point has been illustrated diagrammatically in Figure 2.3. Generally, judgements about the significance of factors have to be refined iteratively as a project develops. This is particularly true when a project is novel and there are few or no relevant data on which to base judgements. At each decision stage the adequacy of the development of the justification of acceptability has to be assessed. Determination of the overall acceptability of a major project, such as a power plant or a new aeroplane, requires the collection and evaluation of an enormous amount of evidence and the integration of analyses of many sub-systems. At each stage of a project attention may have to be focused on different aspects of the decision and often different people are involved with justifying and judging acceptability.

This characteristic metamorphosis in the pattern of actions involved in decision making has been recognized by others. Rosenhead (1989) has recognized the problems in his examination of the principles and prospects for problem structuring methods. Checkland's (1989) soft system methodology is an adaptive form of enquiry that could be applied in helping to understand how the evaluation process associated with a project is likely to develop. In general, risk ranking is more akin to hard system engineering assessment with each factor quantified and the understanding of the system being iteratively refined as knowledge develops. Nevertheless, risk ranking can be adapted to deal with the qualitative statements of expert opinion. It is also possible that a form of Eden's (1989, Eden, in Rosenhead, Chs 2 and 3) cognitive mapping for strategic options development and analysis (SODA) could help define the changing role of an expert in the process of building up an assessment of the significance of a factor.

One important feature a proposer has to include in the justification of the acceptability of a proposal for a major project is a demonstration that a proposal is likely to satisfy all relevant regulatory requirements. The demonstration may, as appropriate, include showing how

1. stresses in structural members will be kept below those allowed by current Codes of Practice;
2. loads on foundations will be kept below the maximum allowed by local soil and rock conditions;
3. pressurized equipment is designed to satisfy legal and insurance requirements;

4. an aeroplane satisfies the requirements of the Civil Aviation Authority;
5. electrical equipment will be designed and installed to conform with relevant electrical regulations.

In cases involving construction work it must be shown that the design of the proposal satisfies all planning and environmental requirements. This may include demonstrating that the design satisfies aesthetic requirements and that all possible discharges to the environment of potentially hazardous materials will be within regulatory limits. It must also be recognized that during the life of a project the understanding of the risks involved and the regulatory requirements may change. A rather dramatic example of the way understanding of the significance of hazards may change is given by the recognition of the hazards associated with asbestos. For many years a variety of products were made utilizing the thermal insulation properties of asbestos. Then it was recognized that exposure to certain types of asbestos could lead to those exposed developing cancer. As a result of this new understanding many claims for compensation were made against manufacturers of asbestos products. It has been reported that a major United States manufacturer of such products considered declaring itself bankrupt to avoid such claims (Selvidge, in Cox and Ricci, 1990).

Proving regulatory criteria are properly satisfied can cause delays in completion of a project and result in additional expense. This suggests that the most effective criteria for ranking the acceptability of technical aspects of a proposal are likely to be those that relate in detail to the technical specification that the particular proposal has to satisfy.

If technical requirements are only specified in qualitative terms two main types of problem are generated:

1. The proposer does not have a precisely defined numerical requirement to satisfy.
2. When there is no quantitative target to satisfy, proof that a proposal is acceptable is a matter of judgement.

It therefore follows that there may be difficulty in proving that all that is reasonably practicable has been done to make the plant or equipment acceptable.

The problems involved in deciding what is acceptable are considerably easier to solve when the nature of any intrinsic risk is completely understood. However, in reality novel projects generally bring in their train new risks that are not fully understood, so some way of judging their acceptability has to be found. It may be unavoidable that for such cases an element of qualitative judgement has to be retained in the criteria, or else it has to be accepted that justification may be substantiated by a specially designed research and development programme. This assumes that it is accepted that the results of research may show that it would be impractical to complete the project. Obvious examples of this approach are the prototype testing of new designs of aeroplanes and motor cars and the testing and efficacy of new medical drugs.

If a proposal involves public demonstration of acceptability, quantitative evidence about the technical nature and level of risk involved will give confidence that at least the risk is understood. When such evidence is not available the impression will tend to be given that the proposer does not properly understand the implications of his submission. In other words the absence of quantitative evidence will clearly suggest that the understanding of the risks associated with a proposal is incomplete. Simply expressing the risk in terms such as 'the probability of failure is low' does not help. For a quantitative statement to be acceptable the data used must be proved to be relevant and the degree of uncertainty associated with it stated. A quantitative statement based on appropriate reliable data is of more help to the decision maker than a qualitative statement that gives no indication of the magnitude of the risk and the uncertainty associated with the estimate. It is therefore logical to aim to have compliance with technical risk acceptability criteria substantiated in quantitative terms. This leads to the questions, 'In what units should technical risks be discussed?', and 'In what units should ranking criteria be defined?'.

UNITS FOR MEASURING TECHNICAL RISK ACCEPTABILITY

There are several units that could be used for measuring technical risk acceptability. The most obvious candidates are the time it takes for the failure of a project and the number of fatalities, as these indicate in a very direct way the harm to human life and the environment that could result. An alternative would be to define the risk in money terms, which is very much the approach of an insurance underwriter. It is appreciated that for many applications money may be the appropriate unit of measurement. However, defining the technical aspects of risk in money terms may conflict with or duplicate the assessment of the economic factors of a proposal. Equally, even describing a risk simply in terms of the number of fatalities is ambiguous, as it would not include allowance for non-fatal casualties and may not include delayed fatalities or give a clear indication of direct and indirect material damage. Perhaps the most important characteristics required of criteria for assessing technical risk acceptability are that they should be easily understood, interpreted and accepted. This may sound trite but it is fundamental, because unless everyone involved in assessing the acceptability of the risk can understand and agree with the meaning of the criteria, there will be no general confidence in the adequacy of the criteria. Criteria are likely to have clearly defined limits of application; for example, criteria aimed at ensuring that the risks associated with chemical plants are acceptable may apply to all chemical plants or only to those manufacturing particular chemicals. Similarly, if the criteria are intended for universal applications it would imply acceptance of the same level of risk regardless of the activity considered. Such uniformity in decision making would be far removed from real life. From the overall criteria, partial criteria can be derived, partial criteria being the criteria that the various subsystems of a proposal have to satisfy. The more complex the proposal the more parts the overall criteria will have to be divided into. The important condition that must be satisfied is that the integrated risk from all the subsystems of the proposal must still satisfy the overall criteria. This means that the criteria that individual subsystems have to satisfy are likely to be more stringent than for the system as a whole.

The discussion so far has dealt essentially with the acceptability of the risks that are an intrinsic part of the hardware that is the subject of the proposal. In this case the term hardware is used in a very loose sense to cover not only all the engineering systems and components involved, but also all the human systems involved. Judging the acceptability of the hardware is quite separate to judging the capability and experience of a proposer, but ultimately the two types of judgement have to be combined.

ORGANIZATION FOR SOLVING TECHNICAL RISK PROBLEMS FOR NOVEL PROJECTS

As already mentioned judging the capability and experience of a proposer is not a simple process. The aerospace industry is one industry which illustrates well the nature of the risks with major projects. It is one industry in which there have been some remarkable successes and also some damaging failures. The failures have included the Comet airliner, airships and the TSR2. The way the Lockheed Corporation deals with new novel projects indicates some of the important characteristics that a capable and experienced proposer would be expected to exhibit.

In 1943 Lockheed formed a unit called the Skunk Works, to concentrate on developing new aircraft (Rich, 1989). This was conceived as a small specialist unit operating almost separately from the main company but able to call on the services of the parent company. Table 5.1 summarizes some of the important projects the Skunk Works has been responsible for.

Kelly Johnson, the man responsible for the Skunk Works, postulated 14 rules for the effective management of novel projects. Five of the rules can be slightly paraphrased so that they describe tests that can be applied to assess the likely effectiveness of any project or proposal implementation team. These are:

1. The head of the project must have control and responsibility for budget, procurement, engineering, manufacturing and security.
2. The number of people involved with the project must be kept to the bare minimum.
3. Records must be carefully kept but paperwork kept to a minimum.
4. There must be monthly cost reviews of funds spent, committed and expected to be spent in the future.
5. Detailed inspection and quality control procedures must be instituted and kept to.

In the example of the Channel Tunnel described in Chapter 1, a very simple view was taken of the form that criteria for ranking technical factors could take. It did not include any allowance for the experiences of the proposer. From the above it can be seen that assessment of technical factors should include assessments of both the technical hardware and the proposer's capability and experience. Such combination of hard and soft assessments is surrounded by many problems, but the temptation to leave the two types of argument separate must be resisted (Tait, 1988).

Table 5.1 Some important projects the Skunk Works has been responsible for

Project	Description	Main parameters	Commercial consequences
P-80 Shooting Star fighter	The world's first operational jet fighter	Prototype completed in 143 days, 37 days under schedule	9000 aircraft built
Saturn low cost passenger aeroplane	Twin-engined high wing airliner	Two prototypes built	Priced out of market by war surplus Douglas C-47
XFV-1 vertical take off aeroplane	Experimental jet prop vertical take off aeroplane	Dual turbine contro-rotating propellers	Navy cancelled project
F104 Starfighter Mach 2 fighter	First operational fighter capable of sustained operation at Mach 2	Two prototypes built in one year	2500 aircraft built
C-130 Hercules transport plane	Military transport plane	Prototypes built	2000 aircraft built
Blackbird reconnaissance aeroplane	Capable of flying at Mach 3 and 80,000 ft. Very low radar cross section	Several versions built	A major technological advance

CRITERIA FOR RANKING THE ACCEPTABILITY OF TECHNICAL RISK FACTORS

It is suggested that a comprehensive assessment of the acceptability of the technical risks of a project could be built up in the way shown in Table 5.2 with the highest ranking score of the four features considered determining the ranking for the technical factor as a whole. The scoring agrees with the score/acceptability relationship described in Tables 1.2 and 1.4 but is modified to include criteria for both technical hardware and the proposer's capability and hardware. For some cases it may be appropriate to simply relate the ranking to the probability of failure and the consequence of failure.

An indication of how quantitative statements about the probability of failure and the consequences of failure can be related to qualitative statements about acceptability is given by the way requirements for acceptability are described for civil aircraft. Figure 5.1 shows how the Airworthiness Authorities Steering

Table 5.2 Technical risk ranking criteria

Feature	Rating	Score*	Rank	Explanation
1. Probability of failure during specified lifetime	Acceptable	1	4	Highest score of the four features determines the overall ranking score and this determines the rank for technical factors. For example, if the highest score of any feature is 5 the overall score will be 5; if the highest score is 14 the overall score will be 14; if the highest score is 2 the overall score will be 2.
	Minor changes required	2	3	
	Major changes required	5	2	
	Unacceptable	14	1	
2. Consequence of failure	Acceptable**	1	4	
	Needs some reduction	2	3	
	Needs major reduction	5	2	
	Unacceptable***	14	1	
3. Capability of proposers	Acceptable	1	4	
	Needs some strengthening	2	3	
	Needs major strengthening	5	2	
	Unacceptable	14	1	
4. Relevant experience of proposer	Acceptable	1	4	
	Needs to be extended	2	3	
	Needs major extension	5	2	
	Unacceptable	14	1	

Notes: *For discussion of scoring system, see Chapter 1 and Appendix 4.
**Risk of premature death of member of the public 1 in 10^7 years.
***Risk of death of member of the public 1 in 10^4 years.

Committee expressed the relationship between quantitative and qualitative statements about acceptability in the Joint Airworthiness Requirements (CAA, 1986). Concorde was the first aircraft for which a full quantitative risk assessment was made. The safety objective that had to be satisfied was that the probability of a catastrophic accident due to a system failure should be less than 1×10^{-9} for each flight hour. Generally the life limitation is set at 60,000 hours, but for large jet transports this may be extended provided a very detailed structural examination is carried out and the condition of the structure is found to be acceptable. In this context it must be remembered that an inspection operation is not 100% perfect; there is only a 50% chance of an inspector detecting a 2-inch long crack. Another view on technical risk acceptability has recently been published by the Health and Safety Executive, which introduced the word 'tolerability' (HSE, 1988).

'Tolerability' is taken as being a willingness to live with a risk so as to secure certain benefits and in the confidence that the risk is being properly controlled. The term is somewhat vague, since the terms 'benefits' and 'properly controlled' are not precisely defined. In 'Tolerability of Risk' the Health and Safety Executive use the term 'risk' to denote the chance of a person having a shorter than normal life. This is a very specific use of 'risk', which has a more general meaning in the rest of this book. Table 5.3 has been constructed to show what the Health and Safety Executive consider to be tolerable levels of risk.

Assessment of the capability and experience of a proposer must to a large extent

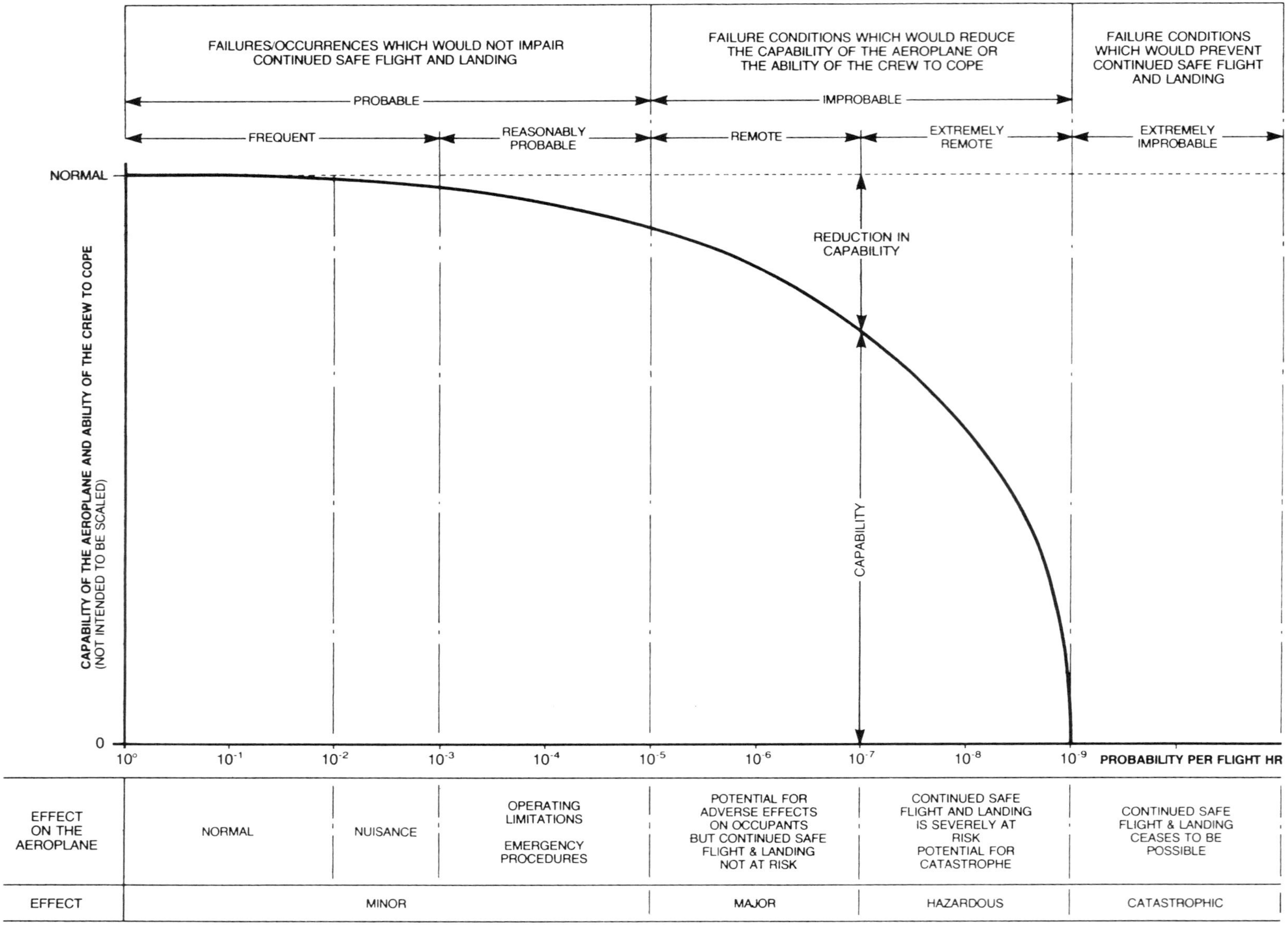
FAILURES/OCCURRENCES WHICH WOULD NOT IMPAIR CONTINUED SAFE FLIGHT AND LANDING
FAILURE CONDITIONS WHICH WOULD REDUCE THE CAPABILITY OF THE AEROPLANE OR THE ABILITY OF THE CREW TO COPE
FAILURE CONDITIONS WHICH WOULD PREVENT CONTINUED SAFE FLIGHT AND LANDING
PROBABLE
IMPROBABLE
FREQUENT
REASONABLY PROBABLE
REMOTE
EXTREMELY REMOTE
EXTREMELY IMPROBABLE
NORMAL
REDUCTION IN CAPABILITY
CAPABILITY
CAPABILITY OF THE AEROPLANE AND ABILITY OF THE CREW TO COPE
(NOT INTENDED TO BE SCALED)
0
10^0
10^{-1}
10^{-2}
10^{-3}
10^{-4}
10^{-5}
10^{-6}
10^{-7}
10^{-8}
10^{-9}
PROBABILITY PER FLIGHT HR
EFFECT ON THE AEROPLANE
NORMAL
NUISANCE
OPERATING LIMITATIONS
EMERGENCY PROCEDURES
POTENTIAL FOR ADVERSE EFFECTS ON OCCUPANTS BUT CONTINUED SAFE FLIGHT & LANDING NOT AT RISK
CONTINUED SAFE FLIGHT AND LANDING IS SEVERELY AT RISK
POTENTIAL FOR CATASTROPHE
CONTINUED SAFE FLIGHT & LANDING CEASES TO BE POSSIBLE
EFFECT
MINOR
MAJOR
HAZARDOUS
CATASTROPHIC

Figure 5.1 Quantitative and qualitative statement of joint airworthiness requirement for acceptability. *Source:* Reproduced with permission of the Civil Aviation Authority.

Table 5.3 Tolerable levels of risk

Group	Risk of premature death per year
Maximum for workers in any industry	1 in 10^3
Maximum for any member of the public from a large-scale industrial hazard	1 in 10^4
Range of risk to members of the public living near a nuclear installation from normal operation	1 in 10^5 to 1 in 10^6
Range of risk to members of the public living near a nuclear installation from any kind of nuclear accident	1 in 10^6 to 1 in 10^7
Risk to average member of the public from normal operation and possible nuclear accidents	less than 1 in 10^7

be subjective. The way the World Bank suggests the capability of consultants is assessed has been mentioned earlier in this chapter and in Appendix 7. The degree of confidence in such assessments must take account of the degree of novelty in the subject of assessment. When a proposal simply repeats some well-established design or process there can be confidence that the capability and experience of the proposer can be judged accurately. But when the project is novel there is little foundation for judgements of capability. An example of such difficulty is the problem of obtaining insurance for novel projects. When the Eiffel Tower was being built it was considered such a departure from existing practice that no insurance company would cover the risk (Marrey, 1988). In a similar way today it would be difficult to obtain insurance cover for processes involving genetic engineering. An indication of the way the insurance industry assesses complex technical proposals like insurance of computer systems is given in Appendix 8.

CONCLUSIONS

The general conclusions that this chapter suggests are:

1. Criteria are proposed for determining technical risk acceptability (as shown in Table 5.2).
2. The proposed criteria give a more comprehensive assessment of the technical acceptability of a proposal than the criteria used in Chapter 1 as the basis for assessing the Channel crossing proposals.
3. The detailed criteria adopted to assess ranking scores for technical factors may have to be tailored to suit each family of proposals.

6 PROBLEMS OF ASSESSING THE ECONOMIC ASPECTS OF RISK

❑ SUMMARY

The problems of assessing the economic aspects of a proposal are examined. Several possible methods of assessment are considered and it is concluded that through-life net benefit is likely to be the most efficacious method of ranking risk acceptability. Criteria for ranking the acceptability of the risks associated with economic factors are proposed.

THE NATURE OF ECONOMIC RISK FACTORS

To simplify the presentation in this chapter the argument about the problems of assessing the economic implications of risk is presented in literal terms and the theoretical aspects of the argument have been consigned to Appendix 9. The wide variety of economic indicators mentioned in Chapter 3 and Appendix 2 that financial institutions use to assess the acceptability of the risks associated with their lending policy, suggest there is no single technique of economic analysis which is universally efficacious in assessing the acceptability of risk. To a certain extent, the banks' procedure could be described as a search for a consensus view without attaching overriding importance to any one factor. Such an approach may be acceptable for assessing the financial risk associated with a major loan to an underdeveloped country. But, the approach would be unnecessarily complex, perhaps even too indeterminate for simpler decisions such as determining the acceptability of financing the purchase of a new ship or a new aeroplane. In the assessment of the Channel crossing options, mentioned in Chapter 1, the economic assessment presented to the decision maker was extremely simple, probably too simple, being based just on estimates of return on investment, cost, and allowance for variation in cost. In this chapter an attempt is made to find the optimum way of assessing the economic aspects of risk acceptability.

METHODS OF ASSESSMENT

Professor Pearce has put the essential features of the problem in the following way:

> If, as economists have repeatedly pointed out for the last two centuries, our wants exceed our capacities to meet them, we must, when choosing one thing, give something else up. This, very simply, is the notion of opportunity cost and an inescapable fact of life . . . What the cost–benefit analyst seeks is a methodology for 'revealing' that underlying valuation.
>
> Pearce, 1981, p. 191

Clearly the heart of the problem is balancing the merits of one form of expenditure against other possible uses for funds.

Various analytical tools have been developed to assist the decision maker in dealing with this problem. Among these tools are: cost–benefit analysis, risk–benefit analysis, risk–cost–benefit analysis, project economic viability, opportunity cost and insurability limits (Berliner, 1982). It is not suggested that these methods give exact results, but only that they reveal something of the nature of the underlying valuation. The choice of method and the factors considered are to some extent related to the constraints of the environment in which the decision has to be made and to the subject of the decision. The decision making inside a small company would be more constrained by factors such as cash flow, debt financing, liquidity and profits than decision making in a government body. Most organizations are subject to constraints on their borrowing. In Britain, the lending policy of banks is, as already mentioned in Chapter 3, subject to control by the Bank of England and the Commission of the European Communities. The Bank of England's criticism of banks' property loans is an example of this type of control (The Times, 1989). Within these constraints the responsible decision makers will aim to ensure that resources are allocated to the most beneficial uses. It is assumed that in building up a picture of costs and benefits both direct and indirect costs and benefits are considered. Attention is drawn to the fact that indirect costs and benefits are often difficult to evaluate and introduce some additional uncertainty into the analysis.

For a completely satisfactory assessment of the cost and benefit aspects of the acceptability of risk the assessment has to include evaluation of the following:

1. the total costs associated with each option;
2. the benefits in money terms associated with each option. It must be recognized that, at least initially, all the benefits may not be expressed directly in quantitative terms and there may be problems in converting qualitative statements about benefits into quantitative statements;
3. the costs in quantitative terms associated with the direct and indirect risks inherent in each option;
4. the errors and uncertainties associated with the estimates of costs and benefits;
5. the overall economic implications of the options considered.

Sometimes the total cost of a project is lightly dismissed as simply being the sum of all expenditures required to bring a project to fruition. Such a definition is misleading, as it overlooks many important indirect costs. Also it overlooks the through-life cost of a project. One option might have a low first cost but very high through-life costs, which would result in the total through-life cost being higher than a high first cost option with low through-life costs. Similar arguments can be applied to the assessment of through-life benefits.

So far the discussion has not touched on the nature of the costs associated with the risks inherent in each option considered. It is important to separate risks from the errors and uncertainties in estimates of costs and benefits. Risks are the expression of the doubts about a proposal achieving its aim while errors and uncertainty refer to the possible variation in the calculation of costs and benefits. Some confusion about the terms stems from phrases like: the risk of a cost overrun. The following examples of possible outcomes from projects makes the meaning attached to risk clearer: a new aeroplane does not fly, a new car engine has a higher fuel consumption than existing models, a new drug is not effective and a bridge fails before it is put into service. The cost of the risk and the loss of benefit in such cases are obvious. The nature of errors and uncertainties can be illustrated by the fact that on average the cost escalation of major civil projects is 50% (Hall, 1980). When a project involves a novel technology the cost escalation can be a great deal more than 50%. The errors and uncertainties apply to the estimate of both costs and benefits. In some ways the errors and uncertainties associated with benefits may be larger than with estimates of costs. The difference is partly due to the ephemeral nature of some benefits and because some benefits are intrinsically hard to quantify. The benefits that are particularly hard to quantify are those connected with social projects, the problem being associated with the difficulty of valuing non-traded goods or services (Irvin, 1978). Examples of non-traded benefits are noise-abatement, pollution control, trade protection and nature reserves. Any attempt to value such benefits reveals the magnitude of the problem. Often assessment of the value of non-traded benefits is based on estimates of willingness to pay for the benefit.

If the comparison of costs and benefits is made in subjective qualitative terms the conclusions tend to be quite artificial. Quantification, or at least ordinal ranking, is necessary for an assessment to have an adequate level of realism (Shrader-Frechette, 1985).

One variation of conventional cost–benefit analysis that has been developed to deal with the element of risk in cost–benefit analysis is risk–cost–benefit analysis. Shrader-Frechette reports that in the 1960s risk–cost–benefit analysis was incorporated into the planning and budgeting procedures of many US federal agencies in the defence, aerospace and energy fields (Shrader-Frechette, 1985). Essentially risk–cost–benefit analysis is a method of weighting and integrating the value attributed to the three factors for each option considered. The integrated values obtained serve as the basis for, what is claimed to be, sounder comparison of each option. Ideally, for complete risk–cost–benefit analysis of a proposal all the implications of the proposal for all involved with the project should be evaluated. In order for such an assessment to be useful there has to be a very detailed understanding of the distribution of risks, costs and benefits. The economic features of a country or the financial performance figures of a company that banks consider when they are assessing creditworthiness give an indication of the range of influences that have to be taken into account in evaluating any economic risk or risk weighting factor.

DISTRIBUTION OF RISKS AND BENEFITS

An important facet of the argument is expressed by the question, 'Who bears the costs and who receives the benefits associated with the activity?'. The argument is fairly simple when the risks, costs and benefits considered are borne entirely by the same party. More generally, the costs and benefits are divided between several parties. This gives rise to the moral question about how the benefits and burdens should be distributed. The following quotation from a congressional hearing goes some way towards identifying a solution to the problem in a way that helps to keep the discussion about the distribution of the burdens of risk in perspective (May, 1982, p. 227)

> The first moral question to be asked is this: 'How ought benefits and risks be distributed?' It is a good rule of thumb to assume that no policy based directly on risk–benefit analysis will automatically distribute benefits and burdens fairly. That will happen only as the result of a deliberate additional effort. A very heavy burden of risk on one group, while another group gains most of the benefits, is clearly inequitable.

The deduction that seems obvious from the above quotation is that the risk and benefits, and their distribution, must be expressed in quantified terms that enable the equity of their distribution to be assessed. It is only when the discussion can be held in numerical terms that the fairness of a proposal can be judged.

THE ANALOGY WITH INSURANCE

Insurance is one commercial way of distributing the burden of risk. The cost of obtaining insurance cover is not a fixed factor as it depends, to some extent, on the state of the market. For example, the view has sometimes been expressed that when insurance rates are high and the insurance markets are 'premium hungry' insurers would cut their premiums, hoping that any losses due to claims greater than premium income would be covered by investment income. On some occasions, employer's liability risks have been accepted at a premium of 60% of the annual claims experienced over the previous five years (Hicks, 1982).

It is important to recognize that the value fixed for insurance purposes may not be the same as the total cost burden (Reed Stenhouse, 1982). Typically indirect losses such as production losses, terrorism, costs of retraining new staff, costs of cleaning up after an accident and investigating an accident are not covered. The insurance value of risk covered assumes the risk is known and understood. If the risk is not understood it would be virtually impossible to obtain insurance cover.

DEVELOPMENT OF CRITERIA FOR RANKING ECONOMIC RISKS

From this broad review of the problems of assessing the economic aspects of risk acceptability assessment, some conclusions can be drawn about the considerations that have to be taken into account in developing criteria for ranking the acceptability of economic factors. The optimum way of assessing the ranking of acceptability of economic factors would be one that gives repeatable, easily explainable and reliable results. These three requirements are mentioned to draw attention to the fact that the assessment technique should, with data of similar quality, give results of similar value to the assessment of any proposals they are applied to. The requirements are quite exacting and are not intended to cast aspersions on the efficacy of methods of economic analysis, but to expose the need to obtain consistent, predictable and easily understandable results. If over the years the methods of analysis used do not give results that are, in general, seen to predict the outcome of proposals accurately the methods will be discredited and decision-making procedures based on them distrusted. For example, the estimating procedures used for the Sydney Opera House and Concorde would be regarded as doubtful. Because in both cases costs escalated to about ten times the original estimate, the estimating errors were massive. Similarly, the estimating procedure used for the Thames Barrier, which cost about twenty times the original estimate, would at best be considered doubtful. The serious escalation of the costs of the Channel Tunnel show how quickly the original estimates of the cost of the project, mentioned at the beginning of this study, can become out of date (Barrett and Byrd, 1989). Not all projects cost more than the original estimate, but the risk of cost overruns are higher with novel projects than with projects that simply repeat an earlier successful proposal.

For two important reasons the requirement of easily understandable results is of vital importance in the design of assessment procedures for economic factors associated with major decisions:

1. Often decisions are exposed to public scrutiny and have to be defended openly to a lay public.
2. The results of the assessment may, as in the case of the Swiss Bank Corporation's Management Brief mentioned in Chapter 3 and Appendix 3, have to be presented to some busy senior executive in a simple, direct, easily understood way.

These requirements do not mean that all the supporting analysis has to be crude and simple. It merely means that the analysis has to result in conclusions that are easily explainable and easily defensible. Accepting that the ranking technique provides a way of presenting the results of analysis in an understanding way, the basic question is: on which economic parameters should the ranking score be based? Possible bases for ranking are reviewed in Table 6.1. In every case allowance has to be made for errors in the data used. The errors may, as already mentioned, be massive.

Basing acceptability on a review of all economic parameters is a special case, which has a useful role in assessing the acceptability of the risks associated with a

Table 6.1 Possible bases for ranking economic factors

Basis	Comment
Review of a company's financial performance data	This is used for assessing the creditworthiness of a company for a loan or the quality of a company as an investment.
Review of all economic parameters	This is appropriate for assessing the credit risks associated with a particular country. It is also appropriate for assessing projects where the cost is a significant proportion of the country's gross national product.
Capital cost	Simple and straightforward, but does not take into account questions like the return on investment or benefit.
Agreed return on investment	Gives an indication of the likely commercial value of the proposal. Can be adjusted to take account of all costs and benefits borne by the public.
Opportunity costs	Gives an indication of the value of alternatives. The problem is to identify all the relevant alternatives.
Cost/benefit	Draws attention to the magnitude of related gains and losses. The problem is comprehensive identification of all costs and benefits involved. Risk/cost/benefit is a refinement of this method.
Non-dimensional comparison of total cost	An ordinal non-dimensional ranking of cost provides a way of comparing options. Only really suitable for use inside an organization.
Through-life costs and benefits	If the assessment is made so that it takes account of all direct and indirect costs and benefits throughout the life of the project it gives a comprehensive assessment of the economic implications of a proposal.
Risk/capital ratio	Needs care to ensure that the calculation of total risk includes all direct and indirect risks. This method indicates whether or not a proposer has sufficient funds to cover all risks.

major project in a country with a poor economic record, or in a country where the cost of the project represents a significant proportion of the country's gross national product.) A company's financial performance data is a fairly conventional basis for assessing a company's creditworthiness for a loan or its value as an investment. But, the method tells nothing of the benefit of the enterprise or the added benefit that will result from making a loan to the company. Considering simple capital cost also ignores many important economic issues like benefit or risk, but the terms could be adjusted by a factor to take them into account. Return on investment can give a more comprehensive view of the economic significance of a proposal providing the calculation of return on investment takes into account the costs, losses and benefits that accrue to people not directly involved in the project being considered. Opportunity cost analysis introduces another dimension, as it attempts to evaluate the comparative value of alternative forms of expenditure. The problem with opportunity cost analysis is identifying all the alternatives that should be considered. Cost–benefit analysis is a very flexible analytical method and can be used to make a comprehensive assessment of all the gains and losses incurred. The intrinsic problems are identifying all the costs and benefits that have to be considered, the degree of uncertainty in the calculation and the life of the project over which the costs and benefits have to be integrated.

None of the methods discussed so far overtly include any assessment of a proposer's ability to pay claims for compensation that may arise during the life of the project. The way claims for compensation due to asbestos induced diseases forced Johns Manville to consider bankruptcy (see Chapter 5), gives a clear indication of the importance of this factor. To save introducing an additional factor into the analysis, it is assumed that estimates of costs include an allowance for either providing adequate insurance cover for all claims for compensation or maintaining sufficient reserves to cover any claims that may arise.

Non-dimensional or ordinal non-dimensional ranking of cost provides a way any project cost options can be compared, but it tends to obscure the amount of money involved. In some cases it might be possible, as in the case of capital cost discussed earlier, to apply the method by adjusting it to take into account indirect losses and benefits.

The most promising of the bases for ranking economic factors can be derived from the through-life cost approach. If the through-life assessment is based on costs and benefits and is calculated by integrating all direct and indirect benefits less all direct and indirect costs, which can be attributed to a project throughout its life, it would give a sound basis for comparing the economic significance of the options that have to be considered. Assessment of all positive and negative, direct and indirect benefits and costs is not without any problems. The costs must include allowance for funding any compensation claims that may arise.

The question that remains is what is the most suitable criteria for assessing the acceptability ranking of economic factors. There is perhaps no single answer. The criteria really have to be adapted to the particular decision being dealt with. But for families of decisions the criteria would be the same. For example criteria based on a review of all economic parameters may be suitable for all cases where the creditworthiness of a country had to be determined, and return on investment would be a sound basis for assessing a modest commercial project. Simply considering the return on investment ignores the influence on national expenditure and is difficult to apply realistically to proposals related to some topics such as defence or social payments. In theory, opportunity cost should give the best indication of the merits of alternatives, but the method is fraught with difficulties as for any proposal all the real alternatives may be hard to identify. Similar limitations apply to

Table 6.2 Possible relationships between economic factors and the ranking score

Acceptability	Economic factors	Score*	Equivalent risk acceptability rank
Unlikely to be acceptable	Through-life benefits – through-life costs, significantly lower than alternatives.	14	1
Only acceptable if risk can be reduced	Through-life benefits – through-life costs, marginally lower than alternatives.	5	2
Yes, subject to detailed adjustments to the proposal being made	Through-life benefits – through-life costs, higher than alternatives but some doubts about errors and uncertainties in data used.	2	3
Yes, without restriction	Through-life benefits – through-life costs, higher than alternatives. No doubts after making due allowance for all possible errors and uncertainties.	1	4

Note. *For discussion of scoring system see Chapter 4 and Appendix 4.

cost–benefit analysis. Any process of determining alternatives must take into account the whole life cost involved and ideally the whole life benefit. Some additional discussion of calculations of through-life cost is given in Appendix 9.

CONCLUSIONS

Given the doubts expressed about the feasibility of finding universal criteria for assessing the ranking that economic factors justify, it is suggested that for many cases ranking of acceptability of the economic factors could be made on the basis of the through-life cost and benefits, the calculation taking into account all direct and indirect costs and benefits. It also has to be accepted that the calculation has to include a factor to allow for the risk of the project not being completed. Such a factor may be a compound factor, which includes allowance for all the features of the economic environment that may cause a project to fail. In Table 6.2 the possible relationships between through-life costs and benefits and the ranking score are set out. It is assumed that the calculation of through-life costs and benefits includes an appropriate factor for compensation claims. It is recognized that simply postulating a ranking criteria does not resolve the moral question of how the costs of benefits should be distributed, answer questions about the macro-economic significance of the proposal, or explain how the calculation should be made. The moral question is partly answered by assessing public reaction to a proposal and this point is discussed further in the next chapter under the heading of socio-political factors.

7 PROBLEMS OF ASSESSING THE SOCIO-POLITICAL ASPECTS OF RISK

❑ SUMMARY

The problem of assessing the socio-political aspects of a proposal is examined. Various methods of assessing socio-political factors are considered. Criteria for ranking the acceptability of the risks associated with socio-political factors are proposed.

THE NATURE OF SOCIO-POLITICAL FACTORS

In this chapter, the problems of assessing socio-political factors are examined, with the objective of identifying the most efficacious procedure for ranking their significance. Because of the nature of socio-political factors the problems involved in assessing their significance in decision making are quite different to the problems of assessing technical and economic factors. Socio-political aspects of a decision are concerned with what ought to be, and such decisions are quite different from technical judgements which are concerned with what can be done.

In the ranking technique, socio-political factors are specified as including all the factors that influence decisions, which are not grouped under the heading of either technical or economic factors. The essential characteristic of this very broad group is that it describes all the shades of public opinion and influence that have to be taken into account in determining the acceptability of a proposal to the public. The spectrum of public opinion ranges from the views of individuals to the views of political parties. For an assessment to be useful to a decision maker it must give him/her a balanced unbiased assessment of socio-political factors related to the public acceptability of a proposal. The importance of such an assessment was stressed in the Layfield report on the public inquiry into a proposal to build a pressurized water nuclear reactor at Sizewell. In the report Layfield drew attention to the need for better communication with the public and better understanding of the public's views about the acceptability of nuclear plant (Layfield, 1987). In other words Layfield considered it was important to take public opinion into account in deciding the acceptability of a major proposal. The need to understand the public's view is not peculiar to proposals relating to nuclear plant but applies to all proposals that have an impact on the public, whether it is the rail link across Kent to the Channel Tunnel, the operation of the Health Service, the construction of a motorway, the siting of an airport or the siting of chemical plant.

QUESTIONS CONSIDERED IN ASSESSING SOCIO-POLITICAL FACTORS

Before examining the nature of the problems inherent in assessing socio-political factors for decision-making purposes, it is useful to consider the views of Merkhofer and Lindblom as their views help to put the problems into perspective. In his study of decision science and social risk management, Merkhofer states

> Social choice theory takes the perspective that the appropriate criteria for social decisions is not the preference of some single decision maker but rather a rational synthesis of the preferences of all those individuals who will be affected by the decision. The theory is thus concerned with finding decision rules or procedures by which preferences specified by individuals may be incorporated into the decision process. (Merkhofer, 1987, p. 65.)

Then in relation to ethical concerns Merkhofer (p. 180) raises two questions that are central to the design of ethical social decision-making systems:

1. Which principles of ethics should be left to individual choice and which should be universally enforced?
2. Should ethical principles be stated in terms of ends or in terms of means?

Merkhofer (p. 202) concludes that:

> Although analysis can help identify alternatives that are 'best' according to some specified criterion, it cannot objectively resolve conflicts of interest . . . Analysis can clarify a decision; it can also obscure it in technical and mathematical abstraction.

Lindblom's outlook on the problem is slightly different as he is concerned with the policy-making process from the political standpoint (Lindblom, 1968). Nevertheless, his views are very relevant to this examination of the problems of assessing socio-political factors, as the type of major decisions being considered often have to be made in the political arena. The particularly relevant points he makes are:

1. Even in democracies not everyone is motivated to vote on issues that may affect them or the interests of the people they represent.
2. Not all the people who may vote are correctly informed about the issues they may vote on.
3. Interest groups are a legitimate way for people to attempt to influence decision making. But the influence of an interest group is no greater than the weight given to it by the proximate policy maker (Chicken and Hayns, 1989). (In the

context of this study, the proximate policy maker could be interpreted as the person presenting an analysis of the decision options to a decision maker.)

The inescapable characteristic of socio-political factors data is that they are soft, in other words they are difficult to quantify with any precision. The available data will be derived from public enquiries, opinion surveys, voting, consultation and epidemiological studies. It has to be appreciated that each survey method has its strengths and weaknesses. An essential prerequisite of any attempt to make a sound assessment of the acceptability of the socio-political aspects of a decision is that everyone concerned, whose opinion has to be considered, has an adequate understanding of the technical and economic implications of the proposal. No honest unbiased assessment of public acceptability can be made unless the nature of the proposal is first explained to the public concerned in terms they understand.

Ideally, views about the acceptability of a project should be collected from all those in the population who could, or think they could, be affected by the project. In practice it is not possible to draw a precise circle around the section of the population concerned about a particular proposal and only deal with the people inside that circle. In mathematical terms it is a 'fuzzy set' of people that have to be considered, so great care is needed in defining the section of the population that has to be considered. At the same time it has to be recognized that there is likely to be a considerable degree of uncertainty about the confidence that can be placed in the views collected.

Once the population whose views must be sought is identified the next question is 'How should their views be obtained?'. Simply asking for a 'yes' or 'no' answer to the question, 'How acceptable do you consider the project is?', only gives a superficial view of the acceptability of the project. It is better to try to build up a feeling for the shades of opinion on a proposal and the alternatives in an iterative way. This procedure could be regarded as a form of the Delphi technique or even arbitration in which a consensus view is built up iteratively.

It is also necessary to recognize that the ideal situation where all the people in the section of the population involved are provided with details, that they understand, of the technical and economic issues involved, can rarely be achieved in practice. Therefore any sample will include people whose knowledge is a mixture of precise fact, belief, various levels of partial understanding and biased views propounded by interest groups. The greater the novelty of the subject the more likely peoples' views are to be coloured by emotional views. Clearly, when there are strong political pressures involved impartial assessment is of paramount importance and the assessor must take care to ensure his assessment of socio-political factors is based on genuine representative views of the population involved. This problem of finding genuine representative views arises in any survey of opinion.

METHODS OF OBTAINING DATA ABOUT SOCIO-POLITICAL FACTORS

Having recognized something of the inherent limitations on the socio-political data that can be obtained the next question to consider is how the data can be obtained. There are four main techniques for assessing peoples' views on acceptability. Each technique has its own special characteristics and is more suitable for some applications than others. The techniques are summarized and their strengths and limitations commented on in Table 7.1, which has been developed from an earlier analysis of assessment techniques presented by Chicken and Hayns (1989). It is only possible to assess acceptability using epidemiological data if there is past experience that exactly matches the proposal being considered. The data must match the proposal being considered both in terms of technical specification and the current state of knowledge and opinion of the group involved. It would be misleading to expect that opinion about the acceptability in the nineteenth century of a lead works in a town would give any indication of opinion in the 1990s about the acceptability of remote siting of a nuclear power reactor. Equally, data about the acceptability of the siting of a bakery give no indication of the acceptability of a factory based on a process employing genetic engineering.

The main problems with the consultation process are ensuring that those being consulted really understand the issue they are being consulted about, that they know the views of any public they represent and are accepted as representing that public. There would be no merit in consulting only farmers if only 10% of the community involved were farmers. It would be more effective to consult a group in which all interested parties are represented in the same proportion as they are in the section of population likely to be affected by the proposal.

Sampling opinion is a statistically valid way of assessing opinion, and is likely to yield more helpful and defensible information than epidemiological data provided, and it is an important proviso, that the sample is properly structured and that the population sampled is the relevant population.

Voting is in many ways the ideal democratic way of assessing the public acceptability of a proposition. However, it is not appropriate for all decisions. It may be appropriate for large decisions in the public sector but not for decisions in the private sector. Voting is generally a very slow and expensive process. Some reduction in cost could be achieved by simply limiting the voting to the region likely to be affected by the proposal; this may simply be a city or country area. If the practice were to become generally adopted it is easy to envisage that the nation's administrative system would become blocked and the decision-making process slowed down.

As already mentioned, the extent to which lay people are willing and capable of making an accurate assessment of the acceptability of a proposal depends on their knowledge of and interest in the proposal and their understanding of its implications. Without an understanding of the significance of the essential features of a proposal the public are in no position to judge its acceptability and any judgement they make would have little value. This does not mean that without proper understanding of the subject the public will not express views. It simply means the

Table 7.1 Techniques for assessing acceptability of socio-political factors

Method	Strengths	Limitation	Comment
Epidemiological studies	Relates what has already been accepted to environment of decision being considered	Past experience may not be relevant to the future. Does not represent a commitment by public involved	Such studies identify past areas of concern, but do not predict present or future concerns or reaction to novel proposals
Consultation	Quick, provided appropriate machinery for consultation already exists. Can give a permanent form of contact between the public and the project and the public and the decision makers	Those consulted may not represent the views of the whole community affected by the proposal in question. May be difficult to organize when national boundaries have to be crossed. Does not represent a commitment by the public involved	The success of this method depends upon those consulted being fully aware of the views of the community concerned and understanding the issues involved. Sometimes it can take two or three years to arrive at a view
Sampling	A sample survey can provide structured evidence about views on acceptability	Does not give everyone a chance to express their views about what is acceptable. Does not represent a commitment by the public involved	The sample surveyed must be taken directly from the population affected by the decision and for the results of the sampling process to really help the decision maker the population sampled must understand the issues involved
Voting	It is the most comprehensive way of establishing the views and wishes of a particular population	Not appropriate for all projects particularly small ones. Expensive and slow to arrange. Unless some form of compulsion is used not everyone will vote. Not necessarily binding on either party involved	If the result is clear it gives the decision maker positive guidance on the action the population consider should be taken. If the verdict is marginal the issue is not efficiently resolved for the decision maker

analyst must be careful to avoid dealing in myths and legends, while at the same time accepting that myths and legends may characterize people's views on a particular subject.

Whatever method of collecting information is used seven essential steps have to be taken. The seven steps are shown in Figure 7.1. The steps as shown might have to be repeated if the proposal is modified or the people questioned do not seem to have understood the implications of the proposal. If a sampling process is used it is possible for the issues to be explained to the people questioned and to include questions that test the understanding they have of the problems involved. It is the responsibility of the analyst to make certain that the people questioned have understood the questions asked. An acceptable decision-making process will be one in which both analyst and public share the view that the implications of a proposal have been fairly explained and opinions correctly assessed.

SURVEYS OF PUBLIC OPINION

Six recent major surveys of public opinion illustrate the capability and the limitations of survey methods: Surrey University study of the perception of the acceptability of risk (Brown *et al.*, 1983), the IAEA/IIASA study of the acceptability of various energy sources (Thomas *et al.*, 1980), the Swedish referendum on nuclear power (OECD, 1984), the two Swiss votes on opposition to nuclear power (OECD, 1984), the Dutch survey of opinion on industrial risks in the Rijnmond area (Chicken and Hayns, 1989) and the European Community surveys of public opinion on the acceptability of various sources of power (CEC

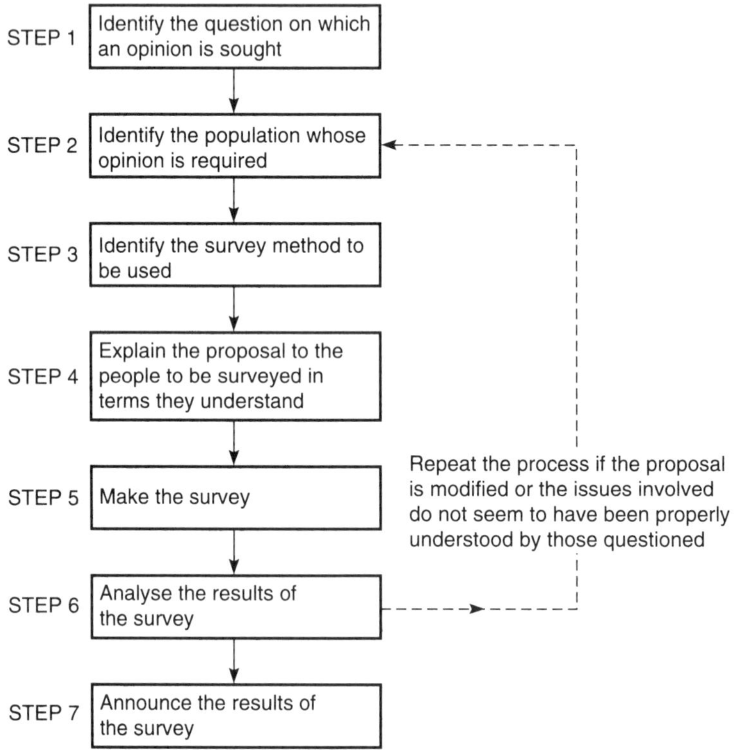
STEP 1
Identify the question on which an opinion is sought
STEP 2
Identify the population whose opinion is required
STEP 3
Identify the survey method to be used
STEP 4
Explain the proposal to the people to be surveyed in terms they understand
STEP 5
Make the survey
STEP 6
Analyse the results of the survey
STEP 7
Announce the results of the survey
Repeat the process if the proposal is modified or the issues involved do not seem to have been properly understood by those questioned

Figure 7.1 Steps in the opinion survey process.

XVII/282/85-EN, 1984). As these surveys have been reviewed at some length (Chicken and Hayns, 1989) the findings and limitations of the methods are summarized in Table 7.2.

CONCLUSIONS

The conclusions that seem to be justified about the problems of assessing socio-political factors are:

1. The socio-political factors related to complex decisions can be evaluated by carefully designed surveys.
2. Changes in opinion that take place over a period as short as two years can be detected by conventional survey methods.
3. Variations in views can be detected over a relatively small geographical area.
4. For an effective survey to be made the nature of the risk must be explained to the population being surveyed.
5. A sample opinion survey does not represent any kind of commitment by the people being surveyed, whereas voting procedures may be binding.
6. For the decision maker considering a major public project there may be considerable uncertainty about the validity of the assessment of public acceptability unless it is based on the results of a voting procedure.
7. For small non-controversial projects surveys of the public's view of the acceptability of a proposal may not be justified.

In a society that lays any claim to being democratic when a decision involves determining the acceptability of a proposal either to the public in general or a particular section of the public, the opinion of the relevant public must be assessed in the most precise terms possible. Ideally, the assessment should be quantitative. Although voting is the most positive way of making such a quantitative assessment, in a binding way, it is accepted that for many purposes a properly designed opinion survey may give an adequate assessment of opinion. For small or local projects consultation procedures may be an adequate way of assessing public opinion about the acceptability of a project.

From the examination of the efficacy of various methods of assessing the acceptability of a proposal in socio-political terms, the conclusions regarding the criteria that should be used for assessing such factors in general and for risk ranking purposes in particular are:

1. The assessment of the acceptability of the socio-political aspects of a proposal should as far as possible be assessed on a quantitative basis.
2. A possible relationship between socio-political factors and the ranking acceptability score is described in Table 7.3.
3. Ranking on the basis outlined in Table 7.3 could be described as being based on an assessment of public opinion about acceptability of the proposal.
4. The approach described in Table 7.3 is rather different to the way the Swiss Bank Corporation assesses political and social factors which was described in Chapter 3 and Appendix 2. The Bank is more concerned to assess the political and social stability of a country and not just the public acceptability of a project.

Table 7.2 Findings and limitations of six opinion surveys

Survey	Design	Findings	Limitations
Surrey University survey of perception of risk	Opinion of 1189 people sought on depth of unease about smoking, nuclear plant, work, air pollution and the home	Average concern 6.5 times average worry and worry 4.2 times average anxiety. Greatest concern smoking. Greatest worry and anxiety the home	Opinion limited to the time at which the views were taken. Did not cover all common risks, for example does not include road risks
IAEA/IIASA Acceptability of various energy sources	Opinion of 224 people sought on acceptability of nuclear, coal, oil, hydro and solar power	Opinion found not to be in favour of nuclear. This correctly forecast outcome of national referendum held shortly afterwards	It represents the lower limit for size of sample
Swedish referendum on nuclear power	Referendum to determine views on nuclear power policy. Preceded by a campaign to educate public	75.7% of the population voted. 58% voted for nuclear power. 38% voted positively against	After Chernobyl opinion changed endorsing the view that a survey is only valid for the time it is taken
Swiss referendum initiatives on nuclear power	Two referenda within three months. One on limiting licences to 25 years and liability to 90 years; the other one was for a modification to the Swiss Atomic Energy Act	The first was rejected by 51.7% to 48.3%. 49% of the electorate voted. The second was supported by 69% but only 37% voted	Although the Swiss are used to referenda, if used frequently interest falls. The method is slow but binding on the government
Dutch survey of risk acceptability part of finding an acceptable site for a major LNG terminal	600 people questioned. Special questionnaire SITE model (sense of insecurity with respect to threat from physical environment)	15% of those asked refused to be interviewed	Findings not binding on government. Only explored shades of opinion
EEC survey of acceptability of various types of power	20 questions to 9911 people throughout the Community on risk of living nearby certain installations; carried out in 1978, 1982 and 1984	Differences in opinion between member states and over the years more people considered chemical and explosives factories more hazardous than a furniture factory	Extent of comparison limited by the range of questions asked

Table 7.3 Possible relationships between socio-political factors and the ranking score

Acceptability	Socio-political factors	Score*	Equivalent risk acceptability rank
Unlikely to be acceptable	Less than 1/3 of the population judged to be in favour of the proposal	14	1
Only acceptable if risk can be reduced	Between 1/3 and 1/2 of the relevant population judged to be in favour of the proposal	5	2
Yes, subject to detailed adjustments to the proposal being made	Between 1/2 and 2/3 of the relevant population judged to be in favour of the proposal	2	3
Yes, without restriction	Over 2/3 of the relevant population judged to be in favour of the proposal	1	4

Note: *For discussion of scoring system see Chapter 4 and Appendix 4.

5. The difference between the Bank's criteria for assessment of socio-political factors and the proposal for risk ranking shows the importance of tailoring the criteria for assessing acceptability to match exactly the requirements of each family of applications.

8 POSSIBLE ALTERNATIVES

❑ SUMMARY

The various methods of assessing risk acceptability are identified and their potential contribution to comprehensive assessment of risks is evaluated.

DEFINITION OF REQUIREMENTS ALTERNATIVE METHODS SHOULD SATISFY

The preceding chapters have concentrated on describing all the factors that have to be considered in making a comprehensive assessment of decision options using a method such as the Risk Ranking Technique and the methods used by financial institutions. In this chapter a critical examination is made of the possible alternatives to those methods. Before launching into the examination of alternatives the perspective from which the examination is made must be identified. Essentially, it is that of the potential user. The aim is to evaluate currently available genera of techniques for assessing decision options to determine to what extent they have the capability to fulfil a comprehensive assessment role, such as that performed by the Risk Ranking Technique, or whether they simply complement or supplement comprehensive assessment in some way.

The ranking technique is considered to fall somewhere between the techniques conventionally considered to be hard quantitative methods and the soft qualitative methods. With rather more precision soft methods can be described as those where the boundaries of the problem involved are ill defined, multi-perspective and with no clear solution. The aim of this examination of alternatives is made clearer by recognition of the fact that the role envisaged for any comprehensive assessment is to summarize, weight and integrate for the decision maker, the conclusions about acceptability justified by detailed assessment of every aspect of each option available. In other words, comprehensive assessment is the last step in the assessment process, as it integrates the results of all the assessments of individual factors.

The typical decision-making situation in which it is envisaged that comprehensive assessment will be used is where an assessment has to be made of the acceptability of various solutions to complex proposals. The circumstances of the decision-making processes are such that the decision maker has to be prepared to defend his/her decision to a large lay public. As part of such a defence it must be demonstrated that all the technical, economic and socio-political factors involv have been considered in adequate depth. Such decision-making situations may found in major public companies, major spending departments of local and nati al governments and inter-governmental bodies. Typical of such decisions are d sions about whether or not to build a new kind of chemical works, decisions ab whether or not to build a power station on a particular site and decisions about the site of a new hypermarket. This description of the potential role of comprehensive assessment is simply to illustrate the characteristics that other techniques should have, to be considered as possible alternatives to comprehensive assessment, and should not be interpreted as limiting possible applications of techniques like risk ranking.

From the description of the role envisaged for comprehensive assessment it is possible to visualize a model of decision making that describes the circumstances in which the role may be played. This is shown diagrammatically in Figure 8.1. From the diagram it can be seen that the decision-making process of interest is

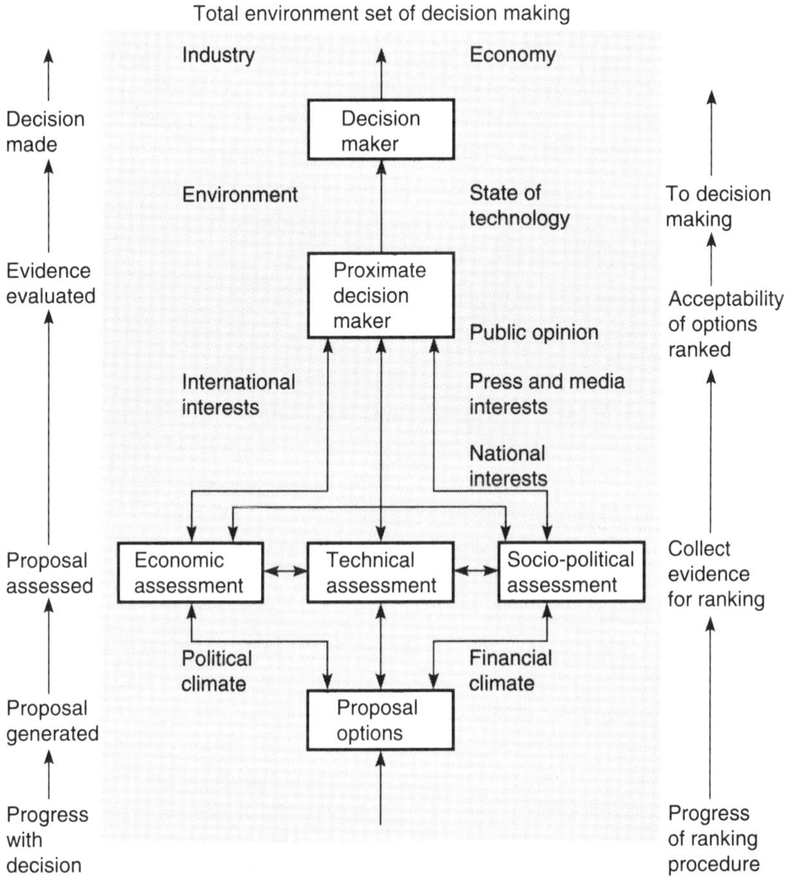
Total environment set of decision making
Industry
Economy
Decision made
Decision maker
Environment
State of technology
To decision making
Evidence evaluated
Proximate decision maker
Public opinion
Acceptability of options ranked
International interests
Press and media interests
National interests
Proposal assessed
Economic assessment
Technical assessment
Socio-political assessment
Collect evidence for ranking
Political climate
Financial climate
Proposal generated
Proposal options
Progress with decision
Progress of ranking procedure

Figure 8.1 Diagrammatic representation of decision-making process.

surrounded by an environmental set containing many factors that may influence and interact with the decision-making process. The diagram also shows that in the environment there will be interactions that will generate proposals; there will be some interactions that will support the proposal and other interactions that will be opposed to the proposal.

At the minimum the decision maker will have two options to consider, one option being to accept a proposal and the other being to reject it. In practice, there are at least two more options: no decision is taken; and the proposal is returned for revision. Once a proposal is generated it will have to be assessed. The comprehensive assessment process should, as already discussed, evaluate the technical, economic and socio-political issues involved and attempt to identify the advantages and disadvantages of each option.

Generally, the assessors are separated, in some way, from the decision makers. This means the findings of the assessors are passed to the decision maker through a proximate decision maker. When all evidence has been collected it is structured for decision making and passed to the decision maker who has the ultimate responsibility for making the decision. In practice the procedure is rarely so simple; there may be many iterative developments in the proposal as it passes between proposer, assessor, proximate decision maker and decision maker. These iterations may be required to take account of changes in technology, better understanding of the relevant technology, changes in the economic climate, changes in the pattern of demand and change in the socio-political climate. It is assumed that the issues involved are not trifling matters; in other words some form of de minimus test has been applied to eliminate trivial issues (Mumpower, 1986). In some cases it may be helpful to use a risk ranking philosophy to determine which risks inherent in the proposal can be ignored.

ALTERNATIVE METHODS CONSIDERED

We now examine possible alternative methods, categorized under three headings: comprehensive alternative methods, supplementary methods and complementary methods. Comprehensive alternatives are those techniques that can entirely replace the ranking technique or any other method of comprehensive assessment. Complementary methods are techniques that could add something to the comprehensiveness of the ranking technique. Supplementary methods are techniques that could overcome deficiencies in the ranking technique. The techniques labelled complementary or supplementary are not complete alternatives to comprehensive assessment as they do not look at all the factors associated with decisions in the comprehensive depth that the ranking technique does, but they may have an important supporting role to play in providing the evidence to rank the acceptability of some factor to be included in comprehensive assessment.

The main characteristics of the comprehensive alternative methods are shown in Table 8.1, those of the supplementary methods in Table 8.2 and those of the complementary methods in Table 8.3.

Table 8.1 The main characteristics of comprehensive alternatives to the Risk Ranking Technique

Possible alternative	Potential role	Limitations
Direct presentation of evidence with guidance on acceptability	Can be used in cases where the decision maker wishes to make his own assessment of the evidence	As it does not include any systematic comparative analysis of the options it does not improve understanding of the significance of the evidence
Direct instruction about acceptability in natural language	Cases where no quantitative justification is considered necessary	Defence difficult without support from detailed quantitative evidence
Review by experts	When a proposal is novel it may be useful to know the degree of support from experts who have some relevant experience	Could be seen as a way of avoiding responsibility for decision. Advice from experts has to be assessed and weighted. The experts consulted should either individually or collectively have an understanding of the technical economic and socio-political issues involved
Public debate	When public participation in the decision making process is judged to be required	May be a slow process. Does not ensure that the decision is universally acceptable. Does not always deal with all the issues involved in a consistent manner
Systems analysis	Can be used to identify interacting factors involved and establish their relative significance	The procedures are more aimed at establishing relationships than producing a quantitative comparison of the significance of the various factors. Can also be considered as a supplementary technique
Statistical methodology such as Bayesian inference or multivariate analysis	May give indication of possible outcomes in cases where the data is inadequate	Findings may be difficult to present to a lay public. Confidence in findings low when the analysis is based on inadequate data
Computerized simulation analysis of the options. Possibly based on a system with either artificial intelligence or an expert system	When all options and uncertainties have to be explored in detail and the interaction between the various factors is known	Confidence in method would have to be established. With a novel proposal it could give misleading results, if proposal is outside the range of the expert systems used. For the system to be effective reliable relevant quantitative data would have to be available

Table 8.2 The main characteristics of supplementary alternatives to the Risk Ranking Technique

Possible alternative	Potential role	Limitations
Soft system methodology	An aid to building up an understanding of the factors and relations that have to be considered. (This influenced the early development of the ranking technique)	It mainly concentrates on identifying the pattern of relationships associated with decisions. It does not normally quantify the significance of relationships
Cognitive mapping	To determine the inter-action of factors and determine their relation-ship with goals about which decisions are required (This also influenced the early development of the ranking technique)	It is more concerned with determining the commitment to action than assessing the merit of particular courses of action
Game theory	Metagame and hypergame approach can be used to explore outcomes of decisions when several organizations are involved in implementing the decision	Simply concerned with deter-mining the most likely outcome of a decision
Risk analysis	Although risk analysis is built into the Risk Ranking Technique, risk analysis can also be used to explore the consequence of the decision and the chance of decision being implemented	Does not necessarily take into account technical, economic and socio-political factors
Probability modelling	Probability modelling can be used to perform a very similar role to risk analysis	Limitations similar to risk analysis. Could be regarded simply as a variant of risk analysis
Multivariate analysis	Can be used to express the relationship between the factors involved in mathematical terms	To be effective really requires considerable quantitative data about factors included in the analysis. Such data may not be available for novel systems
Creditworthiness	To assess proposer's acceptability for a loan to finance a project	Concentrates on determining the creditworthiness of the proposer and in general gives scant attention to other aspects of a proposal

Table 8.3 The main characteristics of complementary alternatives to the Risk Ranking Technique

Possible alternative	Potential role	Limitations
Robustness analysis	To structure the examination of the findings of any quantified analysis including the ranking technique and focus attention on the possibilities of various outcomes in a variety of possible futures	Requires some quantitative data to be available about the factor or factors investigated
Forecasting techniques	To help determine the future significance of the various factors considered	Only relevant when the factors involved in the decision considered have to relate to some time in the future for which the characteristics are predictable
Resource allocation	To assess the merits of the resource allocation of the technical and economic factors available	Justification of the resource allocation tends to be limited to technical and economic factors
Regression analysis	To try to predict the future quantitative significance of every factor from analysis of past experience	Regression analysis can only really contribute to understanding the significance of options when future conditions are expected to relate to past experience
Decision trees	To build up a picture of the relationship between the subsidiary decisions and factors	Comprehensive decision making only deals with the end product of decision trees, as it is concerned with the final decision
Arbitration	For novel projects with arbitration between experts about the values that should be used for factors for which there are no data. Can also be used to establish common ground between various groups in the population	Arbitration only helps to identify the extreme views. The compromise adopted is not necessarily the ideal decision

The comprehensive alternatives described in Table 8.1 are listed in order of the increasing quantitative detail they are structured to take into account in arriving at their conclusions. For example, direct presentation of evidence and natural language presentation of an instruction does not necessarily involve any quantitative statement of the comparative merits of one option as compared with another. The most significant weakness of such approaches is that it is not a prerequisite that they have a rigid structure that requires specific factors to be taken into account in a consistent way. A review of a proposal by experts is likely to be made in very qualitative terms, but it is essential that consultation is structured, as described in Appendix 6, so that the distribution of opinions on all aspects of the proposal being studied can be assessed statistically.

One important variation of the conventional expert consultation approach, that is particularly useful in the context of the decision-making process in a company, is the decision conference. The decision conference is a meeting, which may be a regular meeting, to decide collectively with all the company's experts the best decision to adopt.

Important decision conferences may be held away from the normal working environment to facilitate concentration. This method is used by ICI, who have found that the process of reaching a decision is often helped by using a facilitator (Harvey Jones, 1988). The facilitator is unlikely to be an expert in the subject of the decision, but he will be an expert in helping the group to reach a decision. He will help bring problems to the surface and suggest ways these may be dealt with. Decision conferences can be regarded as a very special form of expert consultation. They are special in the way the range of topics considered is limited and in the way the range of experts consulted is preselected.

Systems analysis can be useful in building a model of the interactions associated with a proposal, particularly the socio-political interactions. Identification of these interactions can lead to detailed quantitative assessment of all the relevant factors. The problem with system analysis is its flexibility, which means that it may be difficult to ensure comparable consistent results, as the analysis does not have to be applied in exactly the same way each time. The influence of systems analysis on the development of the ranking technique is recognized and it could be argued that the ranking technique is a codified application of systems analysis.

Statistical methods including multivariate analysis and computer simulation using expert systems can be applied to give a more refined analysis of options than with the ranking technique, but the success of both methods depends on having good relevant data available. Also when proposals involve some novel process the use of expert systems may be inappropriate as the expert system may not include relevant information from which to construct advice. If appropriate data are available multivariate analysis can be incorporated into a computerized simulation program. In this context it is noted that there are some interesting computer programs being developed using multivariate techniques to assess the acceptability of risk. A particularly relevant development is the RISIKO-DIALOG Program (Jahrsbericht, 1991/92) that is being developed by the St Gallen Institut für Versicherungswirtschaft for assessing insurance risks. It could be adapted for comprehensively assessing a wider spectrum of risks.

ROLE OF ALTERNATIVE METHODS

The exercise of attempting to categorize the various decision-aiding techniques into supplementary or complementary techniques exposes some fundamental limitations to their capability and their potential roles. An important difference between the techniques is that some are based on hard statistical evidence whereas others explore the issues involved in soft qualitative terms. Perhaps the most important difference between the techniques is between those that attempt to assess the significance and impact of all the variables associated with a proposition and those techniques that are simply concerned with exploring the uncertainty associated with a proposition. There is a considerable degree of overlap in some of the techniques, as some are flexible enough to be developed as either supplementary techniques or complementary techniques or even as alternatives to comprehensive assessment procedures like the Risk Ranking Technique. This has resulted in the categorization tending to be arbitrary and artificial.

USEFULNESS OF ALTERNATIVE METHODS

The criterion for assessing the usefulness of the various techniques is whether or not they represent improvement of the logic of the ranking technique or significantly improve the quality of understanding of the factors involved. In making this assessment care had to be taken to avoid encouraging the use of techniques that would obscure the influence of the factors.

We now consider the characteristics of the supplementary methods summarized in Table 8.2. The most difficult method to categorize is soft system methodology. In some ways, because of the comprehensiveness of its nature, it could be considered a complete alternative to comprehensive techniques like the ranking technique. But because it does not attempt to make a quantitative assessment of the significance of the various factors identified as being involved perhaps the most useful contribution soft system methodology can make is at the preliminary stage of assessing a particular decision problem. At that stage soft system methodology could help to identify the interactions that need to be allowed for in the assessment.

The central characteristic of cognitive mapping is production of a map of all the issues concerned with a decision, including driving forces and restrictions. In some ways cognitive mapping could be considered as assessing the balance of pressures for decision options available. It does not attempt to quantify the relative merits of the options.

Game theory, in all its various forms, is principally concerned with exploring all the likely outcomes of a decision and determining which is the most probably outcome (Howard and Bennett, in Rosenhead 1989, Chs 10 and 11). It could be argued that the way game theory explores uncertainty is only slightly different to the way it was suggested, in Chapter 4, that the ranking technique could be used to explore uncertainty.

Risk analysis could be described as an overused term and because it is used in so many ways it can be misunderstood. In the context of this study, it is intended to cover statistically based techniques used to assess the probability of various possible outcomes from a particular course of action (Lindley, 1985; Walpole and Myers, 1989). Such techniques include network analysis. In relation to the Risk Ranking Technique the supplementary role foreseen for risk analysis is in determining the probability of the assessment of the values used for each ranking factor being correct and in the overall ranking being correct. As with game theory exploring the probability of the ranking being correct has been effectively covered by the three-dimensional matrix procedure described in Chapter 4.

The boundary between what is called probability modelling and risk analysis is very unclear and many of the analytical processes have similar forms (Hilton, 1976). This means the comments that have been made about risk analysis also apply to probability modelling.

Multivariate analysis techniques, which are concerned with determining the relationships between sets of variables, are perhaps less widely used (Hilton, 1976; Munford and Bailey, 1989). This may be partly due to the difficulty, particularly with novel projects, in obtaining sufficient data about the relationships between the variables. However, analysis of complex multivariate situations has been tackled (Hilton, 1976), such as those associated with political decisions and, as already mentioned, with the development of the computer program RISIKO-DIALOG for the insurance industry. Such complex models may not simulate the real world exactly. The models may be in error either because they under-identify or over-identify the significance of the variables involved. If there is time, and additional data becomes available, such errors can be iteratively reduced. In relation to comprehensive assessment it would be possible, if appropriate data are available, to allow the significance of variation in the data used to be explored by multivariate analysis techniques. Further discussion of multivariate analysis techniques is given in Appendix 10.

Creditworthiness is a specialist technique developed and used by financial institutions. The method is essentially aimed at determining the proposer's ability to repay a loan or to pay for goods or services. Concern about the technical and socio-political aspects of a proposal are almost incidental and perhaps limited to assessing the proposer's experience in doing what he says he wants to do and assessing his capability to do what he says he wants to. With regard to comprehensive assessment creditworthiness generates information that would be appropriate to include in some cases in the economic part of a comprehensive assessment. Assessing the capability and experience of a proposer, as is explored in Chapter 4 and Appendix 7, could be considered as a variation of this approach.

Differentiating between supplementary and complementary techniques is not as simple and clear as the words suggest. In several cases, particularly forecasting resource allocation, decision trees, arbitration and creditworthiness, it is possible to visualize that on suitable occasions the techniques could fulfil either supplementary or complementary roles. In the discussion that follows attention is concentrated on the complementary role, but where appropriate an indication is given of the potential supplementary role.

The essential feature of robustness analysis is determination of the range of predicted values that result from uncertainty in the data and the futures considered. In many ways robustness analysis represents a form of sensitivity analysis. It has already been demonstrated that a three-dimensional matrix can be used to display the variation in ranking that could be expected from variation in the data that have to be used. The complementary function robustness analysis could play in relation to the ranking technique is as an alternative to a three-dimensional matrix as a way of displaying the consequences of variations in the data used and the future considered.

Forecasting the future is inherently fallible, no matter how good the crystal ball or the oracle that is consulted (Lindley, 1985). Only if there is extensive experience with the subject of a proposal and if the environment in which the proposal is to be realized is exactly the same as past experience is there any chance of correctly forecasting the outcome of a proposal. In the ranking technique, there is an element of forecasting the likely outcome of a proposal, as the duration of the project and return on investment have to be investigated. By their very nature aids to decision making build up their conclusions on estimates of outcomes. To help solve this problem the influence of variations in the data used for ranking can be explored in a systematic way, as already described.

Resource allocation provides a way of comparing and optimizing the benefit or profit from particular courses of action. Generally, the comparison is based on the parameters of total benefit and total cost. The method could perhaps be used as a simplified alternative for assessing the acceptability of economic factors for ranking. If used in such a way care would have to be taken to ensure that benefits were measured in through-life terms. The method does not have the potential for being developed into a comprehensive assessment technique which optimizes benefit in terms of technical, economic and socio-political factors.

To be able to derive the equations for regression analysis there have to be relevant data available that can be used for the derivation of constants. Without such data the equations are no more than intuitive guesses. When the decision involves some novel process for which there are no data, regression analysis has no real role. It could be used for assessing the confidence in some factors. For example regression analysis could be used to estimate the overspend typically associated with government funded novel projects or it could be used to estimate the proportion of the population likely to be opposed to siting a petrochemical plant near a residential area (HSE, 1978). This means that the role of regression analysis in relation to comprehensive assessment is limited to helping to determine the likely magnitude of sub-factors used in the assessment of factor ranking scores in risk ranking.

Decision trees are used in several guises, which can include influence diagrams and event trees. Essentially, the technique helps to structure the decomposition of a decision into its component parts which can then be analysed. Provided appropriate data are available the method can show the significance of the individual components and identify where changes are most required to make a particular option more acceptable. Although the use of a decision tree is mainly in helping to build up an understanding of the significance of the individual factors, it could be constructed in a way that one branch represented technical factors and other branches represented economic and socio-political factors.

Arbitration is a difficult form of analysis to categorize. It can be used to assess the room that negotiating parties have to manoeuvre in order to find a mutually agreeable settlement. The technique could provide a useful basis for assessing the significance of socio-political factors for comprehensive assessment. Also the technique could be used to negotiate acceptance of the final ranking of acceptability with the parties involved in making the decision about which option is most acceptable.

CONCLUSIONS

This brief review of the main types of decision-making aids, which could be considered as offering the decision maker an alternative to the Risk Ranking Technique, suggests several conclusions are justified. The criteria used to determine the justification for the conclusions are:

1. Does the alternative improve the comprehensive assessment of the technical, economic and socio-political factors associated with a particular decision?
2. Is the assessment that the alternative technique gives transparent and easily defensible to both the media and the lay public?
3. Does the alternative give a better assessment of the significance of possible variations in data and the environment in which the decision has to be implemented than the Risk Ranking Technique?
4. Is the alternative flexible and can it be adjusted to give consistent results for various families of decisions?

One important general conclusion that must be recognized is that the efficacy of any technique depends on the quality of the data that can be used. For an assessment to be balanced the data about each option must be of similar quality.

The natural language alternatives such as direct presentation of evidence, direct recommendation, review by experts and public debate do not give results that are inherently more reliable than with risk ranking. The problem with such methods is that they can be biased by the views of the people involved.

Systems analysis does not really justify the title of a comprehensive alternative. The main merit of systems analysis is that it structures the identification of the actions and interactions that should be considered. The method could suggest weightings that should be given to particular factors that have to be considered in arriving at a decision.

Both statistical and computer techniques can help to understand the significance of the data available. In cases where computer simulation is possible it may give insights into the way major parameters of the decision vary. The value of such explorations is of course limited by the quality of the data used and the model used.

Multivariate analysis and comprehensive risk ranking can be considered as members of the same family of statistical methods. Multivariate analysis requires construction of a system of equations that fully describe the decision options. Without relevant data to allow the constants and indices in the various equations to be determined the method really only amounts to a theoretical novelty. If relevant data are available the method could be used to build a computer simulation model of the decision process. The RISIKO-DIALOG program being developed is an example of such a model.

Of the supplementary techniques considered soft system methodology and cognitive mapping mainly have a role in identifying actions and interactions that need to be considered. Game theory, risk analysis and probability modelling are essentially concerned with trying to quantify the possible outcomes of the various options considered. They can also be used to explore the implications of various possible futures. The exploration of possible futures with the Risk Ranking Technique has not been discussed, so far, but exploration of possible futures could simply be considered as a further application of investigating the consequences of variation in data.

Creditworthiness is only an assessment of an organization's financial strength and ability to deal with a certain level of financial commitment; it does not imply any judgement about the value of the work they do. But a variation of the method could be used to assess the capability and experience of a proposer.

Of the complementary alternatives robustness analysis and forecasting techniques can be grouped together since their special contribution is rating the acceptability of options under various possible future environments. These techniques have much in common with game theory, risk analysis and probability modelling already mentioned. Interest in the techniques is not that they endow the analysis of possible future conditions with special accuracy but more that they draw attention to the need for the decision maker to consider the future may be different from expectation.

Regression analysis, including multivariate analysis, assumes future experience will have a form that can be related mathematically to past experience. Even to commence such analysis, relevant data are required. Perhaps the most that can be said for regression analysis is that, if data are available, it may identify possible futures.

Decision trees help to build up a picture of the relationship between subsidiary decisions and the overall view; the efficacy of the method depends on the data available.

Arbitration is a rather different kind of technique and is more related to the natural language techniques mentioned as possible comprehensive alternatives. The special merit of the technique is that with appropriate arbitrators it could provide a way of reaching agreement on how socio-political issues can be solved. The significance of the arbitration is related to the extent to which the arbitrators represent the population involved and are aware of the population's views.

From this examination of possible alternatives to the Risk Ranking Technique for comprehensive assessment, the final conclusion is that apart from computer simulation and multivariate analysis none of the techniques considered is quite as comprehensive. Many of the techniques considered have their own specialist niche even though they are not complete alternatives to comprehensive assessment. Despite this, they often provide valuable insights in their own specialist area.

9 COMPARISON OF THE EFFICACY OF ALTERNATIVE METHODS OF ANALYSIS

❑ SUMMARY

The efficacy of various methods of assessing risk acceptability is tested on three real-life projects, and a practical demonstration of their advantages and disadvantages is given.

METHODOLOGY OF COMPARISON OF ALTERNATIVE METHODS

In this chapter three real-life case studies are presented and used as the basis for comparison of the role and efficacy of the various methods of decision analysis, identified in the previous chapter, with those of the Risk Ranking Technique. The three cases considered are: the proposal to build a new oil refinery on Canvey Island, the proposal to build a liquefied, natural gas terminal at Rijnmond in the Netherlands and the Channel crossing proposal. All three cases are described in Chicken and Hayns (1989), and some aspects of the Channel crossing decision have already been mentioned in Chapter 1. The perspective from which the efficacy of the various methods is made is that of the person responsible for deciding which decision option should be adopted and which method of analysis is most appropriate. The decision maker is likely to be someone at the level of a Chief Executive in an organization or a Minister in Government. It is assumed that the decision maker will wish to have a comprehensive assessment of the acceptability of each option. It is also assumed that the decision maker will have the necessary support staff charged with preparing the detailed assessments required to enable a comprehensive assessment to be made of the acceptability of each option.

The assessment methods considered are:

1. simple direct presentation of the evidence available with guidance about which option is most acceptable;
2. direct natural language recommendations about acceptability;
3. review by experts;
4. public debate;
5. systems analysis;
6. statistical analysis of the options;
7. computerized simulation analysis of the options;
8. soft system methodology;
9. cognitive mapping;
10. game theory;
11. risk analysis;
12. probability modelling;
13. multivariate analysis;
14. robustness analysis;
15. forecasting technique;
16. resource allocation;
17. regression analysis;
18. decision trees;
19. arbitration.

The way the comparison of the various methods of analysis is built up is to first describe the decision cases considered and then examine the way the various methods of analysis could be used as aids to decision making. In examining the methods, particular attention is given to determining to what extent they give a complete and comprehensive assessment of the options the decision maker has to consider. Finally, from the three case studies a series of conclusions is drawn about the merits of each method.

THE CANVEY ISLAND PROJECT

The Canvey Island project involved a proposal by United Refineries Ltd, to build an oil refinery with a capacity of four million tonnes/year on Canvey Island. Canvey Island is located on the North Shore of the Thames, 27 miles east of London. The island measures approximately nine miles by two and a half miles. About 33,000 people live in the area. In the area there are tank storage installations for Texaco Ltd, and for London and Coastal Oil Wharves Ltd. In addition the British Gas Corporation have a methane terminal there. Close to Canvey Island and in the general area covered by the proposed development Shell UK Oil and the Mobil Oil Company have large oil refineries. Additionally, Calor Gas Ltd have a plant for filling cylinders with liquefied petroleum gases. In 1973, outline consent to build the refinery had been granted.

As a result of a public inquiry into the desirability of revoking the planning permission that had been granted in 1976, the Government asked the Health and Safety Commission to make an assessment of the acceptability of the risks associated with existing installations and the cost of the assessment was £400,000 (HMSO, 1978). Three years after the first Canvey Island study report the results of a second more detailed study of the issue were published (HMSO, 1981). It is on the basis of the information published in these two reports that the assessment is made of the potential of the various aids to decision making.

From the first study it was concluded that the risks associated with the various industrial installations would be reduced if certain modifications were made. The conclusion was also drawn that, provided certain design and operational conditions were satisfied, there would be no health or safety objection to the construction of the proposed new refineries. The main objective of the second report, which was published three years after the first, was to show the result of making the modifications identified in the first report and the result of improvements in the data and improvements in the risk assessment methodology. The first report showed the annual risk of death to an individual in the area covered by the study was 7.40×10^{-4} per year. In the second report it was shown that the average risk figure had been reduced to 0.35×10^{-4} per year.

At the time of the first report the acceptability of the level of risk associated with the project was doubtful. The technical risks were not acceptable, as the regulatory body required modifications to be made. The economic aspects of the risks, however, were judged to be acceptable, as the owners of the various installations involved were willing to modify them and to continue to operate them. Concern about the socio-political aspects was high, as it was considered necessary to hold a public inquiry and to commission detailed studies of the significance of the risks.

By the time the second report was issued in 1981, the significance of the various factors related to acceptability of risk had changed considerably. The work done in the three years following publication of the first report allowed estimates of the technical significance of the risks to be reduced, making them more acceptable. The economics of the situation had changed dramatically as United Refineries did not go ahead with the project.

The special characteristics of this case are that there were four main actors who were: the Government, the public, the oil company and the technical assessors who provided the evidence on which the two reports were based. Another important characteristic of the case was that the decision-making process was very slow. It took five years from the time the Health and Safety Commission was asked to prepare the first report to the time the second report was presented. By the time the findings of the second report were announced, United Refineries had lost interest in the development. It was, after all, nearly ten years since they started work on the project and the market and their plans had changed. The Canvey Island case is interesting, as it is one of the first cases in which a quantified assessment of the technical aspects of the potential risks to the public was presented to the proximate decision makers. At the time the first report was being prepared none of the companies on the Canvey Island site had quantified assessments of the potential hazards associated with their plants. This case illustrates the equal importance of the technical, economic and socio-political factors, and that if one factor, like economic acceptability, shows the proposal to be unacceptable the proposal as a whole becomes unacceptable.

Now we consider how the efficacy of the assistance of the Risk Ranking Technique to decision making compares with the possible alternatives when applied to the Canvey Island project. The alternatives are discussed in the same order that they were dealt with in Chapter 8 and as identified at the beginning of this chapter. First, comprehensive alternatives are considered, then supplementary alternatives and, finally, complementary alternatives.

Seven comprehensive alternatives were identified:

1. direct presentation on the basis of evidence;
2. direct natural language recommendation;
3. review by experts;
4. public debate;
5. systems analysis;
6. some form of statistical argument perhaps based on Bayesian inference or fuzzy data analysis;
7. computer simulation.

The problem with direct presentation on the basis of evidence and direct natural language recommendation as compared with the Risk Ranking Technique is that they give the proposer no advance indication of the criteria the decision maker will adopt to determine acceptability. The decision maker might have some quantitative criteria in mind when he makes his decision, or he may adopt a form of subjective reasoning known only to himself. In both cases there is no indication of the range of factors to be considered or weight given to the various factors involved. If these methods had been used in the Canvey Island decision, it would not have been possible to show on what basis the decision was justified.

Review by experts is very close to what actually took place. The experts in practice concentrated on the risk to the public and did not concern themselves with the economics. The socio-political implications were dealt with by Public Inquiry. It could be argued that the review by experts was in the Canvey Island case only advice to the decision maker on the technical acceptability of the proposal and that the decision maker was left with the problem of determining the significance of the other factors. However, ultimately the role of the economics experts was central to the whole decision, as when the proposer decided there was no longer any need for the refinery that was the end of the project.

The Public Inquiry and the public examination of the official reports on the proposal allowed a certain amount of public debate on the acceptability of the technical aspects of the proposal. The debate was not of a form that allowed the public's view to be assessed quantitatively in a way that could be binding on the decision maker.

If the proposer had used systems analysis he might have identified all the factors influencing the decision about the acceptability of his proposal. This would have enabled him to assess the nature of the opposition to his proposal and thus determine the course of action he should follow to avoid or at least minimize the interminable delays he was faced with. Systems analysis does not provide a direct alternative to the Risk Ranking Technique but, by identifying factors concerned, it can help structure the assessment of socio-political factors.

In considering the efficacy of advanced statistical methods compared with that of the ranking technique, it is important to remember that the latter is intended to provide the decision maker with a rational, coherent and consistent way of making decisions which is clear and understandable to the lay public. The most useful role of advanced statistical methods is in helping the decision maker's supporting team to assess the significance of the evidence available. Apart from multivariate analysis the methods do not provide a comprehensive assessment of the proposal of the type given by the ranking technique.

The feasibility of developing a computer simulation as an aid to decision making is a very complex question. If all the information related to a decision is known and the way the variables are interconnected is known a sound simulation model of the acceptability of a proposal can be constructed, which will allow the implications of the uncertainties associated with the variables and interconnections to be explored. The RISIKO-DIALOG program mentioned in Chapter 7 is an example of a simplified form of simulation. Risk ranking could be built into such a program so that it could be explored. With a decision related to a novel project for which there is no substantial body of data, the benefit of computer simulation appears doubtful, as there would be no data on which to base the simulation. In such circumstances the Risk Ranking Technique seems to have the advantage of speed and simplicity over complete and comprehensive computer simulation of the whole decision process.

Six supplementary alternatives to risk ranking were identified in Chapter 8:

1. soft system methodology;
2. cognitive mapping;
3. game theory;
4. risk analysis;
5. probability modelling;
6. multivariate analysis.

The comment on the potential role and comparative value of soft system methodology is very similar to what has already been mentioned under comprehensive alternatives to systems analysis. Soft system methodology can help to identify the factors that should be considered in the assessment of the acceptability of various options. If United Refineries Ltd had identified all the groups who would be concerned with their proposal and had assessed the strengths of the groups and what was required to satisfy them, they might have saved a lot of delay in a decision being reached. In other words, the conclusion is that soft system methodology can help risk ranking by identifying factors that should be considered in building a ranking system, but soft system methodology in no way replaces risk ranking.

Cognitive mapping could, where the decision is novel, aid those assessing the options by helping to identify exactly what criteria are appropriate for determining the acceptability of the options available. Cognitive mapping could be regarded as an aid for helping the decision assessor to decide, for a particular family of decisions, what criteria should be used to assess the options.

Game theory, particularly when mixed motive games are considered, and the Risk Ranking Technique can have roles in which they support each other. The information collected for risk ranking can help the mixed motive game assessor to explore possible outcomes more realistically. The three-dimensional matrix of ranking (Figure 5.1) shows how possible outcomes can be rated. To a certain extent, the essential elements of game theory could be considered as being built into risk ranking. If the potential of risk ranking or game theory had been exploited in the Canvey Island case, perhaps some of the actors would have withdrawn from a very protracted game with a negative outcome.

Risk analysis is a generic term that covers many methods of analysis, most being concerned with attempting to quantify various aspects of the risk associated with a decision, the overall estimate being built up from the various components of the systems involved. Generally, risk is assessed in either technical or financial terms. The Canvey Island reports (HSE, 1978; HMSO, 1981) are good illustrations of the way definition of technical risk acceptability criteria for a particular project may be developed iteratively, and of the time and effort required to develop evidence that the criteria have been satisfied. The Risk Ranking Technique is an attempt to extend conventional risk analysis so that by taking account of the risk or uncertainty associated with the technical, economic and socio-political aspects of a proposal, a comprehensive assessment is built up of the acceptability of the risks involved.

The remarks just made about risk analysis apply equally to probability modelling; for the purpose of this chapter the two terms could be considered as synonymous.

The use of multivariate analysis, particularly in the form envisaged by Hilton (1976), consists essentially of building up a mathematical model for assessing the acceptability of the options related to a particular proposal. Such a mathematical model would be a prerequisite for the construction of a computer simulation of the type mentioned in Chapter 8 as a possible comprehensive alternative to risk ranking. No attempt was made to apply multivariate analysis to the Canvey Island decision, possibly because of the extensive data and analytical effort requirements to construct adequate mathematical models of a complex issue like the Canvey Island decision.

Each of the supplementary alternatives considered could, to a certain extent, help the exploitation of risk ranking methodology to determine the best decision. The soft system related methodologies can assist in identifying the factors that should be considered, and the mathematically related methods can assist the quantification of the significance of the various factors. In practice, risk analysis, using the term risk to mean possible harm to the public, was the only technique applied in the assessment of the Canvey Island case.

Six complementary alternatives to the Risk Ranking Technique were identified in Chapter 8, namely:

1. robustness analysis;
2. forecasting technique;
3. resource allocation;
4. regression analysis;

5. decision trees;
6. arbitration.

By their nature complementary alternatives to risk ranking are not strictly alternatives; more exactly they are methods that add some deeper understanding of the significance of the factors that influence the acceptability of a decision option. Both robustness analysis and forecasting techniques attempt to take account of possible future situations in which the decisions are expected to be effective. The Risk Ranking Technique, as described, is intended to be applied to assessing the acceptability of the various decision options on the basis of their through-life implications, which implies a range of possible futures has to be considered. However, there is no reason why the method cannot be applied to assessing the acceptability of the options under a range of possible futures. The result of considering various possible futures would be a series of three-dimensional matrices distributed along some kind of time continuum. If United Refineries had been able to predict the delays, changes in market conditions and the issues raised by the technical risk assessment, they might not have embarked on the Canvey Island project. Although robustness analysis and forecasting techniques can be used to evaluate acceptability in various future scenarios, there is usually a considerable margin of error in such predictions. This suggests an important advantage of the Risk Ranking Technique, which is that the criteria that have to be satisfied are known in advance. In addition, as already explained, the Risk Ranking Technique can be adapted to assess a variety of futures.

Resource allocation generally attempts to compare the merits of options in terms of the relationship of total benefit and total cost. This approach ignores socio-political problems and questions about the technical feasibility of an option. It assumes the significance of all factors associated with a decision can be measured in money terms. Resource allocation does not really offer a comprehensive assessment of the type offered by the Risk Ranking Technique and it does not seem to be a method that would have helped the Canvey Island decision makers.

Regression analysis and decision trees are tools that the assessor uses to build up the information required for the construction of the risk ranking. The usefulness of regression analysis depends to a large extent on the decision being one of a family of decisions about which there are relevant data. United Refineries should have had sufficient experience in building refineries and been able to predict the kind of delays to expect if they did not present a technically justified case. Decision trees can be used to build up an overall assessment of a project by constructing the tree from the various components that the decision can be decomposed into. Decision trees could, like other methods, have helped United Refineries identify the possible delays they would be faced with if they did not present a fully justified case.

Arbitration analysis might have helped United Refineries to understand their position in negotiations related to obtaining planning permission. This is an aspect of decision making partly covered by the Risk Ranking Technique, which includes an assessment of the socio-political acceptability of a project. Arbitration analysis goes a little further by attempting to assess on what terms negotiators might agree about the acceptability of a proposal. In the context of risk ranking this could be the extent to which public opinion is likely to move towards accepting a particular proposal.

RANK OF ACCEPTABILITY OF THE CANVEY ISLAND PROPOSAL

To complete the picture of the Canvey Island project, in Table 9.1 a ranking of the acceptability of the Canvey Island risks is given. The assessment was made *post hoc* and based essentially on the information given in the Health and Safety Executive Reports. Although the evidence was not ideal, particularly with respect to data on the economic and socio-political aspects, it does show how the ranking technique can give a logical comprehensive analysis of acceptability. The table also shows how the ranking of acceptability can be refined as better data become available, and reflects changes in the pattern of concerns that take place with time. The Canvey Island case also illustrates the tremendous amount of preparatory work that has to be done before a major project can be embarked on and funding is required. It also shows how relatively quickly market conditions can change and demand for a project disappear.

THE RIJNMOND GAS TERMINAL PROJECT

The history of the Rijnmond case is complicated and has its origins in the early 1970s when plans were made to import large quantities of liquefied natural gas (LNG) from Algeria (Kunreuther *et al.*, 1983). The two main contenders for the site were Rotterdam and Eemshaven. The decision involved the Dutch Cabinet, several government departments, the local government authorities of the areas concerned and public meetings. Safety implications and public perception of the acceptability or risk were important factors in deciding which site should be selected. The case is particularly interesting for the fact that local politics appear to have been a more important influence on the final decision than marginal differences in the quantified estimates of the risks to life involved.

Table 9.1 Ranking of the Canvey Island risks

Basis	Scores of sub-factors			Rank
	Technical	Economic	Socio-political	
First report	5	1	5	2 (acceptable only if risks reduced)
Second report	1	5	2	2 (acceptable subject to economic demand improving)

Discussion about which was the most acceptable site can be divided into three rounds. Round A was the period up to the final signing of the contract for the supply of LNG and included the preliminary search for a terminal site. Round B involved the Cabinet and several government departments, and at this stage it was recognized that siting of an LNG terminal involved several issues such as: energy policy, the environment, safety, land use and regional planning. At the beginning of this round Rotterdam was the preferred site and discussions were held with the Local Authorities in the region. These included the Province of Zuid-Holland, Rijnmond Public Authority and the City of Rotterdam. The discussions showed that the Authorities, particularly the Rijnmond Public Authority, were likely to apply stringent safety requirements to any LNG terminal. The involvement of the Rijnmond Public Authority is the reason the decision became known as the 'Rijnmond Decision'. In simple terms, it was considered that discussion of these safety requirements was likely to delay the start of delivering LNG and this led to Eemshaven being considered in more detail as the site for the terminal. Round C was the final round which ended with the Cabinet deciding in favour of Eemshaven.

In April 1978, the Rotterdam and Groningen Local Authorities were each given three months in which to formulate their views on the acceptability of an LNG terminal in their area. During this period there were formal Council debates and public meetings at which the public and interest groups could express their views. The views of the Local Authorities were presented to the Cabinet in June 1978. In August 1978 the Cabinet announced its preference for Eemshaven, primarily on socioeconomic regional industrial grounds. The decision was debated at considerable length in Parliament and finally approved in October 1978.

The view has been expressed that, in part, the reason that the decision went in favour of Eemshaven was that the Governor of Groningen was a skilful politician and a long-standing member of one of the parties in power. In this context the final decision appears to have been guided more by political opportunity than by consistent government policies, strategies or decision procedures. This in many ways underlines the significance of the socio-political factors in any assessment of acceptability. Attention must also be drawn to the fact that the decision was in conflict with the official advice of the Interdepartmental Coordinating Committee for North Sea Affairs (ICONA). The official ICONA report can be criticized because it intentionally did not consider either local risk perception in relation to public and official acceptance of LNG or the political importance attached by some interested parties to the siting of the terminal. In other words, the ICONA report overlooked the major socio-political influences on the decision.

Although ICONA can be criticized for not considering local opinion, it was the only coordinating body that included representatives of all the relevant ministries and in preparing its advice attempted to take account of national policy. ICONA advised that from their evaluation of economics, energy policy and environmental impact they preferred the Maasvlakte site near the Hoek van Holland for the LNG terminal. The ICONA view on the risks associated with the Maasvlakte and Eemshaven sites was that the risks with both sites were approximately equal.

The Local Authorities and the Trade Unions were in favour of Eemshaven. The

Environmentalist Groups, Shipowners Association and Electricity Corporation were against Eemshaven. The Shipowners Association saw some navigation and operational problems could be associated with Eemshaven, while the Electricity Corporation saw some risk to their existing coal-fired power station.

The characteristics of the Rijnmond decision and the scope it presented for assistance from various decision-making aids are quite different from those presented by the Canvey Island case. The Rijnmond decision was centred on socio-political factors, with technical and economic factors being somewhat subsidiary, whereas the Canvey Island decision was initially centred primarily on technical factors. This difference in the characteristics of the Rijnmond decision gives a different pattern to the possible alternatives to the ranking technique. The relative merits of 19 possible alternative methods of analysis have already been shown in relation to the Canvey Island Project, just discussed, so attention is concentrated on the alternatives whose role in relation to the Rijnmond decision is potentially significantly different to their role in relation to the Canvey Island case.

The merit of direct presentational methods is the same in both cases. The role of the review by experts is very different in the two cases. In the Canvey Island case the technical assessment was central to the whole discussion of the acceptability of the proposal. In the case of the Rijnmond decision the advice of the official experts in the form of ICONA was not followed. Perhaps the weakness of the ICONA advice was that it was neither technically specific nor fully comprehensive; it was more a distillation of departmental views. For expert opinion to be respected, it must be seen to be independent and comprehensive.

Public debate and the collection of public views about the Rijnmond decision options was rather more structured than in the Canvey Island case. It seems fair to suggest that the role of public debate in the decision-making process can be unpredictable unless it has been clearly defined. The Risk Ranking Technique attempts to avoid this problem by being specific about the criteria that should be used for judging the acceptability of socio-political factors.

The potential role of statistical methods and computer simulation is judged to be about the same for both the Canvey Island and the Rijnmond cases.

In the Canvey Island case the potential of the six supplementary alternatives to risk ranking was examined. The conclusions drawn about the efficacy of these techniques in the Canvey Island case apply equally to the Rijnmond case.

With the complementary alternatives to risk ranking, the conclusions drawn about each technique in the Canvey Island case are also equally justified in the Rijnmond case. The two cases appear to underline the importance of including some element of testing the possible future merits of a proposal in the assessment of the acceptability of all options. This view draws attention to the possible contribution of robustness analysis and forecasting techniques to assessing how acceptability may vary with time. The Rijnmond case illustrates how the formal arbitration process built into the Dutch procedure was used effectively. The procedure consisted of time limited debate at local level, discussion in Cabinet and debate in Parliament. It is interesting to speculate on the extent to which arbitration analysis would have forecast the outcome and helped the decision maker.

RANKING OF ACCEPTABILITY OF THE RIJNMOND GAS TERMINAL PROJECT

On the basis of the evidence available a risk ranking was made of the Maasvlakte and Eemshaven sites and the results of the ranking are shown in Table 9.2. The technical risk of an accident at Maasvlakte was estimated to be slightly higher than at Eemshaven and there was marginally more political support for the Eemshaven site. The table shows how the Risk Ranking Technique can present a comprehensive assessment of the merits of two decision options. Like the Canvey Island case the Rijnmond case shows how extensive the work is that has to be undertaken to get a project approved before it can be started and major funding can be committed. Anyone financing a major project, or indeed any project, has to be certain that all the preliminary work required to get the project approved has been completed satisfactorily before funding for the project is released.

THE CHANNEL CROSSING

The essential features of the Channel crossing options have already been given in Chapter 1, with a ranking presented in Table 1.6, but to enable the possible role potential of alternative methods of evaluating decision options to be discussed with more confidence, a few more background details of the project are given.

Discussion of a fixed link across the Channel has been going on for nearly 200 years (Ridley, 1985). Following the Anglo-French summit meeting in London in September 1981, an expert study group was established to evaluate the technical and economic arguments for a fixed Channel link. The group advised that they considered the balance of advantage lay with bored twin rail tunnels with a vehicle shuttle. Discussions about the acceptability of the various proposals came to something of a climax at the end of 1985 when the then Transport Secretary, Nicholas Ridley, announced that he was of the opinion that work on the project must start within two years. Ten schemes were submitted, but attention was concentrated on four main proposals. Consultants were employed to analyse the schemes and their reports were presented to the Department of Transport in December 1985. Nicholas Ridley announced that instead of a Public Inquiry there would be extensive public consultation, the basis for this being fifteen-page summaries of each of the proposals. The British and French Governments announced, in Lille on 20 January 1986, that they had accepted the rail tunnel proposal.

Table 9.2 Ranking of the Maasvlakte and Eemshaven sites

Option	Scores of sub-factors			Rank
	Technical	Economic	Socio-political	
Maasvlakte	1	1	2	3
Eemshaven	1	1	1	4

The four main Channel crossing proposals considered were: the Eurobridge, the Euroroute, the Channel Tunnel and the Channel Expressway. In addition, the option of not constructing a fixed crossing was considered. The main technical features of the proposals are summarized in Table 1.3. The technical, economic and socio-political justifications of the ranking of the options are given in Table 1.5.

For building up the ranking of the options the evidence that was used was that given in the official case presented to the British Parliament. There was no attempt in the official case to quantify the magnitude or the probability of the technical risks involved. In the evidence presented attention was not drawn to such facts as, in the Eurobridge proposal, the real experience with the material proposed for the suspension bridge cables was only about one-seventh of the proposed life of the material, and with proposals involving tunnels no justification was given for the acceptability of the explosion risk in such long tunnels. The justification for the scoring of each factor is shown in Table 1.5. Evaluation of the economic implications of the proposals showed that the total cost of the proposals was likely to be a significant factor in the economies of Britain and France. Possible variation in total cost is a factor that has to be considered in any project, as experience has shown that the cost of a major novel project often far exceeds initial estimates. As mentioned in Chapter 1, in quite unrelated projects such as the Sydney Opera House and Concorde, costs escalated to about ten times their original estimates (Hall, 1980). In the case of the Thames Barrier, the actual cost was twenty times the original estimate (Hansard, HMSO, 1985b). In retrospect it seems in the Channel Tunnel project the question of possible variation in cost was treated lightly. Concern about this aspect of the project has been justified by events, as the cost of the tunnel has risen dramatically since work began.

The assessment of socio-political factors seems to have been very elementary. Only minor objections by people living in the area of the terminals were reported in the discussion in Parliament and the press. This is not surprising as no carefully designed survey of public opinion was made. The only surveys made were by local papers and these are considered to be of questionable value.

A special feature of the Channel Tunnel project decision is that although the agreement of two governments was required the project is funded by the private sector. An important limitation of the tunnel decision was that it simply considered the Channel crossing and not all the implications of the crossing, such as the improvements required in connecting road and rail services. The essential features of the decision-making process was that the decision makers were advised by an expert group and had their decision endorsed by a democratically elected Parliament. The weakness of the decision-making process was that it did not detect that the estimates of costs involved were grossly optimistic.

The alternative methods that might have exposed some of the weaknesses in the proposal are public debate, systems analysis, soft system methodology and forecasting techniques. The possible contribution of the other techniques is very similar to that regarding the Canvey Island and Rijnmond cases.

In this case, the Minister reponsible took the decision not to have a Public Inquiry into the proposals, which avoided one type of searching public debate and perhaps shortened the decision-making process. It is possible that a Public Inquiry would have uncovered weaknesses in the economic case, the additional expenditure required for improvements in road and rail services, and the acceptability of the safety of the design proposed.

Systems analysis and soft system methodology generally would have uncovered the wider implications of the proposals and shown the need to recognize the road and rail implications of the Channel crossing. These methods may also have identified the need to consider environmental and safety issues in any decision that claims to take into account a comprehensive list of issues.

Forecasting techniques and robustness analysis could have provided ways of exploring different possible outcomes of the project. Such exploration may have exposed the possibility of a major increase in cost and its implications.

RANKING OF ACCEPTABILITY OF CHANNEL CROSSING PROJECT

The risk ranking of the options given in Table 1.6 simply represents a ranking based on the official case. If there had been access to the detailed assessments on which the official case was based it may have been possible to construct a three-dimensional ranking matrix, of the type shown in Figure 4.2. Such a matrix would have indicated the possible impact on the acceptability of the project of variations in the estimated cost. The Channel Tunnel case shows how important it is to have good quality data on which to base decisions. Unless there is a comprehensive understanding of all the technical problems involved in a project and the cost of their solution the economics of such a project can be put in jeopardy.

CONCLUSIONS

The three case studies have shown the significance of technical, economic and socio-political factors involved in decision making and the role various alternative aids to decision making could have played in the assessment of certain aspects of the cases. The possible contributions of the various methods to the analysis of the three cases considered are summarized in Table 9.3.

In general terms, the systems analysis methods were the only methods offering an additional capability not inherent in the Risk Ranking Technique, the particular advantage of systems analysis being to identify all the factors involved. Computer simulation of the decision process was not used in the three cases considered as there was not a suitable program available. The success of such a method depends on having a model which accurately represents a proposal and on the nature and interactions between all the factors associated with the decision. Building an accurate model to simulate the whole decision-making process associated with a complex project is a long and difficult task and the possibility of achieving adequate precision for a novel proposal is somewhat doubtful. The value of any model or aid to decision making depends on the quality of the data that can be used.

The Risk Ranking Technique can be adapted to adequately explore the acceptability of decision options under a variety of futures by building a system of three-dimensional matrices of rankings for all the variations that need to be considered.

Analysis of that type would fulfil the role of robustness analysis and forecasting techniques.

Table 9.3 Summary of the benefit of alternative decision-making aids to the three cases considered

Method	Possible benefit
Direct presentation of evidence	No advantage
Direct recommendation	No advantage
Review by experts	Useful if experts cover all disciplines involved
Public debate	Would help determine public acceptability
Systems analysis	Would help to identify actors that have to be considered
Statistical analysis	Helps in quantification of evidence provided data are available
Computerized simulation	Within the limits of the model used would allow exploration of uncertainties and options
Soft system methodology	Would help to identify all actors concerned
Cognitive mapping	Helps identify criteria for judging acceptability
Game theory	Would allow possible outcomes to be explored
Risk analysis	Improves understanding of technical and economic risks involved
Probability modelling	Would have a part to play in risk analysis, game theory and computerized simulation
Multivariate analysis	Could be a foundation for computerized simulation and an aid to risk ranking
Creditworthiness	Assessing financial strength of an organization
Robustness analysis	Would help to identify future changes and significance of variation in data used
Forecasting technique	Would help identify possible future changes influencing factors to be considered
Resource allocation	Assessment of alternative uses of resources
Regression analysis	Help understand the significance of data available
Decision trees	Assessment of the significance of the various components of a decision
Arbitration	Finding agreement reached between parties with conflicting views
Risk ranking	Comprehensive assessment of all factors involved

10 COMPARISON OF THE RISK RANKING TECHNIQUE WITH THE METHODS USED BY FINANCIAL INSTITUTIONS

❑ SUMMARY

The methods financial institutions like banks and insurance companies use to assess risk acceptability are examined and their theoretical justification and the extent to which they represent a comprehensive assessment of risk are evaluated.

BASIS FOR COMPARISON

Having examined the construction of comprehensive assessment of risks with particular attention to the Risk Ranking Technique, and attempted to compare its efficacy with that of other decision aids, this chapter concentrates on comparing the merits of the Risk Ranking Technique with the methods used by financial institutions. First the Risk Ranking Technique is compared with the methodologies banking type institutions use. It is then compared with the methodologies of the insurance industry. Although the Risk Ranking Technique is representative of comprehensive assessment methodology, the comparison is not strictly fair, as it was designed to deal with a wider spectrum of issues than financial institutions' assessment procedures. Nevertheless, the comparison shows some important features common to all decision making and some features of both types of methodology that could be improved. The comments made relate essentially to assessment of the acceptability of risks associated with major projects but some comments on the risks internal to an organization are also included.

An important initial assumption that has to be remembered is that the Risk

Ranking Technique was designed particularly for use in cases where the decision process had to be open for public inspection, whereas financial institutions designed their assessment procedures for their own internal use. Financial institutions often regard their risk assessment methods as confidential as they consider they give them a competitive advantage. It also means that the methods of financial institutions and their decisions are not generally subject to the same searching attention that the media gives political decisions. This is really an example of the way the decision-making environment conditions the decision-making process. The decision-making environment is an influence that the assessment technique has to be adjusted to, no matter what form the methodology takes.

It is assumed that the ideal any decision-making aid should aim for is for the aid to be capable of being adapted to decision-making situations over a broad spectrum. In the context of this study the decision-making situations of interest range from the perorating procedures associated with the development of advice for the Cabinet by think-tank like organizations (Blackstone and Plowden, 1988) to a bank deciding to finance the building of an office block in a developing country. Something of the nature of the processes involved in government decisions is described by Professor Nailor in his book on the organization and management of the British Polaris project (Nailor, 1988). The particular relevance of the Nailor study is that it shows how in government decision-making political, economic and technological factors interact to influence decisions. The interaction is rather an *ad hoc* arrangement and not the structured approach that would be required if the logic of the Risk Ranking Technique was followed. The study also shows how protracted some decision-making processes can be, and how the decision-making environment can change in the life of a project.

In the following the comparison of the Risk Ranking Technique with the methods used by financial institutions is built up in five parts:

1. intended roles;
2. coverage of technical, economic and socio-political factors;
3. the nature of the theoretical justification for the methods;
4. an analytical critique of the adequacy of the methods;
5. possible future developments.

The essential features of the comparison are summarized in Table 10.1.

DIFFERENCES IN THE ROLE OF RISK RANKING AND THE BANKS' METHODS

The major difference in the role of the Risk Ranking Technique and the role of the techniques used by financial institutions is that the former is intended to give the decision maker a comprehensive assessment of all the implications of each decision option, which can be defended in public, while the procedures used by banking institutions are generally intended for confidential internal advice to the executive about the credit risks inherent in proposals for loans they consider.

Table 10.1 Summary of comparison of the Risk Ranking Technique with the methods used by financial institutions

Feature compared	Risk Ranking Technique	Methods used by financial institutions
Intended role	Is intended to give an overall assessment of the comprehensive acceptability of major projects. The methods of assessment are in a form that is transparent and justifiable to a lay public	Essentially intended for internal use and in that role to act as the basis for advice to a financial institution's executive on the acceptability of credit risks inherent in proposals
Coverage of technical, economic and socio-political factors	Is designed to give a balanced overall view of technical, economic and socio-political factors involved in each option considered. However, the technique may be used in the mono-factor form to rank acceptability of one factor	The assessments tend to give most emphasis to the economic aspects of options. However, in some cases socio-political and technical issues are considered
Nature of theoretical justification	Ranking requires an assessment of the significance of each factor. The way the assessments are weighted and combined appears to be sound. The main source of uncertainty is the quality of the data that have to be used. The higher the quality of the data, the more reliable the assessment	There is a considerable difference between institutions in the justification of their methods. In many ways their approach could be described as pragmatic. They have identified a number of parameters which by experience they have found gives them a sound indication of the acceptability of proposals
Critique of the adequacy of the methods	The criteria used for scoring acceptability may not be appropriate for every decision and need to be refined	The range of factors considered is more related to assessing creditworthiness of the proposer than the comprehensive acceptability of the proposal
Possible future developments	Broad criteria for ranking factors have been developed. The criteria may have to be adjusted so as to fit a wider spectrum of cases. A computer model could be established to allow options and uncertainty to be explored expeditiously	The theoretical basis for their methods could be refined and assessment of technical, economic and socio-political factors incorporated. Criteria for acceptability could be more clearly defined

The Risk Ranking Technique has been constructed in a way that covers comprehensively all the factors involved in decision making and is transparent to the public. The methods used by financial institutions give the main emphasis to the economic aspects of the decisions considered. For assessment of the acceptability of the technical aspects of a proposal financial institutions tend to rely on expert opinion without having the clearly defined technical criteria that a proposal must satisfy. The financial institutions do not attempt to combine assessment of the technical, economic and socio-political factors into a single overall rating term, but generally consider the factors together when assessing the acceptability of a proposal. Ability to repay debt is the factor of overriding importance.

Attention also has to be drawn to the fact that the ranking technique can be used in the mono-factor ranking form in which the significance of only one factor, such as the economic factor, is assessed. If ranking based only on one factor is compared with the techniques used by financial institutions the only difference between the methodologies is the criteria used to rate acceptability, but this could be harmonized. The design of the ranking technique is focused on assessing the through-life implications on the acceptability of a project. This could be a component of the financial institution's assessment of acceptability. But financial institutions may not be so concerned with estimates of the through-life consequences of a project provided adequate security is given that any loan made can be repaid with interest as required by the loan contract.

Although it is possible to conceive that the criteria for mono-factor risk ranking and financial institutions' methods could be harmonized, such a view would represent a misunderstanding of the roles of the two methods. Risk ranking is intended to provide an overall view of acceptability while the financial institution methods are intended for assessing creditworthiness. However, an element of creditworthiness assessment is incorporated in the Risk Ranking Technique as assessment of the experience and capability of proposers and this could be expanded to incorporate a greater element of the methods used by financial institutions. For example, with the funding of a major project in an underdeveloped country of doubtful stability the country assessment methods of the Swiss Bank could be used, as these would give a greater insight into the financial risks involved.

Of the twenty-five factors the Swiss Bank Corporation assesses, twenty-four are concerned with economic performance of the country and only one is concerned with political risk. This does not mean that political risk is only considered to have one twenty-fifth of the importance of all the other parameters considered. But it does suggest that the financial institutions believe for their purpose a range of economic parameters have to be considered in order to arrive at a justifiable opinion about the acceptability of the relevant economic conditions.

DIFFERENCES IN THE THEORETICAL JUSTIFICATION FOR THE TWO METHODOLOGIES

The differences in the theoretical justification between the Risk Ranking Technique and the methods the financial institutions use are considerable. These differences mainly stem from the differences in the philosophy on which the two approaches are based. The financial institution approach is essentially pragmatic with the results of the assessment presented either in natural language or ranked on a letter coded basis. The Risk Ranking Technique attempts to relate an ordinal index of acceptability to the result of a rigorous scientific assessment of all the issues involved. The methods of weighting and combining factors in the Risk Ranking Technique are clearly defined and defensible and the whole process is transparent. With the ranking technique the proposer has a clear view of the conditions he has to try to satisfy. In the procedures used by financial institutions the targets that a proposer has to satisfy are not so positively stated, as there is a large element of interpretation of evidence. This could be described as the decision maker arriving at a judgement based on experience.

ANALYSIS OF THE ADEQUACY OF THE TWO METHODOLOGIES

The starting point for analysing the adequacy of the two methodologies is to look at the difference in their aims. The methods used by financial institutions are aimed essentially at ensuring that risks which could damage profitability are not accepted, while the Risk Ranking Technique is aimed at the wider horizon of comprehensive acceptability, takes into account all aspects of a proposal and is necessary where the long-term benefit to society needs to be evaluated. The Risk Ranking Technique could easily be adjusted to assess simply the risks financial institutions deal with. However, the methods currently used by financial institutions would require complete remodelling in order to give comprehensive assessment of the acceptability of decision options as is provided by risk-ranking. With any method of assessment the factors assessed and the way their significance is weighted and combined have to match the decision. The weighting and combining of factors is perhaps the most controversial feature of any aid to decision making. For example, in the methods mentioned in Chapter 3, such as the 'Z' test for potential bankruptcy, and in the methods banks use to assess applications for loans, the weighting and combining of factors are pragmatic and are only acceptable because the predictions they give agree fairly closely with experience. There is no justification for thinking the methods will be universally efficacious. Even if the predictions that these methods give fit a particular set of circumstances very well, there is no reason for assuming they will predict outcomes accurately in other circumstances. It is also possible other empirical equations could be devised using quite different parameters which would be equally effective. Can the weighting and combining of factors ever be done on anything but an empirical basis?

Comparing the methods financial institutions use with the comprehensive Risk Ranking Technique does give rise to two intriguing questions which are at the heart of business economics:

1. In arriving at their decisions do financial institutions take a too short term view?
2. Is the profit margin expected from financing projects of any kind too high?

These questions have many implications. Answers to these questions may be related to the way an institution likes to present its accounts and an institution's profit policy. Although computerized accounting methods allow the financial position of a company to be monitored on a daily basis, the main concern is often the annual accounts. Institutions are not free to change the need for annual accounts as these are fixed by company law and tax legislation. But for many major projects and businesses profit in one year is almost irrelevant: major projects may take five or ten years to complete and a business may take five or ten years to become properly established. In the insurance industry it may be three or more years before the pattern of insurance losses is known. If profit can only be judged on an annual basis it represents what could be described as the retail trading syndrome, which works against accepting proposals which when judged on a through-life basis make a more useful contribution to society.

The conclusion that these comments suggest is that when finance of major projects is considered, the whole basis for the proposals must be understood and their long-term viability assessed in detail. The assessment must include the socio-political implications of the project as it is essential to ensure that the organizations involved do not become associated in financing a project that is unacceptable in socio-political terms.

It is easy to suggest that financial institutions should take a long-term view of proposals they consider financing, but financial institutions do not live in a perfectly stable and constant business environment; they are subject to the influence of interest rates, variations in economic activity and inflation. If financial institutions simply float on the sea of economic fluctuations and do not offer a degree of stability in their dealings they could be described as operating in a way that amplifies fluctuations in the economy and working against steady, economic progress.

Attempting to answer these questions gives rise to a whole series of questions such as, 'Is a free economy the perfect answer to economic progress?; Is there really a greater role for the state in the finance of projects for the future well being of the country as a whole?; and In the future is there a greater role of intra-government organizations, like the European Community, in underwriting major projects?'. However tempting it would be to attempt to answer these questions, such a digression is outside the scope of this book. It is sufficient to say that in dealing with any proposal a decision maker must be conscious of the wider implications of his/her decision and the environment he/she is working in, and must be able to defend the criteria used for decision making.

The question of the appropriateness of the profit margin overlaps some aspects of the previous question, while it is appreciated any organization will attempt to maximize its profit margin. A customer buying a financial service has to be aware of the scope that exists in any purchasing situation for bargaining about the costs involved. Large organizations are often in a better position to deal with this aspect of finance than a small company, partly because they have more assets to use as security for borrowing and partly because they probably have their own specialists familiar with the market. In addition, a small organization will, simply because it is small, be regarded by financial institutions as a greater risk and consequently will be expected to pay more for finance. Disproportionate charges for borrowing can result in a company becoming uncompetitive. This factor is important in comparing the competitive position of firms trading nationally and even more important in comparing the performance of companies trading internationally. If the cost of borrowing in one country is lower than in another it will tend to put the country with the lower borrowing costs at an advantage. This leaves the decision maker with something of a moral dilemma: are charges and profits allowed for fair to all? This dilemma is not solved by the methodology of the financial institutions or by the Risk Ranking Technique but could be incorporated in them.

With all the methodologies there is some scope for development, as already mentioned in Chapter 3; the Swiss Bank Corporation iteratively refine their procedures. The comprehensive Risk Ranking Technique was first described in Chicken (1986a), and since then has been progressively refined. A large part of the development has been as a result of applying the technique to specific cases. These cases have shown ways the criteria for ranking factors could be made more potent. There is something of a dilemma about how these criteria should be refined, as postulated in Chapters 5, 6 and 7. One important form of refinement is to tailor the criteria for each specific application, which could be considered as limiting the technique's potential for universal application. On the other hand, tailoring criteria could, with some justification, be considered as merely a way of exploiting the ranking technique's potential. Criteria suitable for universal application may turn out to be so general that the element of critical analysis in the technique becomes so diluted that it no longer represents a useful aid to decision making. An indication of the way such universal criteria could be built up is given by the way Lloyds Bank assess country risk by scoring the acceptability of a range of 25 factors that they consider characterize the risk. It is stressed that it is not suggested that universal criteria should follow the Lloyds Bank form, but merely that for particular applications the usefulness of multi-factor criteria should be investigated. The way the criteria for ranking technical factors include a measure of the proposer's capability and experience, is an example of the way a multi-factor criteria can be developed for judging the acceptability of a single parameter.

To exploit the potential capability of the ranking technique it may be worth developing a computer model that would allow the various weighting and combination systems to be explored expeditiously. Such a model would also allow exploration of the matrices of decision options that develop if a range of uncertainties and possible futures is taken into account. (The RISIKO-DIALOG program, mentioned in Chapter 8, already contains elements of the required program.)

The possible future developments of financial institutions' assessment methodologies are that the theoretical basis of the procedure could be refined particularly in relation to the factors that have to be considered and the way the factors are weighted and combined made less arbitrary. In addition, the procedure could be refined in a way that gives a proposer a clear understanding of what is likely to be acceptable.

COMPARISON OF RISK RANKING WITH THE METHODS USED BY THE INSURANCE INDUSTRY

Having concentrated on comparison of the Risk Ranking Technique with the methods used by banks to assess acceptability of risks, a comparison is now made with the methods the insurance industry use to aid decisions about the insurability of risks. Interest in the methods used by the insurance industry stems from the fact that they have been used for assessing the acceptability of complex risks. The aviation risks that the insurance industry accept are a good example of the complex risks they deal with. Aviation insurers offer products liability insurance. This is insurance cover for compensation for death or personal injury, together with damage or destruction of property suffered by any person through the manufacture, supply or use of aeroplanes. Product liability exists if (Meyrick-Jones, 1986):

1. A product hazard results in accident/incident occurrence causing death or personal injury together with damage or destruction of property.
2. A product hazard results from the handling or use of any product in which there exists any defect, fault or condition that can cause harm.

There are five principal causes that can expose a manufacturer to product liability:

1. Failure by a manufacturer to exercise reasonable care in the design of a product.
2. Failure to exercise reasonable care in the selection of materials used in the product.
3. Failure to exercise reasonable care in the construction of a product.
4. Failure to exercise reasonable care in the testing of a product before it is put into use.
5. Failure to issue warnings and manuals in clear and understandable language as to the safe and proper operation of the product.

The view has been expressed that the aviation insurance market is fragile (Meyrick-Jones, 1986). Doubt has been expressed that the market could withstand a single major catastrophe or a series of minor catastrophes in any one year. In 1986 the maximum limit of liability cover available was US$1 billion and the annual premium income was US$150 million. The insurers attempt to assess trends in losses and to ensure that appropriate funds are available. Four examples illustrate the historical pattern of losses and their magnitude.

1. In 1974, a DC10 belonging to Turkish Airlines was lost due to a cargo door coming off during flight. Result: 346 passenger fatalities and liability settlement of US$54 million.
2. In 1977, two Boeing 747 aircraft collided on a Tenerife airport runway. Result: 550 passenger fatalities and liability settlement US$81,500,000.
3. In 1979, a DC10 crashed due to one engine falling off on take-off. Result: 258 passenger fatalities and liability settlement US$104 million.
4. The last 123 days of 1983 provide the most direct example of how the accident pattern influences premiums. In those 123 days there were 15 total losses and 5

major partial losses valued in total at over US$400 million. The aviation insurance market reacted swiftly and dramatically increased premiums. To provide a basis for decisions about premiums aircraft insurers do have statistical evidence about loss patterns and also knowledge about the quantitative reliability requirements regulators demand aircraft should satisfy. (The regulatory requirements are shown in Figure 5.1.)

In the general sense the criteria for insurability have been defined by Berliner, of the Swiss Reinsurance Company, as consisting of nine parts (Berliner, 1982). The nine parts are:

1. randomness of loss events;
2. maximum possible loss;
3. average loss per occurrence;
4. average period of time between loss occurrences;
5. insurance premium;
6. moral policy;
7. legal restrictions;
8. public policy;
9. cover limits.

The ways in which insurance criteria limit insurability are summarized in Table 10.2. The limits implied are stated in qualitative terms but in practice the limits have quantitative significance. The limits of insurability could be described as defining a set of insurable activities, the set being contained in an environment that includes all human activities. The construction of the set is such that insurable activities includes all risks that fall within the limits defined in Table 10.2. These risks would include direct losses due to natural catastrophes, fires, theft, equipment failure and indirect losses such as loss of production and loss of business.

The definition of direct loss, which is quite important, means in general terms the value of the physical harm done. The harm done may be calculated in several ways; it may be related to original value or current value. The method of calculation is defined in the policy and directly influences the magnitude of the premium. Indirect losses are the losses the insured may suffer as a consequence of a direct loss or some other event. Such losses are often not covered by insurance and some may fall outside the insurable set. There is, however, a fuzzy area in the definition of indirect losses where the quantification of the risk is possible and insurance cover can be agreed.

The following examples illustrate the nature of indirect risks and their insurability. Loss of profit due to business interruption resulting from strikes is an indirect loss that it would be difficult to obtain cover for. One reason for cover not being available is that it would be a form of insurance that could be abused, as the existence of such a policy could be used as a weapon for an employer to use in bargaining with his labour force. In contrast a loss of profits cover could be and often is included in a fire policy. Nationalization is another type of risk that would be difficult to insure against as the premium would be impossible to calculate and there may be legal restrictions against such insurance. Insurance against kidnapping is

Table 10.2 Limits of insurability defined by the criteria for insurability

Criteria	Limits implied
Randomness of loss events	It would be difficult to insure an event for which the loss pattern is completely unknown. The larger the insurer's portfolio of loss events the more likely he is to be able to accept a random event risk
Average loss per occurrence; Average time between loss occurrences	These two criteria are linked with the same limit. The insurer will attempt to balance the sum of his losses, that is: average loss per occurrence × number of occurrences per year expected in his portfolio, with his premium income. (The aviation insurance examples given above illustrate this point)
Insurance premium	The premium is equal to the expected annual loss plus expenses loaded to take account of any uncertainties associated with the proposal
Moral policy	This represents the allowance that has to be made for non-quantifiable actions that may be taken to reduce or amplify risks
Legal restrictions	Limits set by insurance contract law. Limits set by insurance industry's supervisory authorities. Some risks are covered by governments, for example insurance of nuclear reactors
Public policy	The extent to which crime, terrorism and social unrest may change the adequacy of an insurance
Cover limits	These limits the insurer specifies in the policy to ensure that both parties understand exactly what is covered and that the insurer is not exposed to some ill defined unlimited risk

also difficult to obtain as it may be abused. Other risks that fall into the uninsurable category are: cover against civil commotion, speculative entrepreneurial risks and processes involving genetic engineering.

This outline of the procedures used by the insurance industry to assess the acceptability of risks shows that although they do not assess technical, economic and socio-political factors in the same terms as the Risk Ranking Technique they do indirectly make some allowance for them. Technical factors are, to some extent, covered by the randomness of the loss event, the average period of time between loss occurrences and by the maximum loss and average loss per occurrence criteria. Economic factors are partly covered by insurance premium, cover limits and by maximum possible loss and average loss per occurrence criteria. Socio-political factors are partly covered by moral policy, legal restrictions and public policy criteria. Even though the insurance industry takes some account of technical, economic and socio-political factors they do not attempt to directly rank the results of their assessment of acceptability in the way the ranking technique does. However, the amount of cover they are willing to provide and the premium they charge to a certain extent represent the conclusion they draw from their assessment. Premiums do not correlate exactly with risk, as the relationship is subject to modification by market forces.

INTERNAL RISKS

In keeping with the aim of this book the discussion so far has concentrated on the assessment of the acceptability of risks that institutions have an option to refuse. In other words attention has been directed to methods of assessing the acceptability of projects that institutions are asked to participate in bearing at least some of the risks. To complete the picture of risk acceptability a brief discussion is now given of the implications and assessment of internal risks. Internal risks are inside an organization which it has no option but to accept. The internal risks can be considered under five major headings:

1. risks accepted being larger than funds available;
2. fraud by staff and clients;
3. audit risk;
4. natural disasters;
5. terrorism.

The way risks accepted may be larger than funds available has already been hinted at in relation to aviation insurance. In the banking sphere the provisions a bank has to make for foreign countries defaulting on loan repayments and businesses going bankrupt has recently caused many banks embarrassment to the extent that they have had to call on reserves and sometimes had to reduce dividends to shareholders. This raises the question of whether or not the internal controls of an organization are adequate to ensure that the risks accepted are within an organization's financial capability. Sound organizations will try to ensure that their portfolio of risks is kept within the financial capability of the organization. A mono-factor variant of the Risk Ranking Technique using simply the economic factor could be employed to assess the acceptability of a risk in relation to an organization's financial resources. Thornhill has described a check-list that could be used for reviewing the adequacy of the arrangements in an organization for keeping risk portfolio in line with financial capability (Thornhill, 1990). The exact form of the check-list has to be tailored to the particular organization it is applied to.

Fraud, which is really theft, is a very serious financial risk and is much more prevalent than is often assumed. Generally the person perpetrating fraud is an employee of the organization involved. But fraud is also perpetrated by people outside an organization; for example false claims about business activity might be made in order to establish creditworthiness for a loan or unjustified claims for compensation for loss might be made. Table 10.3 shows that 35% of the insurance claims related to computer systems were due to theft and this includes fraud (Chicken, 1989). To a certain extent losses due to fraud can be minimized by careful attention to personnel security and by ensuring that as far as possible operating procedures are made fraud proof.

Table 10.3 Causes of claims for computer system losses (%)

Flood	10.5
Fire	10.5
Lightning	5.25
Theft	35
Sabotage	18.4
Strikes	3.5
Miscellaneous	16.85

Audit risks include fraud of the type already mentioned but they also include failures to detect correctly the magnitude of the risks accepted. This can be simply due to a defect in the auditing organization. Such a defect can mean that the management of an organization is unaware of the magnitude of their true risk exposure.

Natural disasters are an inescapable fact of life. Floods, fires, lightning and earthquakes are always likely to occur but the risk can generally be reduced by careful siting and careful design. Not all flood and fire risks can be considered natural. Broken water pipes can be a cause of flooding and this may destroy vital records. Similarly, fires may be due to a variety of causes. The consequence of a fire may be to put a company out of business until the damage can be repaired and losses are made good. To a certain extent the losses can be mitigated if an organization always has in place an effective disaster recovery plan.

Acts of terrorism including kidnapping can have quite dramatic consequences and the resulting losses may not be covered by insurance. It is possible that a company may lose a very effective chief executive who would be difficult to replace. The pattern of acts of terrorism is quite random, although terrorism may be more rife in some countries than in others. The unpredictability of terrorism makes it difficult to estimate the amount of cover required or the premium that would be justified.

CONCLUSIONS

The comparison of banking and insurance risk assessment procedures with the Risk Ranking Technique suggests several general conclusions about the assessment of the acceptability risk, namely

1. The risk ranking, banking and insurance methods represent three different approaches to assessing the acceptability of risks. Although the methodologies are different, each one strives in its own way to identify criteria for judging acceptability that are effective in the applications they are used for.
2. The Risk Ranking Technique is the only one that attempts to be comprehensive and bring together the assessment of technical, economic and socio-political aspects of a decision into an ordinal rating of the overall acceptability.
3. The Risk Ranking Technique is unique in that it is intended to be transparent to the proposer and give him a clear indication of the requirements that have to be

satisfied in order to be considered acceptable.

4. The theoretical basis for the way the ranking technique builds up a comprehensive ranking of acceptability is defensible. The way the banks and the insurance industry build up their view of acceptability is rather more pragmatic. In all cases the quality of any assessment depends on the quality of the data that have to be used. No assessment technique can pretend to give a sound assessment if it has to be based on uncertain data. In such conditions all that can be said for the Risk Ranking Technique is that it provides a logical structure for the analysis and can be used to present the significance of uncertainties in the form of a three-dimensional matrix.
5. In the forms of analysis considered the criteria used for judging acceptability can be tailored to suit the requirements of particular families of decisions. But this does not mean the criteria are perfect and infallible. The difference between the economic criteria proposed for the ranking technique and the multiplicity of economic parameters banks consider illustrates something of the variation in the range of parameters it may be necessary to consider in some decision-making situations.
6. In the process of determining the criteria that should be used to judge acceptability several very deep moral questions have to be answered about the business ethics that determine what is considered acceptable. Simply identifying the criteria that should be adopted will not instantly change the current ethical basis of business but at least it may show the type of change that could, with advantage, be made.
7. There is still considerable scope for development of the banking, insurance and risk ranking methodologies. Such development should include developing more universally applicable criteria for judging risk acceptability. It is recognized that the search for universally applicable criteria may be an unachievable goal, rather like the search for the philosopher's stone. Nevertheless, it may be possible to identify criteria that are acceptable across a wide range of industry and government.
8. Although attention has concentrated on the way organizations make decisions about the acceptability of the risks that are external to them and they have an option to refuse or accept, there are indications that the risk ranking methodology could be an equally effective tool for assessing the acceptability of the risks that are internal to an organization. These internal risks include those accepted as being greater than the funds available to cover them, that is theft and fraud, audit risks, natural disasters and terrorism.

11 THE OPTIMUM METHOD OF ASSESSING DECISION OPTIONS

❑ SUMMARY

Three real-life and three hypothetical major project decision situations are considered. The risk assessment methodologies appropriate to each stage of the projects are identified. From this assessment optimum methods for assessing decision options at various stages of a project's life are postulated.

THE CONCEPT OF THE OPTIMUM METHOD

In this chapter an attempt is made to answer the most difficult question of this subject, that is, what is the optimum method for assessing decision options? In order to build up an answer to that question six subsidiary questions have to be answered. They are:

1. What will be the environment in which the decision has to be made?
2. What type of decisions has the methodology to be able to deal with?
3. From what range of methodologies will the optimum method be selected?
4. What experience has there been with the methods?
5. What data will be available about the proposal the methodology would be used on?
6. How will the efficacy of the methodologies considered be tested?

From the answers to these six questions an attempt is made to draw conclusions about what is likely to be the optimum method of assessing the merits of a range of decision options. To relate the answers to real-life decision making three real-life projects and three hypothetical cases are considered. The reader might like to consider how they would determine the acceptability of the three hypothetical cases.

THE DECISION ENVIRONMENT

The decisions to be considered are major projects of national importance. The decision about the acceptability of the project will be taken either at ministerial or board level and will be subject to extensive public scrutiny. The people taking the decision will be advised by a competent team with the necessary skills and resources to make the detailed assessments about acceptability. The decision process will consist of five decision steps, shown diagrammatically in Figure 11.1. These steps are: conceptual design, detail design, placing construction contract, construction and operation. At each stage there is the option to abandon the project if it is considered uneconomic or for some other reason unacceptable.

THE TYPE OF DECISION

The essential features of the decisions are that they involve major projects, which by their very nature stretch the resources and capability of all involved. The projects are larger than would fit neatly into the everyday loan decisions of a bank's loans officer. Everyday loans are defined as those the loans officer could decide on his own assessment of a client's proposals, an assessment which possibly includes analysis of the client's balance sheet, profit and loss account, retained earnings account and source and application of funds statement. The assessment procedure may include test ratios of some of the figures to determine the commercial viability of the proposal and proposer (Thornhill, 1990). But such an assessment would not involve evaluation, to any significant extent, of the associated technical and socio-political factors.

RANGE OF METHODOLOGIES FROM WHICH THE OPTIMUM METHOD WILL BE SELECTED

The methodologies considered will be the Risk Ranking Technique, those used by financial institutions as described in Chapter 3 and discussed in Chapter 10 and the alternative methods discussed in Chapter 8.

To set the scene for the evaluation of the three real-life cases they are now briefly described. The cases are from three very different technologies, which helps to illustrate the common problems of all decision-making situations. The cases considered are Concorde, the Sydney Opera House and San Francisco's Bay Area Rapid Transit System (BART) projects.

THREE REAL-LIFE CASES

Concorde

The Concorde supersonic airliner project had its origins in 1956 when the Minister

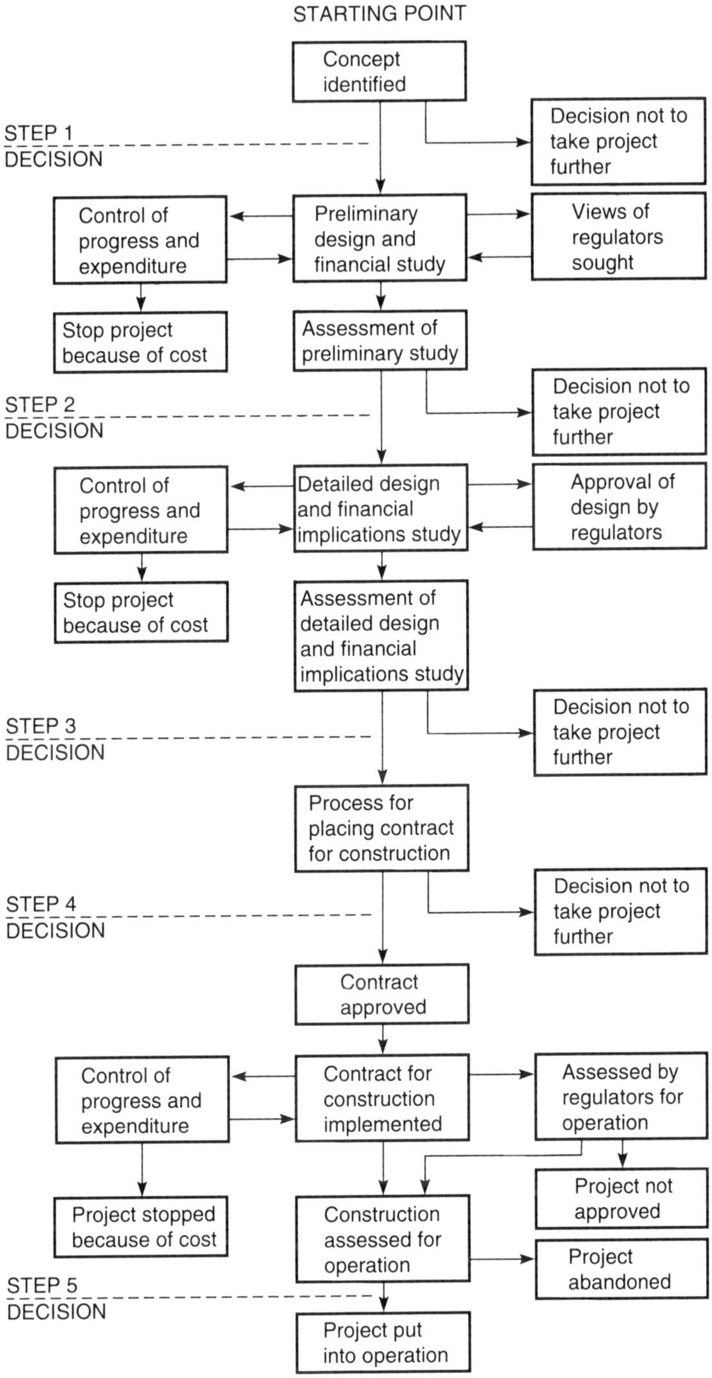
STARTING POINT
Concept identified
STEP 1 DECISION
Decision not to take project further
Control of progress and expenditure
Preliminary design and financial study
Views of regulators sought
Stop project because of cost
Assessment of preliminary study
STEP 2 DECISION
Decision not to take project further
Control of progress and expenditure
Detailed design and financial implications study
Approval of design by regulators
Stop project because of cost
Assessment of detailed design and financial implications study
STEP 3 DECISION
Decision not to take project further
Process for placing contract for construction
STEP 4 DECISION
Decision not to take project further
Contract approved
Control of progress and expenditure
Contract for construction implemented
Assessed by regulators for operation
Project not approved
Project stopped because of cost
Construction assessed for operation
Project abandoned
STEP 5 DECISION
Project put into operation

Figure 11.1 Decision-making process model.

of Supply set up a Supersonic Transport Aircraft Committee to examine the technical feasibility of a supersonic transport aircraft. The committee report published in 1959 argued that the British aircraft industry should start work on two totally new supersonic airliners; one long-range, capable of flying 150 passengers non-stop between London and New York at Mach 1.8 (1200 mph), the other a slower short-haul plane, carrying 100 passengers. It was estimated that there would be demand for up to 500 of the supersonic long-range planes by 1970. In October 1960 the British Aircraft Corporation (BAC) was awarded a design study contract for a 120-seat plane flying at Mach 2.2 (1465 mph). After some revision a 20-page design report was published in October 1962. In November that year the British and French governments signed a Supersonic Aircraft Agreement to share the cost of research and development of a supersonic aircraft. The agreement had no limit of liability, no provision for review and no cancellation clause. It was subsequently accepted that the British Government entered into a binding commitment with an imprecise knowledge of the probable cost. By June 1973 the cost of the project had risen over six times to more than 1 billion pounds. Some of the increased cost was attributed to Concorde being an extremely advanced technological project. As early as 1964 the government was concerned about the escalation in costs and contemplated withdrawal from the project, but were advised that in the agreement with France there was no provision for one of the signatories withdrawing from the project. In 1965 the Boeing Aircraft Corporation announced it would build the 747 Jumbo Jet with 300–400 seats. These aircraft were much more economical to operate than the Concorde, which was ultimately sold to British Airways heavily subsidized. Sixteen Concordes were built, the last one in 1978. The total cost of research and development and production was about 2 billion pounds, which was mainly borne by the British and French governments. Sales nowhere near covered costs, amounting to only a thirtieth of the original estimate. There are many lessons to be learnt from this project, among the more important being:

1. Unless predictions of market size and competition are accurate a company can go bankrupt undertaking a project that introduces financial risks greater than a company can stand.
2. Contracts should always have cancellation clauses in them.
3. Collaborative projects are always more difficult to manage than single organization contracts. By comparison Lockheed's Skunk Works projects, described in Chapter 5, shows how effective a single, dedicated organization can be.
4. Right from the beginning of a project a proposer should be clear where funds are going to come from and how loans will be repaid, including interest payments.

The Sydney Opera House

The Sydney Opera House represents a very different type of technology to Concorde, but is still very dramatic in its own way and had similar financial troubles. In 1954 a committee was set up to determine what kind of opera house should be built. The design was opened to competition and in January 1957, out of 233 entries, the design submitted by a 38-year-old Danish architect, Jorn Utzon, was accepted. The panel, which did not contain a structural engineer, accepted the structural design without any justification of its feasibility being submitted. The original estimate was a cost of AUS$7 million with a completion date of January 1963. The building was completed over ten years later in October 1973 at a cost of AUS$102 million. The rise in price was more than fourteen times the original estimate. Utzon had no experience of supervising any project bigger than one involving medium-sized housing, so it was decided to bring in one of the most experienced firms in Europe, Ove Arup. Arup was made directly responsible to the government of New South Wales. There were considerable delays in the detailed design being completed, partly due to changes in the client's wishes. It took Arup five years to complete the roof design. The contract for the roof was let in 1962 on a cost-plus basis, and the roof was not completed until 1967. Cost-plus contracts are always a risk as there is no commitment to a particular price: by the very nature of the contract they are open ended. Relations between Utzon and Arup deteriorated and in February 1966 Utzon resigned from the project.

One major problem with the project for the Sydney Opera House was that up to 1965 it was under the control of a part-time executive committee, which lacked the resources to evaluate the design in detail or to operate effectively as a client. In the 1965 election the New South Wales Labour government was replaced by a Liberal-Country Party coalition. During the election the escalating cost and delays in completing the Opera House had been a major issue. After the election the government transferred power over payments from the executive committee to the Minister of Public Works. The state provided bridging finance but ultimately the necessary funding was raised by lotteries – not a solution that is generally open to private industry.

The most important lessons that seem to be justified by the Sydney Opera House experience are:

1. When experts are consulted they should have relevant experience. Because the committee that originally accepted the Utzon design did not have experts that understood structural engineering or construction costs, they misjudged the magnitude of the technical problems involved and thus the costs. Also they failed to assess the adequacy of the proposer's relevant experience and capability.
2. The executive committee originally put in control of the project lacked adequate resources and expertise. This error was eventually corrected but had undoubtedly contributed to the delays experienced.

San Francisco's Bay Area Rapid Transport System

San Francisco's Bay Area Rapid Transport System (BART) is again a different technology. In many ways BART is considered as an expensive object lesson that should not be copied. The BART system provided a 71-mile long rapid train service around the San Francisco Bay area. The development really started in 1951 when the Rapid Transit Commission for the Bay area was inaugurated. The commission first made a preliminary study and then in 1953 commissioned a full-scale consultancy study. In January 1956 the consultants presented their report and concluded that:

1. There was a need for a rapid transit system in the Bay area.
2. The route would link existing population centres.
3. The system should be based on conventional trains running on rails.
4. Cost would be between US$586 million and US$720 million. The consultants were clear that operation of the system would require an annual subsidy of perhaps US$38 million.

In April 1959, consultants were appointed to make a detailed design study. They reported in May 1961 and estimated the cost would be US$1.3 billion. After heated discussion between the parties involved it was agreed to shorten the system from 123 miles to 75 miles and this was expected to reduce the cost to US$923 million. In 1962, consultants were appointed to construct the system. The system was considered as novel and unproven as it involved carriages of lightweight construction controlled not by drivers but by computers. The BART Authority had no technical expertise to judge the technical efficacy of the proposals made by the consultants. It was found that traditional railroad manufacturers were not capable of dealing with such advanced designs so aerospace manufacturers were called in and they had to learn about railroads. The control system designed gave rise to many problems and initial operation started with an old system of manual block control. Many problems were experienced with the lightweight cars. Breakdowns occurred due to failures in motors, electronic components, brake systems, door controls and air conditioners. Part of the problem was because the main contractor Rohr had little tradition of controlling and coordinating subcontractors, or, put another way, they simply had poor 'total quality management'.

The original plan was that the system should be complete by January 1971; it was in fact October 1974 before it was finished. The final total cost of the construction of the BART system was US$1.6 billion, which as a percentage increase over the original estimate was small as compared with the other two cases considered. Operating the BART system gave rise to many serious problems. In 1976 the number of passengers carried was only 51% of forecast. The average fare on BART was 72 cents and the costs US$4.48 per trip leaving US$3.76 to be covered by subsidy. The total annual subsidy required was very close to the consultant's original estimate of US$38 million. The concern about the project is that as the system is under-used and making a loss, the money could have been spent in a different way that would be of more benefit to the people in the Bay area.

The lessons from the BART case are very similar to those from the Sydney Opera House, namely that the client should have his own team of experts for assessing the magnitude and significance of the problems involved in a project that incorporates novel technology and suppliers working outside their previous experience.

IMPLICATIONS FOR DECISION MAKING IN THE ABOVE CASES

These three cases provide many important lessons for decision makers. In Table 11.1, the general nature of problems experienced in the three cases considered are summarized.

Model of project decision making

Having identified something of the complex nature of the type of major decisions being considered in this study, the model of the decision-making process as

Table 11.1 General nature of the problems experienced in the three cases considered

Project	Completion date	Delay in completion	Ratio final cost/ initial cost estimate	Comment
Concorde	1978	About 5 years due to major design modification	13	In addition there were losses due to operation of Concorde that had to be covered. There seems to have been no progressive updating of the estimate of the market for the plane. Technical and financial control not coordinated
Sydney Opera House	1973	10 years	14.6	Original decision taken on the basis of inadequate understanding of the technical and financial implications of the proposal. The experience and capability of the proposer was not assessed. Management problems on site
San Francisco Bay Area Rapid Transit System (BART)	1974	3.75 years	1.7	Client did not have technical or financial capability to judge proposals. Experience and capability of suppliers not effectively assessed. Traffic for system only half that estimated. System requires continuing subsidy

presented in Figure 11.1 can be discussed. The model is more comprehensive than that presented as Figure 2.3, but follows the same general pattern. It is also intended that the model is consistent with the decision-making processes associated with the three cases just considered. Perhaps if all the checks allowed for in the model had been properly followed in the three cases the outcome would have been happier.

In the model, as in real life, the starting point for the decision process is identification of a concept. This may take place in many different ways including as a result of pressure from customers, market assessment inside an organization, political pressures, the need to exploit new technology or some defence requirement. The concept may be rejected immediately or funds may be provided to make a preliminary design and financial study. In the model the terms 'design' and 'financial study' are used rather loosely. Design is intended to cover design of both engineering systems and service systems. The financial study should cover all costs, including implementation of project, the cost of further development of the concept and evaluation of the likely through-life net benefit of exploiting the concept. At each step in the project progress must be monitored to determine whether or not it is being kept within the specification on which the decision about its acceptability was made. If the project deviates from specification its acceptability will have to be reconsidered.

Even at the conceptual stage there should be preliminary discussion with the relevant regulatory authorities to determine if any special requirements are likely to be imposed. Such a procedure is vital with any novel project, or any project that contains features that are a departure from established practice. When the preliminary study is complete it will have to be assessed to determine if it is worthwhile to proceed with a detailed design and financial implication study. The assessment must consider the proposal in terms of the acceptability of technical, economic and socio-political factors involved. The economic assessment at this stage should include an evaluation of the availability and cost of the funds required to bring the project to fruition. Possible sources of funds would assess in their own way their willingness to be involved with the project. For this the Risk Ranking Technique would be an appropriate tool. At such an early stage in a project all the necessary data for risk ranking are unlikely to be available, but the technique imposes a logical structure on the assessment and ensures that all the relevant factors are considered. If the project goes ahead the ranking of acceptability can then be refined as more data become available.

If a project goes to the detailed design stage similar management controls will have to be exercised and acceptability assessments made, with a built-in option to cancel the project if it deviates from specification. The ranking of acceptability should at this stage be quite refined as it is on the basis of assessment at this stage that major financial resources will be committed. The greater the confidence that can be established in the various estimates the more likely the project is to justify funding and to be a financial success.

Assessing which tenderer should be given the construction contract involves consideration of the capability and relevant experience of the tenderers. In a major project it is not just the competence of the major contractor that is of concern but the competence of all the subcontractors. The experience of Rohr in the BART project, mentioned earlier, illustrates the kind of problem that can arise. This emphasizes the fact that judging the capability and experience of contractors is not something that can be taken lightly. The assessment must determine whether or not the contractor has the effective total quality assurance procedures in place.

All through the life of the project there must exist the option to abandon it. There is no merit in building a plant that produces a product for which there is no adequate demand. Similarly, if the regulators will not approve an installation it must either be modified to satisfy their requirements or, if that is not an acceptable solution, the project must be abandoned.

ASSESSMENT OF THREE HYPOTHETICAL CASES

Having set out the decision-making process the model is now used as an aid to explore the decision-making processes likely to be associated with three imaginary

Table 11.2 Data for the 1000-seat aircraft project

Name of project
The 1000-seat, long range aircraft project

Nature of the project (specification)
The project is to design, test and manufacture a 1000-seat aircraft that will have a range of 15,000 miles and a life in excess of 100,000 flying hours. A speed of Mach 0.95 (sub-sonic), a service ceiling of 14,000 metres. A cargo variant to be capable of carrying 100 tons of cargo. Capable of landing and taking off from existing airport runways.

Organization of project
The project to be undertaken by a single company set up specially for the purpose with half the £50 million capital provided by the government and half by a single major aircraft manufacturer. The government would underwrite commercial bank loans up to £500 million. In the long term, development costs are to be recovered and an adequate return made on the investment. Whatever technical resources the company needs that are not available from the company's own resources are to be bought in at ordinary commercial rates.

Timescale
- One year for a preliminary design study.
- Three years for detailed design study and all research and development work required.
- Two years to build a prototype.
- One year for test flying and certification of aircraft.

If after eight years there were not enough orders to make a viable commercial proposition the project would be wound up.

Problems anticipated
1 airlines are unwilling to buy a 1000-seat aeroplane;
2 airport owners are unwilling to adapt their airports to handle 1000-seat aircraft;
3 countries are unwilling to adapt their transport facilities to the needs of airports handling 1000-seat aircraft;
4 the insurance market is unwilling to insure an aeroplane carrying 1000 passengers;
5 100,000-hour life cannot be achieved.

Table 11.3 Data for the prestige concert hall for Europe

Name of project
The prestige concert hall for the European Community

Nature of the project (specification)
To build a prestige concert hall for the European Community that can be used for all major theatrical and musical productions including full-scale operas. The building also to be suitable for conferences and exhibitions. The layout to be arranged to include seating for 3500 people, with adequate provision for rehearsal rooms and smaller productions.

The site of the building has not yet been decided but it must be located in such a way that it has good communications with all major centres of population in the community.

Organization of project
The Commission of the European Community is to establish a project committee with responsibility for building the concert hall. The Commission will pay for the hall and for its running. It is stipulated that all contracts must be open to tenders from all member states, as is common practice.

Timescale
- One year to find a suitable site.
- Two years to design the building.
- Three years to build and commission the building.

Problems anticipated
1 finding a site that is acceptable to all member states;
2 obtaining planning approval to build the concert hall on the agreed site;
3 obtaining the required quality of construction and finish;
4 a non-technically qualified committee managing the project.

proposals. Although the cases are imaginary it is hoped that the reader will be able to associate them with real-life projects. The three cases are: a 1000-seat aircraft with a 15,000-mile range, a prestige concert hall for the European Community and a unified high speed rail system for Europe. The projects are in the realms of possibility and each is endowed with many potentially controversial aspects. Each of the projects has arrived at the conceptual stage and in the following the various problems the decision maker will be faced with in the process of the projects being brought to fruition are explored. The essential features of the projects are summarized in the form of data sheets. Table 11.2 is the data sheet for the 1000-seat aircraft; Table 11.3 is the data sheet for the prestige concert hall; Table 11.4 is the data sheet for the high speed rail system for Europe.

In each case there is some governmental involvement either at the national level or the European Community level, so it is not difficult to envisage the type of political considerations that must be taken into account. The aircraft project is the nearest to being a private sector venture. The concert hall is completely a Community project and from the outset beset by problems of getting the various member states to agree. Politically, the high speed rail system project is likely to be the most difficult as governments are likely to be doubly involved. In most cases the national railways are state owned and the European Community Commission will be involved with a cash commitment and a political interest in the project. In determining what action to take the Commission will have to take into account a difficult set of pressures from the various national governments involved.

Table 11.4 Data sheet for high speed rail system for Europe

Name of project
The high speed rail system project for the European Community

Nature of the project (specification)
To establish a unified high speed rail system for passengers and goods linking all cities in the European Community with a population of one million or more. The intention is to ease pressure on the roads and airlines and to speed the transport of goods around the Community. It is expected the trains will operate at 200 mph. In some cases the service will be operated in conjunction with existing services but it is expected it will require its own special tracks and separation from existing tracks.

Organization of project
All railway companies in the Community would cooperate to establish a new company charged with the responsibility of establishing and operating the high speed rail system. The companies would put up £5 billion in capital and the Commission would put up another £5 billion. If further capital is required it would be raised commercially.

Timescale
- Two years to agree routes.
- Four years to build tracks and install signalling equipment.
- Six years to design and build rolling stock, stations and marshalling yards.

If after four years the routes had not been agreed and a start made on laying track the Commission would have the right to withdraw the funds it provided.

Problems anticipated
1 railway companies not willing to collaborate on the scale envisaged;
2 railway companies cannot provide the required capital;
3 routes cannot be agreed;
4 design and reliability problems with rolling stock and signalling equipment.

In examining the decision processes in each project the decisions that have to be made at two representative steps in the overall plan are evaluated. It is assumed that in each case the project organization identified has been established, is fully operational and committed to performing the first task in the programme.

PRELIMINARY STAGE OF PROJECT ASSESSMENT

At the end of the preliminary stage ranking acceptability has to be made on the basis of mainly qualitative evidence, but consistency in the ranking is essential. The criteria defined earlier in Tables 5.2, 6.2 and 7.3 are not entirely appropriate, so slightly different ones have been adopted for this demonstration, as set out in Table 11.5. Although it is stressed the criteria are designed just for demonstration purposes, the need to design special criteria does underline the fact that the criteria used for ranking must be appropriate to the particular application.

In practice the whole organization will not be devoted just to the first task; there will be some preliminary work on the later tasks proceeding in parallel. Nevertheless, at the end of the first task a decision is likely to have to be made about whether or not to proceed to the second step. Figures 11.2, 11.3 and 11.4 show how the data available at the end of the first step in each project are incorporated into the ranking process assessment of the acceptability of moving to

Table 11.5 Ranking criteria for the three imaginary projects

Rank	Technical (definition)	Economic criteria	Socio-political criteria
4 Acceptable	Original specification met	Economic return requirements satisfied	No public or political opposition to the project
3 Acceptable with minor changes	Additional work required to satisfy specification	It will take longer than expected to earn an acceptable return	Some public opposition to the project
2 Acceptable with major changes	Extensive additional work required to satisfy specification	Additional funding required which may make project uneconomical	Serious public opposition to the project. It may not be possible to reduce opposition
1 Unacceptable	No way to satisfy specification or acceptable variation of it	Economic targets unlikely to be satisfied	Extensive opposition to the project that cannot be placated

the second step. Figure 11.2 shows how the ranking can be built up at the end of the preliminary design stage of the 1000-seat aircraft project. Figure 11.3 shows how the ranking can be built up at the end of the preliminary design stage of the prestige concert hall project. Figure 11.4 shows the ranking at the end of the preliminary design stage of the high speed rail system project.

As these are imaginary cases it is not clear exactly who will be the decision makers. In the cases of the 1000-seat aircraft and the high speed rail system projects it is tempting to imagine that the chief executive of the company involved would be the decision maker, but as there is government money in the projects it is likely that there will be a government committee somewhere that has at least to agree with the decision and a Minister who would have to be convinced about the justification for the decision. The Minister is likely to have to defend the project both in Parliament and in the Cabinet. In a rather similar way the prestige concert hall will have to be defended through the European Parliament. It is also possible that the projects will have to be defended in some investigative enquiry by the media. The public defence of the projects will cover the technical, economic and socio-political aspects, so it is important to apply the ranking technique methodology consistently from the beginning of project life and to iteratively refine the analysis as the projects proceed.

From Figures 11.2, 11.3 and 11.4 it can be seen that the ranking technique structures the analysis of the projects by requiring technical, economic and socio-political factors to be assessed in parallel and an overall assessment of acceptability made by integrating the assessment of individual factors. In the assessment of the hypothetical cases no attempt is made to evaluate the significance of variation in

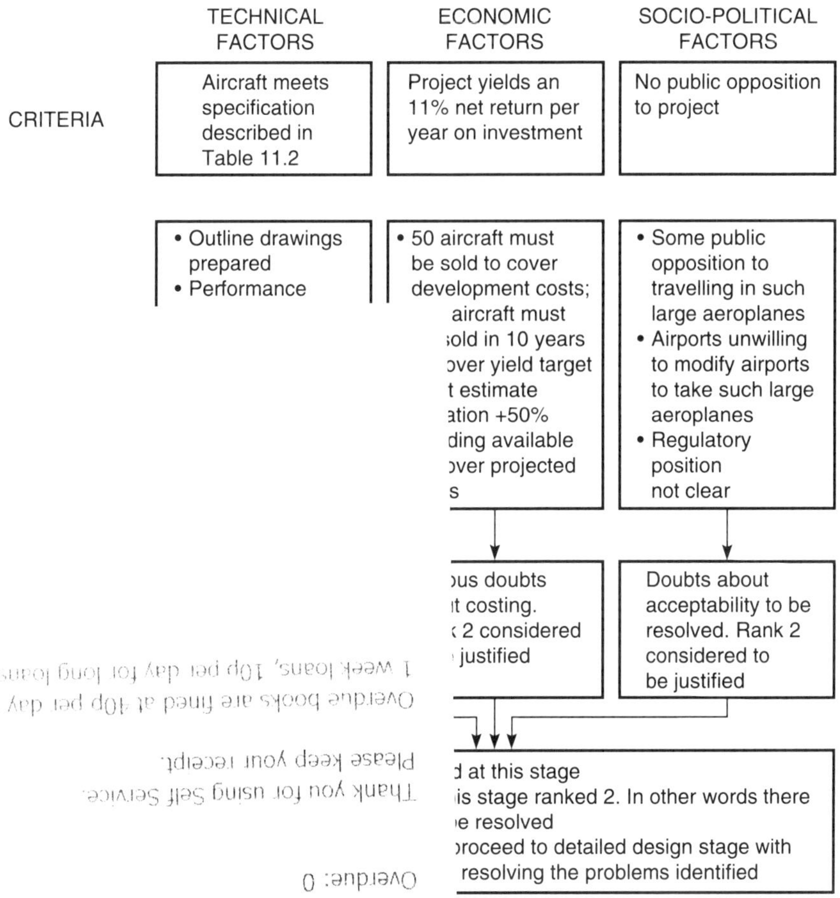
TECHNICAL FACTORS
ECONOMIC FACTORS
SOCIO-POLITICAL FACTORS
CRITERIA
Aircraft meets specification described in Table 11.2
Project yields an 11% net return per year on investment
No public opposition to project
• Outline drawings prepared
• Performance
• 50 aircraft must be sold to cover development costs;
aircraft must
sold in 10 years
over yield target
t estimate
ation +50%
ding available
over projected
s
• Some public opposition to travelling in such large aeroplanes
• Airports unwilling to modify airports to take such large aeroplanes
• Regulatory position not clear
ous doubts
t costing.
2 considered
justified
Doubts about acceptability to be resolved. Rank 2 considered to be justified
d at this stage
is stage ranked 2. In other words there
e resolved
proceed to detailed design stage with
resolving the problems identified

seat aircraft project at the end of the
esign stage.

justified could be made using the proce- n Table 4.3. Essentially, the table shows change the ranking of a particular factor he acceptability of the proposition was

ASSESSMENT

ion of the three imaginary projects. In acceptability of the projects would be visors to the decision maker, so that ediately of any significant changes in demonstration only a second ranking situation of the critical step 4 decision

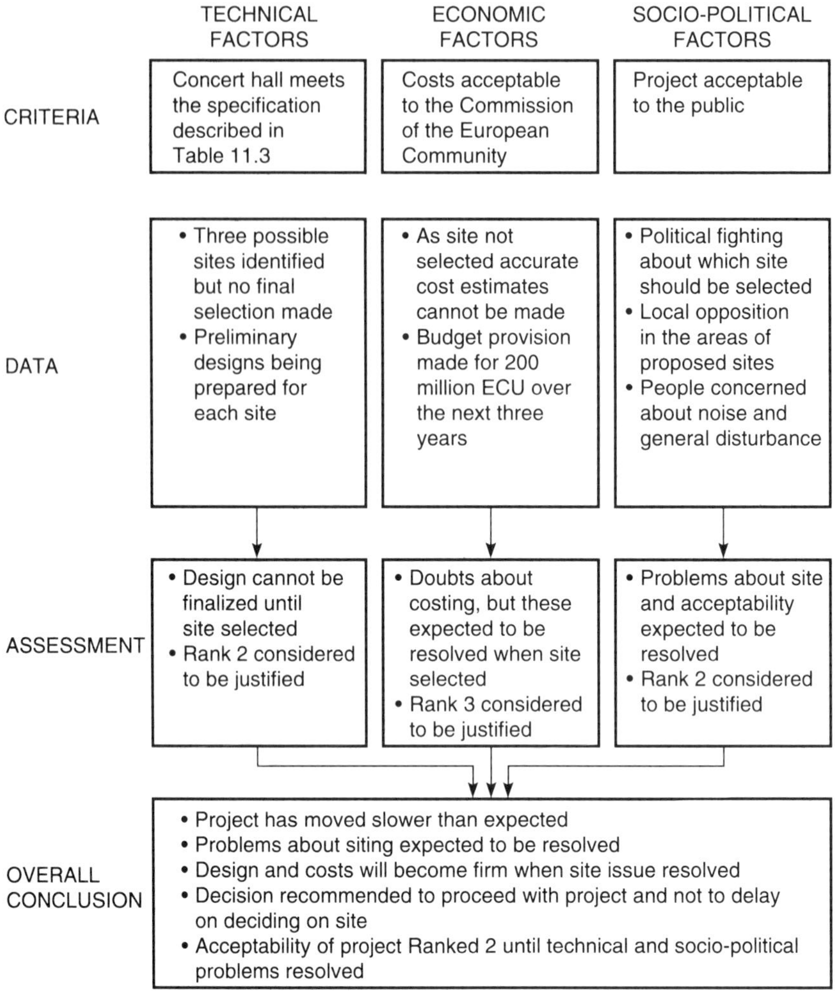
TECHNICAL FACTORS
ECONOMIC FACTORS
SOCIO-POLITICAL FACTORS
CRITERIA
Concert hall meets the specification described in Table 11.3
Costs acceptable to the Commission of the European Community
Project acceptable to the public
DATA
• Three possible sites identified but no final selection made
• Preliminary designs being prepared for each site
• As site not selected accurate cost estimates cannot be made
• Budget provision made for 200 million ECU over the next three years
• Political fighting about which site should be selected
• Local opposition in the areas of proposed sites
• People concerned about noise and general disturbance
ASSESSMENT
• Design cannot be finalized until site selected
• Rank 2 considered to be justified
• Doubts about costing, but these expected to be resolved when site selected
• Rank 3 considered to be justified
• Problems about site and acceptability expected to be resolved
• Rank 2 considered to be justified
OVERALL CONCLUSION
• Project has moved slower than expected
• Problems about siting expected to be resolved
• Design and costs will become firm when site issue resolved
• Decision recommended to proceed with project and not to delay on deciding on site
• Acceptability of project Ranked 2 until technical and socio-political problems resolved

Figure 11.3 Assessment of the prestige concert hall after the first year of the project.

(see Figure 11.1), which is the decision as to whether or not the project should be committed to its major expenditure. This implies that the source of funding is secure and that those making the funding available are confident the project satisfies their lending criteria. Also it is the stage at which everybody responsible for the finance of the project would need to be convinced that financial targets such as a return on investment are achievable. The assessment is made in the same style as the preliminary assessment presented in Figures 11.2, 11.3 and 11.4. Figure 11.5 shows the ranking assessment at the start of the major contract expenditure for the 1000-seat aircraft project. Figure 11.6 shows the ranking assessment at the start of the major contract expenditure for the prestige concert hall project. Figure 11.7 shows the ranking at the start of the major contract expenditure for the high speed rail system project. Compared with the end of the preliminary design stage just

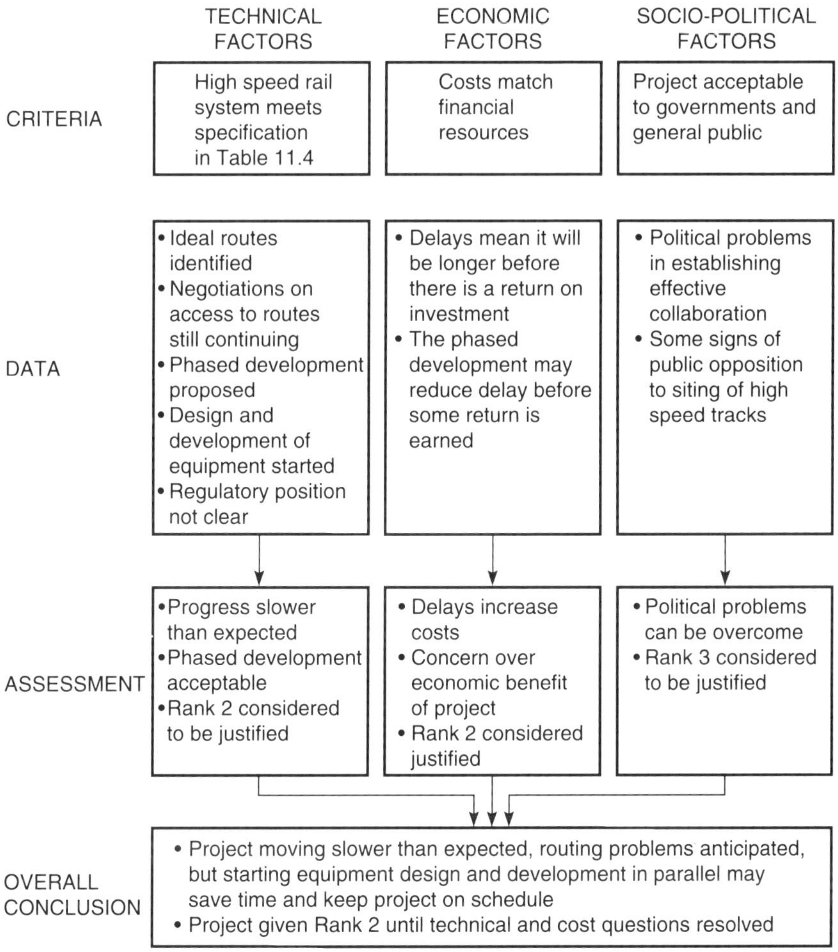
TECHNICAL FACTORS
ECONOMIC FACTORS
SOCIO-POLITICAL FACTORS
CRITERIA
High speed rail system meets specification in Table 11.4
Costs match financial resources
Project acceptable to governments and general public
DATA
• Ideal routes identified
• Negotiations on access to routes still continuing
• Phased development proposed
• Design and development of equipment started
• Regulatory position not clear
• Delays mean it will be longer before there is a return on investment
• The phased development may reduce delay before some return is earned
• Political problems in establishing effective collaboration
• Some signs of public opposition to siting of high speed tracks
ASSESSMENT
• Progress slower than expected
• Phased development acceptable
• Rank 2 considered to be justified
• Delays increase costs
• Concern over economic benefit of project
• Rank 2 considered justified
• Political problems can be overcome
• Rank 3 considered to be justified
OVERALL CONCLUSION
• Project moving slower than expected, routing problems anticipated, but starting equipment design and development in parallel may save time and keep project on schedule
• Project given Rank 2 until technical and cost questions resolved

Figure 11.4 Assessment of the high speed rail system project after the first two years of the project.

prior to major contract expenditure the data about the project should be more comprehensive and precise.

The assessment for the step 4 decision shows some significant developments in the projects and the emergence of some characteristic problems. The 1000-seat aircraft project exudes an air of confidence that all problems will be solved during the test flying programme. It would not be unusual for major problems to appear during test flying. Such problems are expensive to solve and delay delivery of aircraft to airlines. For example, it may be that airlines are unwilling to take up their options to buy the aeroplane when they see airports are unwilling to adapt their airports to deal with such large aeroplanes. However it is judged that overall the risks inherent in the project have decreased and the ranking can be improved from 2 to 3.

Confidence in the prestige concert hall project has also increased. As the socio-

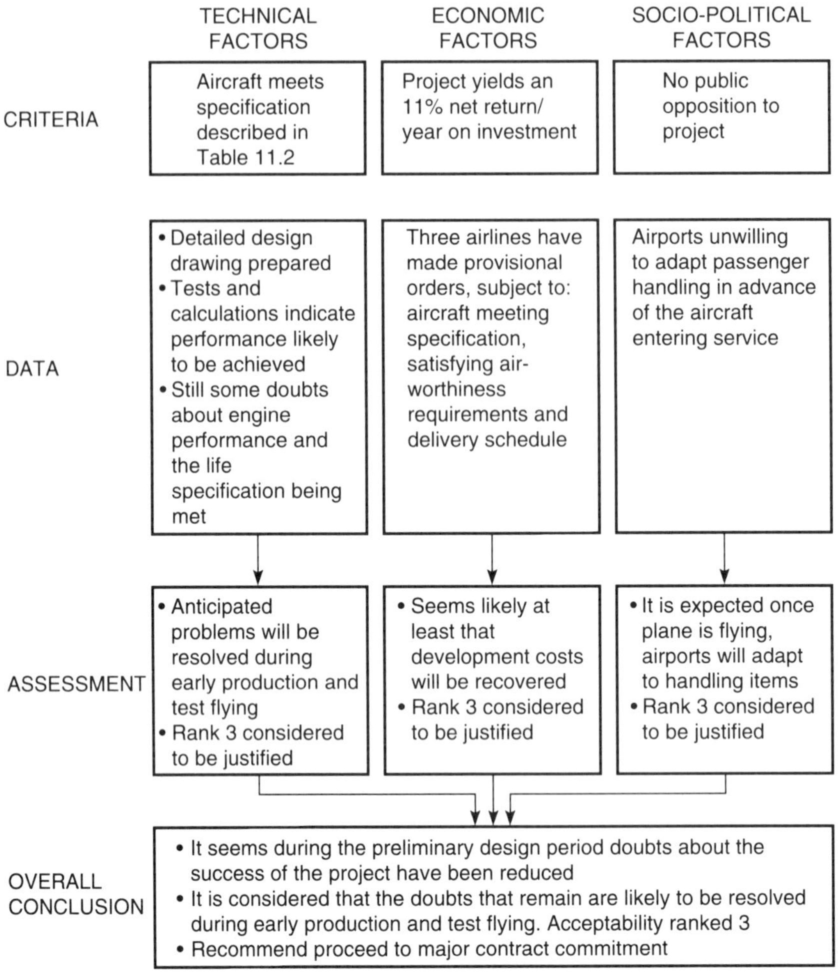
TECHNICAL FACTORS
ECONOMIC FACTORS
SOCIO-POLITICAL FACTORS
CRITERIA
Aircraft meets specification described in Table 11.2
Project yields an 11% net return/ year on investment
No public opposition to project
DATA
• Detailed design drawing prepared
• Tests and calculations indicate performance likely to be achieved
• Still some doubts about engine performance and the life specification being met
Three airlines have made provisional orders, subject to: aircraft meeting specification, satisfying air-worthiness requirements and delivery schedule
Airports unwilling to adapt passenger handling in advance of the aircraft entering service
ASSESSMENT
• Anticipated problems will be resolved during early production and test flying
• Rank 3 considered to be justified
• Seems likely at least that development costs will be recovered
• Rank 3 considered to be justified
• It is expected once plane is flying, airports will adapt to handling items
• Rank 3 considered to be justified
OVERALL CONCLUSION
• It seems during the preliminary design period doubts about the success of the project have been reduced
• It is considered that the doubts that remain are likely to be resolved during early production and test flying. Acceptability ranked 3
• Recommend proceed to major contract commitment

Figure 11.5 Assessment of the 1000-seat aircraft project prior to major contract commitment.

political acceptability is now rated 4 it can be considered that the overall ranking of 3 is really at the most acceptable side of Rank 3. The project is rather different to the other projects in that the Commission of the European Community assumes direct responsibility for all costs, so funding does not have to be raised on the commercial market; also the project does not have to earn a return on the investment made. However, it must be recognized that in a project like a prestige concert hall cost escalation of some sort is almost inevitable. Some contracts may have clauses in them which allow prices to be adjusted for inflation. Also there will be additional costs for vital items not foreseen in the original design. Such adjustments are not likely to prejudice completion of the project, but to be a source of embarrassment for members of the European Parliament particularly those concerned with budget issues.

The pre-major contract ranking analysis of the high speed rail system exposed a

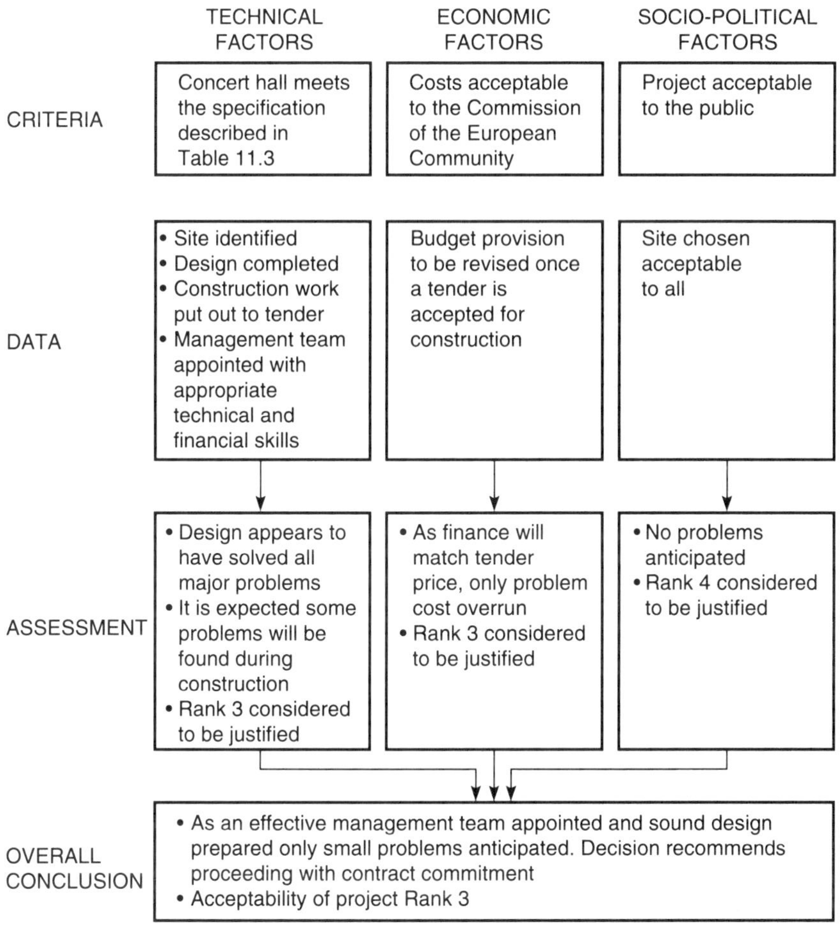
TECHNICAL FACTORS
ECONOMIC FACTORS
SOCIO-POLITICAL FACTORS
CRITERIA
Concert hall meets the specification described in Table 11.3
Costs acceptable to the Commission of the European Community
Project acceptable to the public
DATA
• Site identified
• Design completed
• Construction work put out to tender
• Management team appointed with appropriate technical and financial skills
Budget provision to be revised once a tender is accepted for construction
Site chosen acceptable to all
ASSESSMENT
• Design appears to have solved all major problems
• It is expected some problems will be found during construction
• Rank 3 considered to be justified
• As finance will match tender price, only problem cost overrun
• Rank 3 considered to be justified
• No problems anticipated
• Rank 4 considered to be justified
OVERALL CONCLUSION
• As an effective management team appointed and sound design prepared only small problems anticipated. Decision recommends proceeding with contract commitment
• Acceptability of project Rank 3

Figure 11.6 Assessment of the prestige concert hall project prior to major contract commitment.

very different picture and one that exposes a number of issues that give cause for concern, perhaps even alarm. No improvement in the post-preliminary study ranking of 2 appears to be justified. Technical problems with the prototype train have been identified and not resolved, and the possible need for additional funding has also been identified. Moreover, it has been recommended that the management team must be strengthened. If additional capital has to be raised, this must be done in the private sector on a commercial basis. There is no clear indication that the project will earn a significant return and this may give problems in raising additional capital. As the project does not appear to be financially attractive it may be given a poor rating by the financial organizations asked for funding. The result of this is that if funding is made available it would only be at a high interest premium and on early repayment terms. However, as the Commission of the European Community is a major partner in the project they may be willing to either contribute more capital or act as a guarantor for loan repayment. The need for the

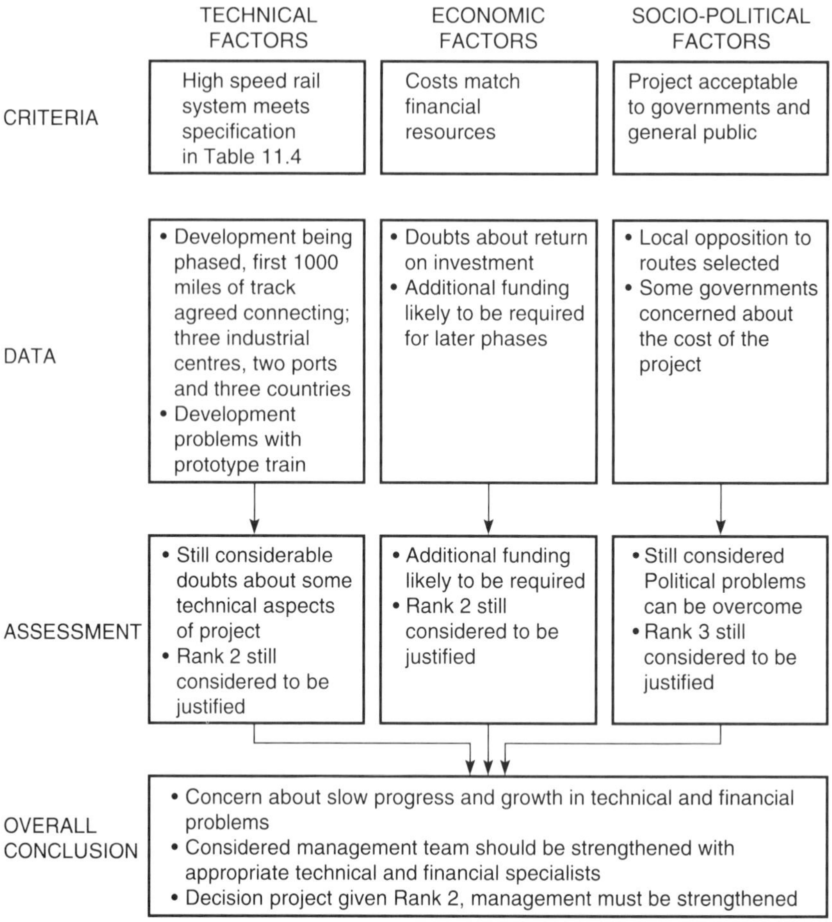
TECHNICAL FACTORS
ECONOMIC FACTORS
SOCIO-POLITICAL FACTORS
CRITERIA
High speed rail system meets specification in Table 11.4
Costs match financial resources
Project acceptable to governments and general public
DATA
• Development being phased, first 1000 miles of track agreed connecting; three industrial centres, two ports and three countries
• Development problems with prototype train
• Doubts about return on investment
• Additional funding likely to be required for later phases
• Local opposition to routes selected
• Some governments concerned about the cost of the project
ASSESSMENT
• Still considerable doubts about some technical aspects of project
• Rank 2 still considered to be justified
• Additional funding likely to be required
• Rank 2 still considered to be justified
• Still considered Political problems can be overcome
• Rank 3 still considered to be justified
OVERALL CONCLUSION
• Concern about slow progress and growth in technical and financial problems
• Considered management team should be strengthened with appropriate technical and financial specialists
• Decision project given Rank 2, management must be strengthened

Figure 11.7 Assessment of the high speed train system project prior to major contract commitment.

management team to be strengthened is a very serious matter. The management of an international team is always difficult and the management of a new high technology particularly difficult. The team needs to include managers with the relevant technical and financial skills. The indications from the analysis are that the project will take longer to complete and cost more than originally envisaged. Because of the nature of the sponsors the project is likely to be kept alive. The ranking of the project as Rank 2, acceptable but with major problems to be solved, really reflects the true position.

In practice the ranking would be kept up to date throughout the life of the projects until they become operational and financially self-sustaining. It is possible that the prestige concert hall and the high speed rail system would never become self-sustaining, but once they become operational the management responsibility would be different. In the operational phase it is possible that the managers would use a variant of the ranking technique to help judge the continuing acceptability of the project's operation.

EFFECTIVENESS OF THE RISK RANKING TECHNIQUE

The question of how effective the Risk Ranking Technique has been shown to be in assessing the three imaginary projects can now be examined. The technique has given structure to the analysis of acceptability. In the particular cases considered the assessment had to be made in qualitative terms mainly because the data available were in that form. Another important reason for the assessment being just in qualitative terms was that there was no single quantitative parameter for judging the overall acceptability of the various factors. This problem is particularly well illustrated by the technical criteria that the 1000-seat aircraft had to satisfy, which included specific size, speed, range, life and airworthiness requirements. In the example, no data were given of the extent to which the five requirements were satisfied, so an overall judgement was made of the acceptability of progress towards satisfying the requirements. In practice there would be some hard data on progress made towards satisfying requirements. For a real-life case it would be possible to identify all the sub-factors and rank them, and take the worst rank to symbolize the status of the group as a whole. Another approach would be to average the ranks, but this might give a slightly optimistic impression by suppressing the worst ranks. In any project it is the problem areas that have to be identified as they give the most trouble and generally require the most attention.

If the rankings are plotted against time the resultant graph gives an indication of the progress that a project is making. Is it becoming more or less acceptable, in other words, are the problems growing or being eliminated? In Figure 11.8 graphs are given of the rankings derived for the three imaginary projects. Comparison of the three graphs shows clearly that although the acceptability of the 1000-seat aircraft project and the prestige concert hall project has improved there has been no improvement in the acceptability of the high speed rail system project.

Having examined three major real-world projects, established a model of decision making and assessed the acceptability of three imaginary projects, the

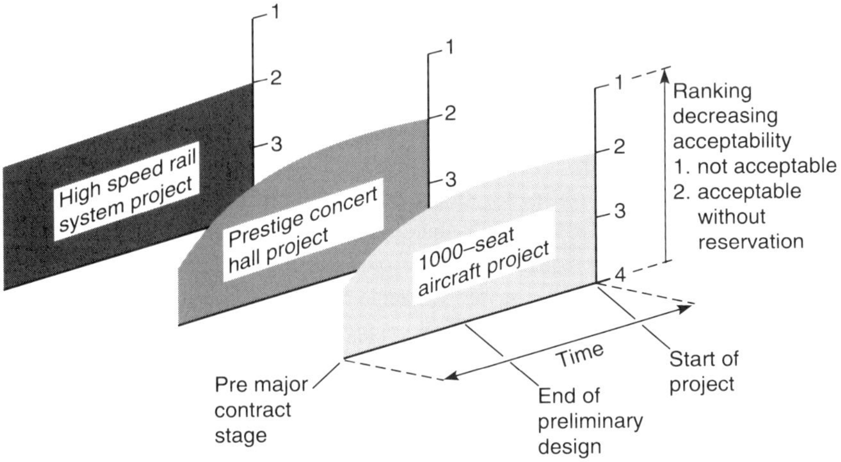
1
2
3
High speed rail system project
1
2
3
Prestige concert hall project
1
2
3
4
1000–seat aircraft project
Ranking decreasing acceptability
1. not acceptable
2. acceptable without reservation
Time
Pre major contract stage
End of preliminary design
Start of project

Figure 11.8 Graphs of the rankings of the three imaginary projects.

Table 11.6 Characteristics of major project decision phases

Phase	Characteristics
1 Preliminary exploration of concept	No data about the project. Project discussed more in terms of an idea. Preliminary design – calculations experiments – surveys suggest project worthwhile Decision making on a subjective basis
2 Detailed design of project	Data starts to emerge. Quantification of essential parameters develops but with quite a large measure of uncertainty Decision making becomes more objective as it can be based on quantified data
3 Decision to prepare for construction of the project	Economic implications become clearer. Costs can be defined with greater precision. It can be determined whether or not the project is acceptable to regulatory bodies and in socio-political terms Decision making can be based on better data
4 Construction of the project	The project becomes a major financial commitment Decision making concerned with determining whether or not the project meets all goals set for it
5 Putting the project into service	Proof becomes available about whether or not the project is acceptable in technical, economic and socio-political terms Objective decision making possible on the basis of good quality quantitative data

common features of the decision-making processes associated with them can be identified. The three real-world projects considered showed the magnitude of the cost variation that may occur in different types of project, and how the market for the output of the project may change dramatically before it is complete. The sales of the supersonic airliner were only one-thirteenth of the original estimate of sales. Utilization of the San Francisco Bay Area Rapid Transport System turned out to be only about half the original predictions and the system has to be very heavily subsidized. Clearly, in the three cases considered there was room for much tighter control not only of financial aspects of the projects but of the whole management. The best decisions in the world can be destroyed if there is not an effective management system to implement them. Any really sound decision-making process must include assessment of the relevant skill and capability of all involved with the project and this includes both management and contractors. The need to assess the capability and experience of proposers was identified as an integral part of the process of ranking technical factors (see Table 3.7). In this context the term 'capability' is taken to include both technical skill and organizational capability.

Table 11.7 Summary of decision assessment methodology appropriate to decision making at each stage of a project

Phase	Appropriate decision assessment methodology
1 Preliminary exploration of concept	At this stage there will be a shortage of data on which to build up a quantified assessment. Decision will be based more on a combination of expert opinion and direct recommendation. Decision making can be structured using the Risk Ranking Technique
2 Detailed design of project	Quantified data will start to become available and it will be possible to start building up a comprehensive assessment of acceptability using the Risk Ranking Technique. If computer simulation of the proposal is used it will be possible to explore options and uncertainties associated with the decision
3 Decision to prepare for construction of the project	At this stage there will be a major commitment of funds and a fairly accurate comprehensive assessment of acceptability can be made using the Risk Ranking Technique as there will be sufficient data available to make all the necessary supporting assessments
4 Construction of the project	At this stage the magnitude of variation in real costs becomes known and acceptability can be assessed with considerable precision
5 Putting the project into service	With the construction of the project complete a decision can be made about putting it into operation. This decision should be based on a comprehensive assessment of all the factors involved. For such an assessment the Risk Ranking Technique is an appropriate tool

From the cases considered it can be seen that at each step in the project the decision-making process has its own characteristics and problems. The main characteristics of these steps are summarized in Table 11.6, and in Table 11.7 the decision assessment methodologies appropriate to each step in the project are summarized.

CONCLUSIONS

The conclusions that appear to be justified regarding the phases in decision making are:

1. During the life of a project the data available change from virtually none at the conceptual stage to fairly comprehensive at the end of the project.
2. At the conceptual stage decisions have to be based mainly on opinion.
3. Then as the project proceeds and more data become available the assessment of acceptability can be refined and made more accurate.

Assuming the aim is to have a comprehensive assessment of acceptability of decision options, it is suggested that the optimum method to use throughout a project's life is the Risk Ranking Technique. The technique provides a consistent structure for overall assessment of acceptability. It is recognized that it will have to be supported by other techniques; for example, at the conceptual stage expert opinions are significant and at the design stage the techniques for detailed assessment of the various factors are important. Whichever techniques are used the assessment will have to be iteratively refined as the project proceeds and more accurate data become available.

12 CONCLUSIONS

❑ SUMMARY

Conclusions are drawn about the ideal methodology for assessing decision options and the conditions necessary for sound decision making. The conditions required include: good quality data; a comprehensive assessment of the technical, economic and socio-political factors involved; and that the proposer has the required experience and capability to implement a decision.

CONCLUSIONS ABOUT DECISION MAKING IN GENERAL

Generally no decision is free from risk and it is the decision maker's task to determine which decision will combine the lowest risk and the highest benefit. In addition the decision maker has to ensure that the regulatory constraints on risk are not contravened. These constraints apply equally, but in different ways, to the financial and technological aspects of proposals. Banks are constrained by regulation to the amount of financial risk they can accept in relation to their assets. Insurance companies have to balance the risks they accept with their potential premium income. Proposers of technological projects besides having to live within the limits of their financial resources generally have to satisfy some regulatory authorities about the acceptability of the technical risks involved. All decisions are also constrained by the subtle and sometimes intangible constraints of socio-political factors.

In order to determine which decision option will give the most acceptable result, many aspects of the issues involved have to be assessed. At the top level of decision making, which is the main subject of this book, the decision maker will be concerned to have a comprehensive assessment of all the technical, economic and socio-political factors involved. As has been shown the Risk Ranking Technique is one way of helping the decision maker to arrive at a decision by providing him with a structured comprehensive assessment of all the factors involved. The technique also provides the decision maker with a consistent way of comparing the significance of the specialized assessment of one factor with the assessment of other factors. For example, is a favourable technical assessment likely to be negated by problems in financing the project?

CONCLUSIONS FROM ASSESSMENT OF METHODS USED BY FINANCIAL INSTITUTIONS

In the earlier chapters the efficacy of the technique was compared with that of other aids to decision making including the methods used by financial institutions like banks. The comparison with other decision-making aids showed that the comprehensive nature of the assessment required for risk ranking makes it of more universal assistance in decision making than most other methods considered, also helping to put the findings of other methods of assessment in perspective.

The comparison of the Risk Ranking Technique with the methods used by financial institutions, was not just a comparison of similar aids to decision making but rather of different approaches to the problem. For understandable reasons banks concentrate on the economic aspects of the risks they are asked to accept. For example, the Swiss Bank Corporation in assessing the acceptability of making a loan to a developing country considers twenty-four economic criteria whereas the Risk Ranking Technique determines the ranking of the acceptability of the economic aspects of a risk on the basis of the assessment of a single economic parameter. But evaluation of the single parameter requires a considerable amount of supplementary assessment. Also, the ranking technique gives technical, economic and socio-political factors equal weight. If required the ranking technique could be modified to incorporate assessment of more economic parameters and to give economic factors more weight. One factor in the Country Risk Assessment procedure that the Swiss Bank Corporation use is assessment of political and social stability on a ten-point ranking scale. No special weight is attached to this factor, but doubtless it influences the advice the proximate decision maker gives the decision maker. Attention is drawn to the fact that Lloyds Bank rank the results of their assessment of the significance of the parameters they consider in determining acceptability. In other words, Lloyds Bank attempt to put their findings in ordinal form while the Swiss Bank Corporation, apart from socio-political factors, use qualitative terms like improving or deteriorating to describe the conclusions from their assessment. Assessment of technical issues tends to be treated separately by the banks and if it cannot be done 'in house' the advice of outside specialists is sought. In building up their view of the acceptability of a proposal, banks assess in a qualitative way the relevant experience and capability of the proposer. This is a feature of decision making that has also been incorporated into the Risk Ranking Technique. The conclusions that seem to be justified from the comparison of the procedures adopted by financial institutions with risk ranking are:

1. The Risk Ranking Technique gives a more comprehensive assessment than the procedures used by financial institutions.
2. The financial institutions give more weight to assessment of economic/financial issues than is given by the Risk Ranking Technique in its general form, but the latter can be tailored to suit specific applications.
3. Both the procedures used by the National Westminster Bank and the Risk Ranking Technique make allowance for the experience and capability of the proposer.
4. In some of the banks' procedures, it is overtly accepted that parts of the data to be used will be based on judgement and other parts will be based on statistics. This difference is not so clearly expressed in the Risk Ranking Technique but

has to be taken into account when designing the rank scoring criteria to be specified for a particular application.

5. None of the methods takes into account the capability of the financial institutions themselves to accept all the financial risks involved. It is tacitly assumed that institutions will keep within the required risk asset ratio and that insurance companies will keep the risks they cover adequately supported by premium income.
6. Attention is drawn to the importance of the information on which decisions are based being transparent. If the information obscures the truth any decision based on it is likely to be of doubtful value.

CONCLUSIONS FROM ASSESSMENT OF THEORETICAL CONSIDERATIONS

In Chapter 4 an attempt was made to build a theoretical justification for the ranking technique. From this examination of the theoretical basis of ranking the following conclusions are considered to be justified:

1. The design of the ranking scale appears to give an adequate distribution of the possible views on acceptability.
2. The method of weighting and combining the technical, economic and socio-political factors seems acceptable and can if necessary be varied to match special decision-making situations.
3. The criteria used for scoring the significance of the economic, technical and socio-political factors may be adjusted to suit particular special families of decisions.
4. The conclusions from ranking are not absolute. There is by the very nature of the subject a degree of uncertainty associated with each stage of the process.
5. In some cases, particularly when relevant quantitative data are available, conventional statistical methods including multivariate analysis, fuzzy data analysis and computer simulation can be applied to give a better understanding of the significance of the associated uncertainties.
6. A matrix form of presentation of the ranking of options can be used to give the decision maker a clear picture of the acceptability of the options and of the significance of uncertainty in the data used. Implications of possible future scenarios can be explored by building ranking matrices for them.
7. The methods of fuzzy data analysis can be used to assess the likely significance of factors described in qualitative terms. Such methods require the data to be collected in a way that ensures a consistent pattern of words is used to describe the level of significance of each factor that needs to be considered, and the findings can be refined as better data become available.

CONCLUSIONS ABOUT THE ASSESSMENT OF TECHNICAL, ECONOMIC AND SOCIO-POLITICAL FACTORS

From the critical assessment made of the way the ranking technique should assess technical, economic and socio-political factors the following general conclusions were reached about the risks inherent in any project:

1. The technical aspects of risk that should be included in any comprehensive evaluation of the acceptability of risk should be based on an assessment of:
   (a) the probability of failure to satisfy specification for a project sometime during specified lifetime;
   (b) the consequences of failure;
   (c) capability of proposer;
   (d) relevant experience of proposer.

   Including the capability and experience of the proposer in the ranking of the technical aspects of a proposal overcomes the criticism of earlier simpler versions of the Risk Ranking Technique.
2. The assessment of the economic aspects of risk is somewhat complicated by the wide range of parameters that could be used. Financial institutions may consider many economic or financial performance parameters when assessing the acceptability of a proposal. For major engineering projects economic acceptability may be evaluated on the basis of a simple financial performance parameter. It was concluded that for general purposes the difference between through-life costs and benefits would be an appropriate criterion for ranking economic factors of many major projects. At the same time, it was appreciated that at the assessment stage of a predominantly financial proposal or a project that involves risks beyond the financial resources of the proposer, a wider range of economic/financial indicators may have to be assessed to rank the acceptability of the proposal.
3. The assessment of the problems associated with ranking socio-political factors drew attention to the difficulty of quantifying the views about a proposal of all those who may be affected by it. Regardless of the problems involved in determining such views, no assessment can be considered comprehensive unless it incorporates an evaluation of the views of the relevant public. It is proposed that the ranking of the acceptability of socio-political factors associated with a proposal should be based on an assessment of the support for the proposal from the population that may be affected by it. It is recognized that in some circumstances arbitration procedures may be an appropriate way of achieving acceptability in socio-political terms. A prerequisite of such a procedure is that the arbitrators and the people they represent have an adequate understanding of the significance of the proposal.

CONCLUSIONS ABOUT ALTERNATIVES

From the examination of possible alternatives to the Risk Ranking Technique there are a number of quite important conclusions drawn. The conclusions are:

1. The natural language alternatives, such as direct presentation of evidence, direct recommendation, review by experts and public debate, do not give results that are inherently more reliable than the risk ranking. The problem with such methods is that they may be very biased.
2. Systems analysis does not really justify the title of a comprehensive alternative. The main merit of systems analysis is that it structures the identification of the factors and interaction that should be considered. The method may suggest factors, particularly socio-political factors, that should be included in any analysis of decision option and the weighting that should be given to them.
3. Statistical and computer techniques can both help to understand the significance of the data available and allow insights to be developed into the way major parameters of the decision may vary. Some computer techniques can allow the consequences of various decisions to be explored by simulation techniques. The value of such explorations is of course limited by the quality of the data used and the adequacy of the computer model.
4. Of the supplementary alternatives considered, soft system methodology and cognitive mapping mainly have a role in identifying factors and interactions that have to be considered.
5. Game theory, risk analysis and probability modelling are essentially concerned with trying to quantify the possible outcomes of the various options considered. They can also be used to explore the implications of various possible futures. The exploration of possible futures with the Risk Ranking Technique has not been attempted so far, but an indication has been given above in point 6 (p. 139) of how the ranking technique could be used to explore future scenarios.
6. Multivariate analysis could simply be considered as a subset of statistical analysis. In a theoretical sense it is attractive as it involves building up a system of equations that fully describe the decision-making process. Without relevant data to allow the constants and interactions in the various situations to be determined, the method would really only amount to a theoretical novelty. However, such analysis would be a vital component of any model for computer simulation of decision outcomes.
7. Creditworthiness assessments only give an indication of a proposer's ability to repay a loan; they give no indication of the value of the project for which the loan is required.
8. Of the complementary alternatives, robustness analysis and forecasting techniques can be grouped together as their special contribution is rating the acceptability of options under various possible future environments. These techniques have much in common with game theory, risk analysis and probability modelling already mentioned. Interest in the techniques is not that they endow the analysis of possible future conditions with special accuracy but more that they draw attention to the need for the decision maker to consider that the future may be different from expectation.
9. Regression analysis, like multivariate analysis, assumes future experience will have a form that can be related mathematically to past experience. To even start on such analysis relevant data are required. Perhaps the most that can be

said for regression analysis is that if data are available it may suggest possible futures. But the method is not relevant to the assessment of novel projects for which there are no data.

10. Decision tress help to build up a picture of the relationship between subsidiary decisions. The efficacy of the method depends on the data available.
11. Arbitration is a rather different kind of technique and is related more to the natural language techniques mentioned as possible comprehensive alternatives. The special merit of the technique is that with appropriate arbitrators it could provide a way of assessing the significance of socio-political factors.

CONCLUSIONS FROM TESTING THE RISK RANKING TECHNIQUE

The testing of the alternatives to the Risk Ranking Technique on three major decisions appears to reinforce the conclusion that none of the alternative techniques considered is quite as comprehensive in concept as ranking. Although some of the techniques may be used as alternatives they are not so rigorous and would not give such consistent results as the Risk Ranking Technique. From the direct comparison of the procedures used by banks and insurance companies and the assessment of the three real-life case studies, the conclusions about risk ranking that appear to be justified are:

1. Although the risk ranking approach and the methods used by banks and the insurance industry are different, they all strive to identify criteria for judging acceptability that are efficacious in the application of interest.
2. The Risk Ranking Technique is the only technique that attempts to be comprehensive and bring together the assessment of the technical, economic and socio-political aspects of a decision into a single number rating of the overall acceptability.
3. The Risk Ranking Technique is transparent to all concerned including the public, giving everyone a clear indication of the criteria adopted for assessing acceptability and the degree of acceptability justified by particular evidence.
4. The theoretical basis for the way the ranking technique builds up a comprehensive ranking of acceptability is defensible. The way the banks and the insurance industry build up their view of acceptability is rather more pragmatic. In all cases the quality of any assessment depends on the quality of the data that have to be used. No assessment technique can pretend to give a sound assessment if it has to be based on uncertain data. In such conditions all that can be said for the Risk Ranking Technique is that it provides a logical structure for the analysis and can present the significance of uncertainties in the form of a series of matrices.
5. In all the forms of analysis considered the criteria used for judging acceptability can be tailored to suit the requirements of particular families of decisions. But this does not mean the criteria are perfect and infallible. The difference between the economic criteria proposed for the ranking technique and the multiplicity of economic parameters banks consider illustrates something of the

variation in the range of parameters it may be necessary to take into ac some decision-making situations.

6. There is considerable scope for development of methods of assessin tive merits of decision options. Such development should include: universally applicable criteria for judging acceptability, combined te various approaches and building a computer model of the assessment pr that would allow variations in data and possible futures to be explored expeditiously.
7. Although the study concentrates on the way organizations make decisions about the acceptability of the risks that are external to them and have an option as to whether or not they accept them, the risk ranking methodology is equally effective as a tool for assessing the acceptability of the risks that are inescapable and internal to an organization. These internal risks include: commitments being accepted that are greater than the funds available to cover them, theft, fraud, and audit risks.

OVERALL CONCLUSIONS

The overall conclusions that this comparison of aids to decision making justifies are that sound decision making requires that the technical, economic and socio-political issues involved are thoroughly investigated, and that the Risk Ranking Technique is an effective tool for making a comprehensive assessment of these issues, all of which have to be considered in determining the acceptability of major projects. The other aids to decision making considered are either designed for very special purposes, such as banking or insurance decisions, or are subsidiary but useful aids to the overall decision-making process. There is no reason why the Risk Ranking Technique cannot be adapted to assessing a wide range of families of specialist decisions, provided appropriate criteria are specified for ranking each factor. The technique would give as consistent and reliable assessments as the data that have to be used allow.

The final comment that must be made is that no aid to decision making can ensure that the best decisions are effectively implemented. If the organizations involved do not maintain the necessary capability throughout the life of a project there are likely to be doubts about its satisfactory completion. Projects may fail if economic changes prevent financial institutions from providing finance, or a contractor goes bankrupt, or a government department is not reorganized in the way required to allow it to implement a decision.

GLOSSARY

WORDS AND PHRASES

ACP countries A group of African, Caribbean and Pacific countries receiving aid from the European Community.

additive rules Applies to unions of events such that:
$P(A\ B) = P(A) + P(B) - P(A \cap B)$.

alternative hypothesis Accepts the possibility of several values of a parameter.

autonomous robots Robots capable of operating independently and making their own decisions about the action they will take.

BART San Francisco's Bay Area Rapid Transit system.

Bayes approach (or Bayesian analysis) A way of dealing with a subjective degree of belief of probability, but can be used when there is some objective evidence available. The Bayesian approach provides a way of refining estimates of probability based on initial knowledge ('prior' probability) by taking account of additional data to give a posterior distribution.

bridging finance Short-term finance to cover the period between the finance being required and the main funding being available.

cognitive mapping A form of soft system analysis aimed at determining how people interact with the decision-making process.

combination Is the number of ways of selecting r objects from n without regard to order and is expressed as:

$$\left\{\begin{matrix} n \\ r \end{matrix}\right\} \text{ which equals } \frac{n!}{r!(n-r)!}$$

complement the complement of a subset is the part of a sample space that remains after deduction of the subset of interest.

comprehensive decisions Decisions involving consideration of technical, economic and socio-political factors.

conceptual need The initial demand that leads to a proposal being developed to satisfy the need.

conditional probability The probability of event B occurring when it is known that event A has occurred and is denoted by $P(B \mid A)$.

cost–benefit analysis (CBA) An assessment of the potential costs and benefits of a project which allows a comparison to be made of the return with alternative investment.

cost overruns Claims that a tenderer makes for payments to cover costs that were not allowed for in the original contract price.

de minimus test Discarding data that have no significant impact on the subject being discussed.

Delphi technique Finding a consensus view by iterative consultation with experts.

direct loss Loss suffered by people or plant directly involved in an accident.

direct risk Probability of direct loss, sometimes expressed as monetary value of direct loss.

Dixon test Method of eliminating outliers or wild data.

ECU European Currency Unit = approximately £0.78 in 1993.

end decisions Decisions about the acceptability of a proposal as a whole.

event A subset of a sample space.

experiment Any process that generates a set of data.

fusion reactors Reactors that derive their energy from the fusion of two light nuclei to form a single heavier nucleus.

fuzzy analysis Analysis of the significance of fuzzy data.

fuzzy data Data that are not clearly defined and may be qualitative.

fuzzy set A set of elements whose limits are not clearly defined.

game theory A methodology for assessing the implications of various strategies.

hard data Precise quantitative data directly relevant to the proposition being assessed.

indirect loss Consequential losses from an accident, such as loss of production, harm to people outside the site and loss of customers.

indirect risk Probability of indirect loss sometimes expressed as the monetary value of indirect loss.

intersection The subset containing the parts of other subsets in a particular sample space that are common to each other.

joint probability distribution Is the distribution of probabilities associated with possible values of two random variables.

jump jet A jet engined fixed wing aircraft capable of vertical take-off.

LNG Liquefied natural gas.

Mach number Ratio of speed to the speed of sound.

maxi-min return Choosing the decision option that has the largest minimum return.

mini-max criterion Option selected is the one with the lowest maximum risk (sometimes confused with mini-max regret criterion).

mini-max regret criterion Defines the most acceptable project as the one which would involve the greatest loss of gain if given up.

minimum criterion Choosing the decision option whose maximum risk is the lowest.

multiplication rule If an operation can be performed n_1 ways and for each of these n_1 ways a second operation n_2 can be performed, the total number of operations is the product of n_1 and n_2, that is $n_1 n_2$.

multivariate analysis Construction of a series of equations that together describe how the factor of interest behaves under various circumstances.

mutually exclusive Events that have no elements in common, i.e. $A \cap B = \varnothing$

natural language Describing something in words rather than numbers.

null hypothesis Specifies the exact value of a parameter.

objective data Data based on observation or measurement (*see also* quantitative data).

objective view Based on quantitative scientific evidence.

opportunity cost Cost of foregone alternatives. This is a way of saying that, as resources are always limited, having more of one thing means having less of something else.

optimum decision The decision that will produce a result that fulfils or most nearly fulfils the criteria set for acceptability.

outlier A data point that does not belong to the set of data being considered (*see also* wild point).

parameter space The set containing all possible values of the parameter.

permafrost area Area that is permanently below the freezing temperature of ice.

permutation The number of ways of arranging n objects which is equal to $n!$ The number of permutations of n distinct objects taken r at a time is $nPr = n!/(n-r)!$

probability The likelihood of an event in a statistical experiment. The probability is defined in real numbers ranging from 0 to 1. Therefore $0 \leq P(A) \leq 1$.

probability density function Function that describes the distribution of probabilities associated with possible values of a particular function.

proximate decision maker A close advisor to the decision maker.

Public Inquiry A British practice which involves a Government Minister appointing a leading figure, generally with a legal background, to conduct an inquiry into some controversial subject and advise him on the most appropriate course of action. The person appointed to conduct the inquiry may be supported by specialist advisors. The inquiry takes evidence from all interested parties and it is open to any member of the public to present their views.

qualitative data Data based on opinion expressed in non-quantitative terms (*see also* subjective data).

quantitative data Numerically expressed data based on observation, measurement or calculation (*see also* objective data).

ranking Ordering the significance of decision options and the sub-factors that have to be considered.

ranking scales An ordinal measure of the acceptability of a particular option or sub-factor.

recursive No direct or indirect feedback.

regression analysis A method of finding a mathematical relationship between variables.

relative frequency The probability justified in the long run.

risk The probability of an undesired outcome. In economic arguments it can mean the undesired outcome expressed in monetary terms (*see also* direct risk, indirect risk and total risk).

robustness analysis An analytical method for assessing the implications of uncertainty about possible outcomes (*see also* sensitivity).

semantic differential technique A method of assessing opinions by rating them, on an agreed scale, between pairs of adjectives describing the attribute of interest.

sensitivity The responsiveness of the results of an analysis to changes in the data used (*see also* robustness analysis).

social cost–benefit analysis (SCBA) Method of assessing public sector investment in Third World countries which calculates net benefit as being equal to resulting exports less imports and domestic inputs.

soft data Qualitative data or data of doubtful validity or relevance.

soft system analysis A methodology for identifying the factors and relationships to be considered in the analysis of organizational systems.

statistical inference Statistical methods to predict from one set of data the data for another set of circumstances.

subjective data Data based on opinion.

subjective probability Probability based on intuition, personal belief or other indirect information.

subjective view Non-specialist views, such as public opinion (*see also* qualitative view).

supersonic Faster than the speed of sound measured by Mach number: Mach 1 = speed of sound; Mach 2 = twice the speed of sound.

tolerability A level of risk people are willing to take in order to achieve certain benefits. (The British Health and Safety Executive use this term as a way of identifying acceptability of a risk.)

total quality management procedures A form of management structure devoted to fully satisfying customer requirements at minimum cost.

total risk The sum of the direct and indirect risks.

true points Data points that belong to the set of data being considered.

uncertain data Data about which there is no indication of the associated probability distribution.

uncertainty Doubt about the validity of either qualitative or quantitative data.

union An event (subset) which contains all the elements contained by two or more subsets.

universal set A set that contains all activities associated with or influencing life.

utiles A measure of the value of the outcome of a policy decision which can be measured in money terms or a non-dimensional characteristic.

utility An analyst's measure of a proposal's benefit compared with the benefit that would result from spending the money involved in different ways.

Venn diagram Shows diagrammatically the sample space as a rectangle and subsets of values as circles inside the rectangle.

weighting A constant a factor is multiplied by to adjust the significance of the factor into its correct relationship with other factors.

well-proven technology A technology that has proved in practice to be reliable.

wild point A false data point that can be confidently neglected (*see also* outlier).

MATHEMATICAL SYMBOLS

$\mid$ Means given that, e.g. $P(X \mid A)$ is the probability of X, given also that there is some evidence the probability should be A.

$\varnothing$ Denotes a null set, that is a set that contains no element at all.

$'$ Denotes the complement of a subset in a particular sample space, e.g. A' denotes the complement of subset A of a particular sample space.

$\cap$ Denotes the intersection between two events (subsets), e.g. $A \cap B$ is the event (subset) containing all elements that are common to both A and B.

$\cup$ Denotes the union between two events (subsets), e.g. $A \cup B$ is the event (subset) containing all the elements that are contained in A and B.

***n*!** n factorial $= 1 \times 2 \times 3 \ldots \times n$

P(A) The probability of A.

μ Mean value.

APPENDICES

APPENDIX 1: BANK OF ENGLAND'S RISK WEIGHTING

Summary

The weightings and conversion factors that the Bank of England specifies should be used to determine the value of assets for calculation of the allowable level of lending are described.

Risk weight categories for capital adequacy: on-balance-sheet items

1 Category 0% weighted

(a) cash and claims collateralized by cash deposits placed with the lending institution (or cash deposits and similar instruments issued by and lodged with the reporting institution) and meeting the conditions set out in the Bank's reporting requirements for 0%;
(b) gold and other bullion held in own vaults or on an allocated basis;
(c) claims[1] on Zone A[2] central governments and central banks including claims on the European Community;
(d) claims guaranteed by Zone A central governments and central banks;[3]
(e) claims on Zone B central governments and central banks denominated in local currency and funded in that currency;
(f) claims guaranteed by Zone B central governments and central banks, where denominated in local currency and funded in that currency;[3]
(g) certificates of tax deposit;
(h) items in suspense;[4]

2 Category 10% weighted

(a) holdings of fixed-interest securities issued (or guaranteed) by Zone A central governments with a residual maturity of one year or less, and floating-rate and index-linked securities of any maturity issued or guaranteed by Zone A central governments;
(b) claims collateralized by Zone A central government fixed-interest securities of any maturity;
(c) holdings of securities issued by Zone B central governments with a residual maturity of one year or less, and denominated in local currency and funded by liabilities in the same currency;

(d) loans to discount houses, gilt-edged market makers, institutions with a money-market dealing relationship with the Bank of England and those Stock Exchange money brokers which operate in the gilt-edged market, where the loans are secured on gilts, UK Treasury bills, eligible local authority and eligible bank bills, or London cash deposits.

3 Category 20% weighted

(a) holdings of fixed-interest securities issued (or guaranteed) by Zone A central governments with a residual maturity of over one year;
(b) claims collateralized by Zone A central government fixed-interest securities with a residual maturity of over one year;
(c) holdings of Zone B central government securities with a maturity of over one year denominated in local currency and funded by liabilities in the same currency;
(d) claims on multilateral development banks and claims guaranteed by or collateralized by the securities issued by these institutions;
(e) claims on credit institutions incorporated in the Zone A and claims guaranteed (or accepted or endorsed) by Zone A-incorporated credit institutions;
(f) on-balance-sheet claims in gold and other bullion on the non-bank market making members of the London Bullion Market Association;[5]
(g) claims on credit institutions incorporated in Zone B with a residual maturity of one year or less and claims of the same maturity guaranteed by Zone B credit institutions;
(h) claims secured by cash deposited with and held by an agent bank acting for a syndicate of which the reporting institution is a member;
(i) claims on Zone A public sector entities and claims guaranteed by such entities. In the United Kingdom, these comprise local authorities and certain non-commercial public bodies;
(j) claims on discount houses and claims which are guaranteed (or accepted) by discount houses which are unsecured, or secured on assets other than specified in 3(d) above;
(k) cash items in the process of collection.

4 Category 50% weighted

(a) loans to individuals fully secured by a first priority charge on residential property that is (or is to be) occupied by the borrower or is rented;
(b) loans to housing associations registered with the Housing Corporation, Scottish Homes and Tai Cymru that are fully secured by a 'first priority' charge on the residential property which is under development and fully secured by a charge on the housing association's residential property that is being let, and where the project attracts Housing Association Grant (HAG). If HAG is not available, such loans must be fully secured by a 'first priority' charge on residential property that is being let;
(c) mortgage sub-participations, where the risk to the sub-participating bank is fully and specifically secured against residential mortgage loans which would themselves qualify for the 50% weight;

(d) holdings of securities issued by special purpose mortgage finance vehicles where the risk to the security holders is fully and specifically secured against residential mortgage loans, which would themselves qualify for the 50% weight, or by assets which qualify for a weight of less than 50%,[5] as long as the mortgage loans are fully performing, or origination of the vehicle;

5 Category 100% weighted

(a) claims on the non-bank private sector;
(b) claims on credit institutions incorporated in Zone B with a residual maturity of over one year;
(c) claims on Zone B central governments and central banks (unless denominated in the national currency and funded in that currency);
(d) claims guaranteed by Zone B central governments or central banks, which are not denominated and funded in the national currency common to the guarantor and borrower;
(e) claims on commercial companies owned by the public sector;
(f) claims on Zone B public sector entities;
(g) premises, plant, equipment and other fixed assets;
(h) real estate, trade investments[6] and other assets not otherwise specified;
(i) aggregate net short open foreign exchange position;
(j) gross deferred tax assets.

Credit conversion factors for off-balance-sheet risk

Credit conversion factors should be multiplied by the weights applicable to the category of the counter party for an on-balance-sheet transaction.

Instruments		Credit conversion factor (%)
A	direct credit substitutes, including general guarantees of indebtedness, standby letters of credit serving as financial guarantees, acceptances and endorsements (including 'per aval' endorsements, i.e. endorsed for availability;	100
B	sale and repurchase agreements and asset sales with recourse where the credit risk remains with the bank;[8]	100
C	forward asset purchases, forward deposits placed and the unpaid part of partly-paid shares and securities,[8] and any other commitments with a certain drawdown;	100
D	transaction-related contingent items not having the character of direct credit substitutes (e.g. performance bonds, bid bonds, warranties and standby letters of credit related to particular transactions);	50
E	short-term self-liquidating trade-related contingent items (such as documentary credits collateralized by the underlying shipments);	20

F	note issuance facilities and revolving underwriting facilities;[9]	50
G	other commitments (e.g. formal standby facilities and credit lines) with an original[10] maturity of over one year;	50
H	similar commitments with an original[10] maturity of up to one year, or which can be unconditionally cancelled at any time;	0
I	endorsements of bills (including 'per aval' endorsements) which have previously been accepted by a bank.	0

Multi-options facilities and other composite products should be disaggregated into their component parts; for example, into a credit commitment, note issuance facilities, and so on, and each component part should be converted according to the above classification. However, components carrying the lowest credit conversion factors should be disregarded to the extent necessary to ensure that the total value of all the components does not exceed the value of the facility.

Notes on text

1. Other than securities issued by these bodies.
2. Zone A includes OECD countries plus those with special lending agreements with IMF. Zone B countries are all other countries.
3. Including lending under Export Credit Guarantee Department (ECGD) bank guarantee and equivalent schemes in other Zone A countries, but excluding lending against the security of ECGD insurance cover.
4. Where such items do not represent a credit risk but rather a position risk as detailed in the guidance notes to the form Bank of England, BSD1.
5. Until 1 January 1993, from which time such claims will be weighted to 100%.
6. Excluding: (i) holdings of capital instruments issued by credit institutions which will be deducted from total capital; and (ii) holdings of capital instruments of other financial institutions which must be deducted according to Article 2(12) and (13) of the Own Funds Directive.
7. This is a proxy weight for bank's foreign exchange risk, and will remain in effect until an international framework for capturing foreign exchange risk is agreed. Includes the net short open position in gold, silver, platinum and palladium.
8. These items are to be weighted according to category of the issuer of the security (or the borrower in the underlying loan agreement) and not according to the counter-party with whom the transaction has been entered into. 'Reverse repos' (i.e. purchase and resale agreements where the bank is the receiver of the asset) are treated as collateralized loans, with the risk being measured as an exposure to the counter-party. Where the security temporarily acquired attracts a preferential risk weighting, this is recognized as collateral and the risk weighting of the loan accordingly reduced (e.g. a Zone A government security).

9. To be applied to the total amount of the institution's underwriting obligations of any maturity. Where the facility has been drawn down by the borrower and the notes are held by anyone other than the reporting institution, its underwriting obligations must continue to be reported as the full nominal amount. (Own holdings of notes underwritten are, however, deducted from the overall value of the commitment, because they are weighted as an on-balance-sheet item.)
10. Banks may report on the basis of residual maturity until the end of 1992 to assist data collection.

Reference

Bank of England (1990) Bank of England's Notice to Institutions authorized under the Banking Act 1987, Implementation in the United Kingdom of the Solvency Ratio, BSD/1990/3, December.

APPENDIX 2: SWISS BANK CORPORATION'S RISK ASSESSMENT AND CREDIT ASSESSMENT PROCEDURES APPLIED TO FICTITIOUS COUNTRIES

Summary

Illustrations of the Swiss Bank's Country Risk Assessment Methodology with definition of the terms used.

Developing Country Risk Assessment

	INDICATORS		1984	1985	1986	1987	Estimate 1988	Outlook 1989
DOMESTIC ECONOMY	1. REAL GDP GROWTH	%	5.2	3.1	1.2	-4.5	-3.2	1.5
	2. Investment / GDP — International average: = 25%		25.6	24.9	24.1	18.5	14.7	↗
	3. INVESTMENT EFFICIENCY (1:2) — critical level ≤ 0.2		0.23	0.19	0.13	-0.02	-0.11	→
	4. INFLATION (Period average)	%	18.5	22.3	24.9	52.6	18.2[1]	↗
	5. MONEY SUPPLY GROWTH (End of period)	%	22.8	18.5	19.6	6.9	9.8[1]	→
	6. REAL DOMESTIC CREDIT CREATION	%	16.8	27.9	37.2	-15.0	-9.4[1]	up
	7. Fiscal Balance / GDP	%	-3.5	-5.1	-2.5	-1.8	-1.7	↘
EXTERNAL ECONOMY	8. COMPETITIVENESS (Real Exchange Rate) INDEX 1980 = 100		109.5	105.4	85.6	84.0	80.0	↗
	9. TRADE BALANCE (Goods)	US$bn	-1.84	-2.95	-3.24	-2.40	-0.80	↗
	10. EXPORTS (Goods + Services)	US$bn	8.60	8.10	8.15	8.30	9.10	↗
	11. IMPORTS (Goods + Services)	US$bn	10.81	11.95	12.54	11.40	10.30	up
	12. CURRENT ACCOUNT BALANCE	US$bn	-1.95	-3.55	-4.12	-2.60	-0.90	↗
	13. Exports / GDP	%	23.0	20.7	23.5	21.5	23.0	→
	14. EXPORT CONCENTRATION (high = critical) [2]	%	33.4	35.2	36.7	35.6	35.0	→
	15. IMPORTS FROM SWITZERLAND	SFr.m	104.2	110.3	117.9	106.2	105.0	↗
DEBT	16. TOTAL EXTERNAL DEBT (Public + Private)	US$bn	16.8	20.9	25.1	27.3	28.0	↘
	17. INTERNAT. RESERVES (Excl. Gold)	US$bn	3.12	1.94	0.95	0.81	1.00	↗
	18. EXTERNAL DEBT SERVICE	US$bn	2.45	2.71	2.96	2.82	3.40	↘
	19. External Debt / Exports — critical level ≥ 150%		195	258	308	329	308	↗
	20. External Debt Service / Exports — critical level ≥ 25%		28.5	33.4	36.3	34.0	37.3	↗
	21. Interest-Adjusted Current Account / Interest Payments	%	-25	-67	-84	-13	67	↗
	22. International Reserves / Imports — critical level ≤ 3 mths		3.5	1.9	0.9	0.9	1.2	↗
	23. POLITICAL RISK	points (1–10)	7	7	7	6	6	→
	24. Recorded Unemployment Rate	%	11.2	10.5	11.0	13.4	13.5	→
	25. Per capita GDP Growth	%	2.8	0.7	-1.1	-6.8	-5.5	-0.8

Definition of Terms used in Country Risk Assessment

We use three symbols as visual aids to monitoring risks:

= **Ratio** has gone beyond an empirically determined **critical level** (applies to indicators 3, 19, 20 and 22)

= **Value** or **ratio** has deteriorated very sharply within a 12-month period **(critical change)**

= **Ratio** both exceeds critical level and has undergone **critical change** within a 12-month period

Outlook: → = unchanged ↗ = improving ↘ = deteriorating Asterisk * = Estimate NA = Not available

Note: The suggested critical values apply to **developing** countries only and do not necessarily reflect similar risks in the case of **industrialized** countries.

1. **Real GDP growth:** Change in Gross Domestic Product over a 12-month period in %, adjusted for inflation (i.e. in volume terms); growth measure.

2. **Investment ratio:** Gross fixed capital formation (fixed investment) as % of GDP or GNP. The higher the ratio, the higher the potential economic growth. International average: 25%.

3. **Investment efficiency:** 3-year moving average of real GDP growth (no. 1) divided by the average investment ratio (no. 2) for same period. The higher the value, the more efficient the economy; critical **level** ⩽ 0.2 on average. (Note: values will tend to be lower for more developed countries.)

4. **Inflation:** Change in consumer prices as an annual average in %. One measure of the quality of economic policy.

5. **Money supply** (M1 or other monetary control variable): Annual % change in money supply. Measure of monetary policy and early indicator for future inflation.

6. **Real domestic credit:** Annual % change of the domestic component of money supply (= M2 minus Net Foreign Assets), deflated by consumer price inflation. Measure of domestic monetary disequilibrium (in comparison to real GDP growth) and early indicator for balance-of-payments developments and exchange-rate changes.

7. **Fiscal balance as % of GDP:** General or (if unavailable) central government surplus or deficit as % of GDP. Fiscal policy measure. Since structural (permanent) deficits are more important than cyclical peaks and cross-country comparability is lacking, critical values are not determined.

8. **International competitiveness index (Index of real effective exchange rate):** Compares domestic with foreign inflation, adjusted for exchange-rate changes. Domestic inflation: GDP deflator. Foreign inflation: Trade-weighted changes of GDP deflators of major trading partners, adjusted for exchange-rate changes. A decline in the index (= a real devaluation) indicates an increase in competitiveness.

9. **Trade balance:** Exports minus imports of goods, in bn US$. Goods are valued at their prices as they leave the exporting country, i.e. f.o.b., without costs of insurance and freight. Chief determinant of the current-account balance (see no. 12).

10./11. **Exports and imports:** Exports and imports of both goods and services (e.g. tourism, transportation, interest), in bn US$.

12. **Current account balance:** Trade balance + balance of services + balance of unrequited transfers, in bn US$; a deficit shows the extent of a country's dependence on foreign resources to satisfy domestic demand, to be financed (a) by drawing down international reserves (see no. 17) and/or (b) by additional borrowing abroad (no. 16).

13. **Share of exports in GDP:** Exports of goods and services (see no. 10) as % of GDP. Index of the openness of the economy, indicating (a) the allocation of domestic resources to the tradable sector and the country's ability to service its external debt and (b) the country's vulnerability to foreign demand shocks.

14. **Export concentration**

    Either: Share of main commodity exports in total exports. Main commodity exports (food and other agricultural products, raw materials and metals) as % of total exports. High value indicates high vulnerability to fluctuations in international commodity market conditions.

    Or: Merchandise exports to main customers (countries) as % of total merchandise exports. High value indicates dependency on a few major customer markets.

15. **Imports from Switzerland:** Goods imports from Switzerland in m Sfr.

16. **External debt:** Total external debt (gross) of the reporting country in bn US$ at end of year. Includes short- and long-term debt, IMF lending and interest arrears.

17. **International reserves:** Total official international reserves at end of year, excluding gold. Foreign exchange, Special Drawing Rights, IMF reserves. Liquidity measure.

18. **External debt service:** Interest payments due on total debt + amortization payments due on medium- and long-term debt.

19. **External debt/Exports:** Total external debt as % of export receipts (goods & services). An important debt capacity indicator, since external debt ultimately has to be repaid out of export revenues. Critical **level:** ⩾ 150; critical **change:** approx. 25% increase within a year.

20. **Debt-service ratio:** Annual interest and amortization payments on total external debt as % of export receipts (goods & services). Short-term liquidity measure. Critical **level:** ⩾ 25%; critical **change:** approx. 50% increase within a year.

21. **Interest coverage:** Current account balance net of interest payments to foreign creditors, as % of interest payments. Indicator of debt-servicing capacity. **100% or more** indicates net current account revenues technically sufficient to cover all interest obligations. **0 or less** indicates net current account revenues technically too small to pay any interest.

22. **Import cover:** Official reserves at year-end (no. 17) divided by average monthly imports (see no. 11). Measure of how long imports could be financed from international reserves. Critical **level:** ⩽ 3 months; critical **change:** approx. 50% decrease within a year.

23. **Political risk:** Social and political situation rated on a scale of 1–10 with regard to creditworthiness. Scores **1 to 3:** no foreseeable/low risks; **4 to 6:** acceptable/moderate risks; **7 to 9:** high/higher risks; **10:** unacceptable/extremely high risks.

24./25. **Optional indicators:** Any readily available risk-related indicator or any country-specific indicator.

Industrial Country Credit Risk Assessment

COUNTRY X

Sector	INDICATORS		1989	1990	1991	1992	Estimate 1993	Outlook 1994
FUNDAMENTALS	1. REAL GDP GROWTH	%	2.1	0.7	-2.5	-0.8	0.7	1.4
	2. GROSS INVESTMENT/GDP	Int. avg.= 25%	23.4	22.1	19.2	19.2	19.1	↗
	3. INFLATION	%	7.8	9.5	5.9	3.7	2.1	3.8
	4. MONEY SUPPLY GROWTH	%	18.3	15.9	7.9	4.6	3.9	up
	5. UNEMPLOYMENT RATE	%	6.2	5.9	8.3	9.9	10.8	11.4
	6. GENERAL GOV'T. BALANCE/GDP	critical deficit ≥ 3%	0.9	-1.3	-10.2	-11.1	12.0	→
	7. SHORT-TERM INTEREST RATE	%	13.8	14.6	11.1	9.0	5.0	→
	8. LONG-TERM YIELD OF GOV'T. BONDS	%	9.6	11.1	9.9	9.1	7.8	→
	9. COMPETITIVENESS INDEX	1990=100	98.7	100.7	108.1	107.7	95.0	up
	10. DEVIATION FROM PPP **(DM/national currency)**	%	14.4	12.3	18.8	15.9	4.4	→
	11. INDUSTRIAL PRODUCTION	%	0.5	-0.6	-3.0	-0.3	1.6	3.2
	12. REAL AVERAGE EARNINGS INCREASE		1.7	0.6	1.9	1.3	0.8	1.5
EXTERNAL SECTOR	13. EXPORTS (GOODS AND SERVICES)	US$ bn	320.6	380.4	375.6	397.9	414.2	up
	14. IMPORTS (GOODS AND SERVICES)	US$ bn	-348.7	-401.0	-384.6	-424.2	-448.4	up
	15. CURRENT ACCOUNT BALANCE	US$ bn	-35.59	-29.39	-11.44	-20.84	-18.72	→
	16. NET DIRECT INVESTMENTS	US$ bn	-4.95	14.90	3.51	4.0	6.0	↗
	17. NET EXTERNAL FINANCIAL ASSETS/GDP	%	13.2	0.7	3.6	4.0	0.5	down
	18. NET INTEREST INCOME/EXPORTS	%	-2.0	-3.2	-3.5	-2.0	-2.5	down
	19. INVISIBLE BALANCE	US$ bn	4.8	3.2	7.0	9.0	8.0	→
PUBLIC SECTOR	20. PRIMARY BUDGET/GDP	%	3.3	1.0	-0.9	-4.5	-5.8	down
	21. NET INTEREST PAYMENTS/TOT. EXPEND.	Int. avg.= 6.5%	6.3	5.7	4.7	4.7	5.3	up
	22. GROSS TOTAL PUBLIC DEBT/GDP	critical level ≥ 60%	37.0	34.9	36.5	41.9	47.4	up
	23. GROSS FOREIGN PUBLIC DEBT/GDP	%	6.1	5.4	5.4	5.0	5.0	→
	24. FOREIGN CURRENCY DEBT/TOTAL PUBLIC DEBT		4.1	4.5	5.0	5.5	5.8	↗
BUSINESS SECTOR	25. CORPORATE PROFIT GROWTH	%	5.9	4.3	1.1	0.2	2.0	↗
	26. INTEREST PAYMENTS/CORPORATE INCOME	%	24.0	26.7	27.0	24.5	19.0	down
	27. DEBT/EQUITY (140 largest corporations)	%	36	43	44	44	44	down
	28. BUSINESS FAILURES	1989 = 100	100	149	274	387	down	down
	29. HOUSEHOLD FINANCIAL LIABILITIES/INCOME		88.6	90.3	90.9	86.2	80.0	down
	30. POLITICAL RISK	points 1–10	2	2	2	2	2	2

Definition of terms used in Industrial Country Credit Risk Assessment

We use three symbols as visual aids to monitoring risks:

= **Ratio** has gone beyond a **critical level**

= **Value** or **ratio** has deteriorated very sharply within a 12-month period (**critical change**)

= **Ratio** both exceeds critical level and has undergone **critical change** within a 12-month period

Outlook: → = unchanged ↗ = improving ↘ = deteriorating

* = Estimate NA = Not available

1. **Real GDP growth:** Change in Gross Domestic Product over a 12-month period in %, adjusted for inflation (i.e. in volume terms); growth measure.

2. **Gross investment/GDP:** Gross fixed capital formation as % of GDP (or GNP). The higher the ratio, the higher the potential economic growth. International average: 25%.

3. **Inflation:** Change in consumer prices as an annual average in %. One measure of quality of economic policy.

4. **Money supply** (M1 or other monetary control variable): Annual % change in money supply. Measure of monetary policy and early indicator for future inflation.

5. **Unemployment rate:** Ratio of the totally unemployed in labour force in %.

6. **General Gov't. balance/GDP:** General or (if unavailable) central government surplus or deficit as % of GDP. Fiscal policy measure.

7. **Short-term interest rate:** 3-month Euro-currency interest rate or any other key money market interest rate. Monetary policy indicator.

8. **Long-term yield of Gov't. bonds:** Long-term treasury bond, if possible 10-year maturity. Indicator of capital market conditions.

9. **International competitiveness index (index of real effective exchange rate):** Compares domestic with foreign inflation, adjusted for exchange-rate changes. Domestic inflation: GDP deflator. Foreign inflation: Trade-weighted changes of GDP deflators of major trading partners, adjusted for exchange-rate changes. A decline in the index (= a real devaluation) indicates an increase in competitiveness.

10. **Deviation from PPP:** % deviation of the exchange rate from its purchasing power parity value. A negative sign indicates a potential overvaluation of the currency (devaluation risk). A positive sign stands for an undervaluation. Indicator of currency risk and international competitiveness.

11./12./19./24./29. **Optional indicators:** Any readily available risk-related indicator or any country-specific indicator.

13./14. **Exports and imports:** Exports and imports of both goods and services (e.g. tourism, transportation, interest), in bn US$.

15. **Current account balance:** Trade balance + balance of services + balance of unrequited transfers, in bn US$; a deficit shows extent of a country's dependence on foreign resources to satisfy domestic demand, to be financed (a) by drawing down international reserves (see no. 17) and/or (b) by additional borrowing abroad (no. 16).

16. **Net direct investments:** Covers all net inflows of equity investment on a balance-of-payments basis. Portfolio investment inflows are not part of direct investment.

17. **Net external financial assets/GDP:** Indicates country's external asset position as % of GDP. A negative sign stands for net indebtedness.

18. **Net interest payments/Exports:** Annual net interest payments on net external debt as % of export receipts (goods & services).

20. **Primary budget/GDP:** Overall general government balance less interest payments on public debt, as % of GDP. Measures sovereign cash flow before any allowances for interest payments.

21. **Net interest payments/Total expenditures:** General gov't net debt interest payments as % of total gov't expenditures. Total expenditures are defined as current receipts minus net lending.

22. **Gross total public debt/GDP:** Domestic and external debt owed by or guaranteed by general government as % of GDP.

23. **Gross foreign public debt/GDP:** External debt owed by or guaranteed by general government as % of GDP.

25. **Corporate profit growth:** Annual % change in corporate profits. If not available, cash flow.

26. **Net debt interest payments/Cash flow:** Measure of corporate sector income gearing.

27. **Debt/Equity:** Corporate sector's borrowed capital as % of its own capital.

28. **Business failures:** Bankruptcies in corporate sector, specified in terms of percentage change or in relation to new business creation or outstanding bank loans.

30. **Political risk:** Social and political situation rated on a scale of 1-10 with regard to creditworthiness. Scores **1 to 3:** no foreseeable/low risks; **4 to 6:** acceptable/moderate risks; **7 to 9:** high/higher risks; **10:** unacceptable/extremely high risks.

APPENDIX 3: STRUCTURE OF THE SWISS BANK CORPORATION'S EXECUTIVE MANAGEMENT BRIEF ON THE CREDITWORTHINESS OF A COUNTRY

Typically a creditworthiness brief discusses outlook and risk analysis, politics, domestic economy, trade account and balance of payments and external debt. The brief concludes with advice to the Executive about the implications of the findings of the risk monitoring exercise for the Bank's lending policy towards the country involved.

Under the heading 'Outlook and Risk Analysis' the brief gives an assessment of the political stability of the country and an assessment of six indicators of economic stability. These are: population, GDP, current account balance, total external debt, international reserves and exchange. The way each of the indicators appears to be developing is estimated in qualitative terms such as rising, unchanged and depreciating.

Discussion of political factors covers results of elections, the programme of the party elected, unrest, strikes, trade union activities and developments in international trade and economic collaboration.

The discussion of domestic economy tends to focus on assessing the prospects for economic growth in the years ahead. In building up an assessment of the prospects for economic growth attention is given to the magnitude of inflationary pressures and the way they are dealt with.

The assessment of trade accounts covers balance of payments, trade prospects, external financing and exchange rate policy. In the assessment attention would be given to whether or not exports were growing.

Discussion of external debt is the last section of the brief, but perhaps the most important. The brief would comment on the debt-to-exports ratio and whether the situation is sustainable or not. Also the brief would comment on the reality of the country being able to service its debts.

APPENDIX 4: ADDITIONAL COMMENT ON THE SCALING OF RANKING FACTORS

Summary

This appendix examines the problem of designing ranking scales and assessing the options available.

The nature of the problem

Scaling of ranking factors, as mentioned in the main text, could be described as a subjective attempt to identify the decision that would result in the optimum distribution of resources. In their discussions of distributive justice, Braybrooke and Lindblom (1963) drew attention to the fact that even Aristotle recognized that many factors influenced the equitable distribution of resources. In some ways it could be argued that an infinite range of factors have to be considered in determining which decision option will yield the optimum distribution of resources. The Risk Ranking Technique is an attempt to rationalize for the decision maker the number of factors and the number of levels of acceptability that have to be considered.

The four levels of acceptability were chosen as a way of grading acceptability on the basis of the intrinsic properties of each proposition considered. In Figure 4.2 in the main text, it was shown how a three-dimensional matrix of ranking would result from variation in the data used. In the diagram the mean ranking is shown evenly spaced between the upper and lower limits. Such even distribution suggests the data may follow a normal distribution, an assumption that may be misleading. Reflecting on the magnitude of cost escalation, mentioned in Chapter 1 of the main text, suggests that in reality the data may be skewed and that a distribution other than normal may be more appropriate. A possible description of the data could be a Weibull distribution with a suitable parameter. Such refinement of the analysis may not be justified by the quality of the data available.

A three-dimensional matrix, of the type shown in Figure 4.2, really only represents a snapshot of the decision options as they appear at a particular time. With the passage of time the components of the factors involved in the ranking matrices will tend to change, as will the composition of the matrices. The influence of time on the ranking matrices could be described diagrammatically as a series of matrices distributed along a line representing a time continuum. In many decision-making situations, a decision has to be made at a particular time on the basis of the information then available, so exploration of changes with time is not necessary. However, there are decisions in which changes with time have to be considered. These decisions are of two main types:

1. Decisions that have to be repeated over time.
2. Major decisions which take many years to come to fruition and in that time needs and the environment surrounding the decision change.

In both cases, at the time the decision is made care will have to be taken to ensure that, as far as is practical, time related changes have been allowed for.

Examples of such changes are:

1. When a bank makes a loan to a particular country, it will evaluate whether or not the economic strength and political stability of that country has changed significantly since it was last made a loan by the bank.
2. Before an insurance company accepts a risk, it will first assess what factors have changed since it last accepted that kind of risk.
3. Adequacy of allowance for changes in borrowing conditions such as interest rate or repayment condition changes.
4. Before a company embarks on a major construction project lasting several years, it will have to decide whether or not the project will still be wanted when it is complete.

Possible methods of ranking

Having summarized how the Risk Ranking Technique allows for variation in the data and the environment of decision making, attention can now be turned to justification of the ranking scales postulated and justification of the proposed method of scoring acceptability proposed. The system of scoring proposed was intended to characterize the degree of acceptability of each of the four grades of acceptability specified. It has been argued in Chapter 4 that four ranking steps would give an adequate classification of the various shades of acceptability and at the same time avoid a neutral middle-ground grade. The selection of a 1, 2, 5, 14 scoring scale was purely arbitrary and intended to grade the acceptability of each factor in a way that would ensure adverse rankings would not be obscured in the overall ranking.

The attribute that is scored is acceptability. The length of the scale chosen was chosen quite arbitrarily, but criteria were specified for determining which grade a particular factor should be allocated. Although the criteria specified for determining Ranking Grade and Score are generally described in numerical terms, they cannot be measured with precision. For example, it is very difficult to measure the capability and relevant experience of a proposer, such judgements remaining subjective.

Nevertheless, the structured approach of the Risk Ranking Technique provides a consistent way of relating qualitative information to numerical representation. Building up the ranking process includes two important analytical disciplines, which are ordering the data available and making some ordinal measure of the significance of the data. The specification of criteria for scoring provides the ordering of the measurement. The form of ordinal measurement adopted is non-dimensional, a form chosen to enable the measurements from disparate factors to be combined. If only one factor, such as economics, was being considered it would be possible to contemplate the significance of the factor being measured in dimensional terms. In the case of economics, money would be an appropriate unit of measurement.

Critical analysis of scoring methods

One problem with the type of scoring system proposed arises from the environment that normally surrounds the particular type of decision making being considered. The problem is that data for some parts of the assessment of acceptability may be qualitative and for other parts quantitative. In other words, the quality of the data that have to be used may be variable. The qualitative data may arise from consulting experts about acceptability. Some of the procedures that can be adopted in such cases to ensure the results are as consistent as possible are described in Appendices 5 and 6. Presentation of the variation in the quality of the data used can be achieved with the three-dimensional ranking matrix that has already been described.

In making a critical assessment of the adequacy of the scoring scale, consideration must be given to possible alternatives. Three alternatives are considered: a linear scale, the quadratic/Bier scoring rule and a variation of the β measure of systematic risk.

Linear scale

A simple 1, 2, 3, 4 linear scale, while giving a satisfactory identification of each factor in each option, tends to obscure the significance of adverse ranking of a single factor. Table A4.1 shows how the significance of an individual adverse ranking can be obscured in the overall ranking. For the linear ranking system postulated, for illustrative purposes, it is assumed that:

1. A factor that is unlikely to be acceptable would have a score of 4 and a Rank 1.
2. A factor that is only likely to be acceptable if the risk can be reduced would have a score of 3 and a Rank 2.
3. A factor that is only acceptable subject to some additional control would have a score of 2 and a Rank 3.

The total score range of the overall rankings would be:

Rank 1, total score 10–12	Rank 2, total score 7–9
Rank 3, total score 4–6	Rank 4, total score 3

As a linear ranking score scale can lead to the significance of some adverse factors being obscured, a linear ranking scale is considered unacceptable.

Quadratic/Bier scoring scale

The quadratic/Bier scoring systems are for the purpose of this study considered to be similar as both are based on a quadratic scoring scale, and can be expressed as

$$\text{score} = (1 - P)^2 \times 100 \qquad \text{Equation 1.}$$

where P is the probability of a statement being true.

In risk ranking, options are graded under four headings, which is different to the quadratic/Bier concept. Simply to follow the quadratic distribution of scores it is assumed that each grade can be represented by the centre point of each quartile

Table A4.1 Examples of overall ranking based on a linear scale

Option	Factor score	Overall rank	Comment
1	Technical 2 Economic 2 Socio-political 2	Total score 6 giving an overall ranking of 3	The Rank 3 fairly reflects the individual scores
2	Technical 2 Economic 4 Socio-political 2	Total score 8 giving an overall ranking of 2	In this case the adverse economic ranking is obscured
3	Technical 4 Economic 1 Socio-political 1	Total score 6 giving an overall ranking of 3	In this case adverse technical ranking is obscured
4	A factor that is acceptable without restriction would have a score of 1 and a Rank 4		

between 0 and 1. The centre points give P the series of values 0.125, 0.375, 0.625 and 0.875. Using these numbers with equation 1 would give the score series 76.56, 39.06, 14.06 and 1.56. Reversing the numbers and rounding gives the series 2, 14, 39 and 77. To illustrate the efficacy of the scoring system it has been applied to, the pattern of options is described in Table A4.1 and the results are shown in Table A4.2. With the quadratic scale, the total score range for the overall rankings would be:

Rank 1, total score 81–231 Rank 2, total score 43–117
Rank 3, total score 18–42 Rank 4, total score 6

The quadratic/Bier ranking scale does not offer any advantage over the linear scale and can give ambiguous ranking.

β scale

If the risk was being measured purely in financial terms it might be possible to devise a scale based on the β coefficient which is used as an indication of the nature of the risk/return relationship associated with a particular investment. The greater β the greater the risk associated with that investment. A β equal to unity suggests that the return on an investment fluctuates proportionately to the market's average return. If β is less than one, the fluctuation is less than the market's. β does not appear to be an appropriate measure for a comprehensive ranking scale as it does not seem directly applicable to measure technical and socio-political factors.

The Risk Ranking Technique scale

Finally, to complete the review of possible scoring scales, the ranking scale used in the main text is tested against the pattern of decision options used to test the linear and quadratic/Bier scales. In the main text, the scoring scale 1, 2, 5, 14 was used.

Table A4.2 Examples of overall ranking based on a quadratic/Bier scale

Option	Factor score	Overall rank	Comment
1	Technical 14 Economic 14 Socio-political 14	Total score 42 giving an overall ranking of 3	The Rank 3 fairly reflects individual scores and gives the same result as the linear scale
2	Technical 14 Economic 77 Socio-political 14	Total score 105 giving an overall ranking of 2 or 1	Overall ranking uncertain and the adverse-economic ranking may be obscured
3	Technical 77 Economic 2 Socio-political 2	Total score 81 giving an overall ranking of 2 or 1	Overall ranking uncertain and the adverse technical ranking is obscured

This gave a total score range for overall ranking of:

Rank 1, total score 16–42   Rank 2, total score 7–15
Rank 3, total score 4–6   Rank 4, total score 3

The results of the main text scoring scale are given in Table A4.3.

Table A4.3 Test of the main text scoring scale

Option	Factor score	Overall rank	Comment
1	Technical 2 Economic 2 Socio-political 2	Total score 6 giving an overall ranking of 3	The Rank 3 fairly reflects individual scores as did the linear and quadratic/Bier scales
2	Technical 2 Economic 14 Socio-political 2	Total score 18 giving an overall ranking of 1	The Rank 1 draws attention to the importance of most critically ranked factor
3	Technical 14 Economic 1 Socio-political 1	Total score 16 giving an overall ranking of 1	The Rank 1 draws attention to the importance of the most critically ranked factor

Conclusion

The ranking scoring scale used in the main text has the advantage compared with the other scales considered, that it does not reduce the significance of the most critically ranked factor or introduce ambiguity into the ranking.

References

Braybrooke, D. and Lindblom, C. E. (1963) *A Strategy of Decision*, The Free Press, New York, p. 258.

Brown, R. V., Kahr A. S. and Peterson, C. (1974) *Decision Analysis for the Manager*, Holt Rinehart and Winston, New York, pp. 425–37.

Chicken, J. C. and Hayns, M. R. (1989) *The Risk Ranking Technique in Decision Making*, Pergamon Press, Oxford, p. 83.

Koutsoyiannis, A. (1982) *Non-Price Decisions*, Macmillan, London, pp. 611–35.

Lindley, D. V. (1985) *Making Decisions*, 2nd edn, John Wiley, London, pp. 21–9.

Luce, R. D. and Krumhansal, C. L. (1988) *Measurement scaling and psychophysics.* Published in *Stevens' Handbook of Experimental Psychology*, Vol. 1, 2nd edn, John Wiley, New York, pp. 3–4.

Van Horne, J. C. (1989) *Financial Management and Policy*, 8th edn, Prentice-Hall, Englewood Cliffs, NJ, pp. 64–8.

Walpole, R. E. and Myers, R. H. (1989) *Probability and Statistics for Engineers and Scientists*, 4th edn, Macmillan, New York.

APPENDIX 5: A GENERAL DESCRIPTION OF BAYESIAN AND FUZZY ANALYSES

Summary

The nature and the potential role of Bayesian and fuzzy data analyses are examined. Particular attention is given to identifying the practical limitations of both methods.

Introduction

An analyst trying to assess the acceptability of a complex novel project is faced with the difficult problem of finding a way to measure acceptability even though there are few or no relevant quantitative data. Without quantitative data classical statistical methods of calculating probability are of little direct use.. The analyst is faced with three options: to resort to qualitative analysis using natural language terms to describe acceptability, to use some form of synthesis of quantitative data or use a codified method of statistical inference such as Bayesian or fuzzy analysis.

Simple description of acceptability in natural language, that is, non-mathematical, can give rise to many problems even if the terms used are codified and used in a consistent manner. Ideally, the terms used should be related to some quantitative statement of acceptability, but given that no relevant data are available establishing such a relationship is not easy and certainly not precise. One good example of an attempt to relate qualitative statements of acceptability with satisfying a quantitative criteria of acceptability is given by the Civil Aviation Authority (CAA) requirements that a civil aircraft has to satisfy (see Figure 5.1 in the main text). These requirements relate qualitative descriptions of accident severity and frequency to quantitative statements of acceptability. The main CAA document specifies that satisfaction of the requirements has to be demonstrated experimentally in a precisely defined way that builds up statistically acceptable evidence that the criteria will be satisfied. In other words, the final decision about the acceptability of a design is deferred until the acceptability is proved experimentally. A decision maker does not always have the opportunity of waiting for experimental proof before making a final decision. However, the procedure does suggest that when relevant quantitative data are not available any decision about acceptability should be kept under review until the validity of a decision can be justified in quantitative terms.

An alternative to making a decision purely on a qualitative view is to attempt to synthesize the quantitative characteristics of the feature of interest from data on components similar to those from which the feature is made. The synthesizing process can be applied both to complete systems and the individual components that make up complete systems. Synthesis does not produce error-free results. For simple engineering systems it has been suggested that for instrument systems the ratio of observed failures to failures predicted by synthesis there is a 96% chance of the ratio being within a factor of 4 of the median value.

The American space agency NASA stated that it was not able to use numerical assessment for its fault analysis as the data base it had was so small it would not produce precise failure rates. The problem was exacerbated by the fact that although the NASA programme is massive the differences in configuration between each space shot make comparison of the data obtained from each shot of little value. In the financial area quantitative data about the significance of the risks involved in novel financial projects are equally difficult to establish and banks and insurance companies tend to adopt either a qualitative or a non-dimensional ordinal way of assessing the acceptability of risks. Such methods can be loosely described as inferring the risk acceptability. So the next step is to examine what the formal methods of statistical inference have to offer as an aid to determining risk acceptability when there are few or no data available.

Statistical inference

The starting point for any examination of statistical inference must be the work of the eighteenth-century English clergyman, Thomas Bayes. Fuzzy analysis has its origins in the form of analysis that Bayes originated, so there is no excuse needed for giving considerable emphasis in the discussion that follows to Bayes methods. Inference involves extrapolating from the known to the unknown. The following quotation from Sir Ronald Fisher (1953) *The Design of Experiments* helps to put the arguments that follow into perspective. 'We may at once admit that any inference from the particular to the general must be attended with some degree of uncertainty, but this is not the same as to admit that such inference cannot be absolutely rigorous, for the nature and degree of the uncertainty may itself be capable of rigorous expression.'

Bayesian analysis

In mathematical terms Bayes' rule can be expressed as follows:

If events B_1, B_2, ... B_k constitute a partition of a sample space S, where $P(B_i) \neq 0$ for $i = 1, 2, \ldots\ldots k$, then for any event A in sample space S such that $P(A) \neq 0$,

$$P(B_r \mid A) = \frac{P(B_r \cap A)}{\sum_{i=1}^{k} P(B_i \cap A)} = \frac{P(B_r)P(A \mid B_r)}{\sum_{i=1}^{k} P(B_i)P(A \mid B_i)}$$

for $r = 1, 2, \ldots\ldots\ldots k$.

In other words Bayes' rule specifies a way of determining the conditional probability of an event given some of the other relevant data.

The Bayesian approach is intended to be applied to the analysis of distributions appropriate to problems for which the data are initially subjective. Subjective data represent belief about what the relevant parameters should be, rather than hard quantitative data such as the results of observation. A typical example of subjective data would be expert opinions about the acceptability of a novel project. Starting from an initial position, or prior position, when there is some subjective view about the data and their distribution it is possible to calculate the prior mean and prior variance. Then with the addition of some objective data it is possible to refine the prior view into a better estimate of the distribution. The refined distribution, known as the posterior distribution, does need a data input to make it any improvement on the prior distribution. Essentially the process involves extrapolation and because it involves extrapolation there must still be some uncertainty about the conclusions. But it is important to remember that the Bayesian process is iterative, that is the results become more certain as more data are obtained.

The Bayesian approach can be applied to determination of: means, correlation, regression, contingency tables and analysis of variance. Essentially in all applications of the Bayesian approach the problem lies with identification of prior conditions and related basic data. This underlines the difficulty of assessing the acceptability of really novel projects for which there really are no data. It is just in this area that classical statistical methods are at their weakest as they make no allowance for the role of subjective data. The decision maker often has to make his decision on the basis of subjective data, so what else has Bayesian analysis to offer? In the context of decision making the Bayes estimator and Bayes risk have to be considered.

Assuming that the decision maker is concerned to make the correct decision an attempt must be made to evaluate the benefits resulting from a correct decision and any penalties that may result from making a wrong decision. The criterion that can be used is for the decision function $\bar{\theta}$ to have the least penalty when the incorrect action is taken. The next step is to introduce a loss function L whose value depends on the true value of parameter $\bar{\theta}$ and action A.

The functional relationship is $L(\bar{\theta}; A)$ and for decision making problems a loss function of the form $L(\bar{\theta}; A) = |\bar{\theta} - A|$ can be used or if two or more decision functions have to be considered $L(\bar{\theta}; A) = (\bar{\theta} - A)^2$.

Since A is unknown, the set of all possible values is known as the parameter space. For each possible value of A the loss function will have a different value.

A risk function R can be defined for the decision function as $R(\bar{\theta}; A)$ and this in turn defines the expected value E of the loss function in the following way:

$$R(\bar{\theta}; A) = E[L(\bar{\theta}; A)]$$

If a decision has to be made between two options $\bar{\theta}_1$ and $\bar{\theta}_2$ and the mini-max criterion is adopted then the decision option $R(\bar{\theta}; A)$ that is selected is the one that has the lowest maximum risk. Determination of the expected value may be very complicated, a fact belied by the simplicity of the expression $E[L(\bar{\theta}; A)]$.

In considering which choice to make between the options available a term called a Bayes' estimator is sometimes used. The estimator B is the Bayes risk x, the decision function which gives a minimum value. For example, if $\bar{\theta}_1$ and $\bar{\theta}_2$ are decision functions then if $B(\bar{\theta}_1) < B(\bar{\theta}_2)$ it follows that $\bar{\theta}_1$, is the better decision.

Relevance to practical decision making

Now to consider a practical example of a decision involving a public inquiry. Public inquiries call for a tremendous amount of detailed information and take a year or more to reach their verdict. In inquiries there are usually many groups presenting their cases and the chairman of the inquiry has to make his decision on the basis of the evidence they present. The arrangement is analogous to any decision-making process – the chairman of the inquiry could be equated to the chief executive of a company or a government minister. The influence of a particular group on the final decision has been characterized in the following way:

x_1	=	a	+	b_2x_2	+	b_3x_3	+	b_4x_4	+	. . .	b_nx_n	+ E
the chance of winning or losing	=	constant	+	contribution of groups favoured argument	+	contribution of size of group	+	contribution of nature of group		+	contribution of all other factors considered	+ error

While such a regression equation is attractive as a theoretical expression a considerable amount of evidence is required to convert it into a practical tool for estimating influence. Even without the additional evidence the equation can help structure subjective analysis of a group's influence.

The diagram in Figure A5.1 shows how Bayes' theorem can be used to iteratively refine an estimate of a proposal winning support in a mixed group of decision makers.

Bayes' theorem is expressed as:

$$P(H_1 \mid A) = \frac{P(A \mid H_1)P(H_1)}{P(A)}$$

wherc

$P(A|H_1)$ = likelihood
$P(H_1)$ = prior probability
$P(A)$ = sum of products of likelihood and prior probability for relevant calculations
$P(H_1|A)$ = standardized likelihood score obtained by aggregating A's likelihood and prior probability

The result of the calculation is a statement about the probability of a particular proposal winning support from a mixed group of decision makers, the probability being between 0 and 1. Equally the calculation shows the probability of the group losing. As with all Bayesian analysis the more data there are about the performance of the group of interest the more the estimate of success or failure can be improved.

In the context of the discussion in this book the question that has to be answered is whether or not it is possible to have a prior distribution that expresses complete ignorance.

Assuming that the prior distribution can be described as

$$f(\pi) = C'\pi^{a-1}(1-\pi)^{b-1}$$

where:

$f(\pi)$ is the function governing the unknown population proportion π and $0 < \pi < 1$

$$C' \text{ is a constant} = \frac{(a+b-1)!}{(a-1)!(b-1)!}$$

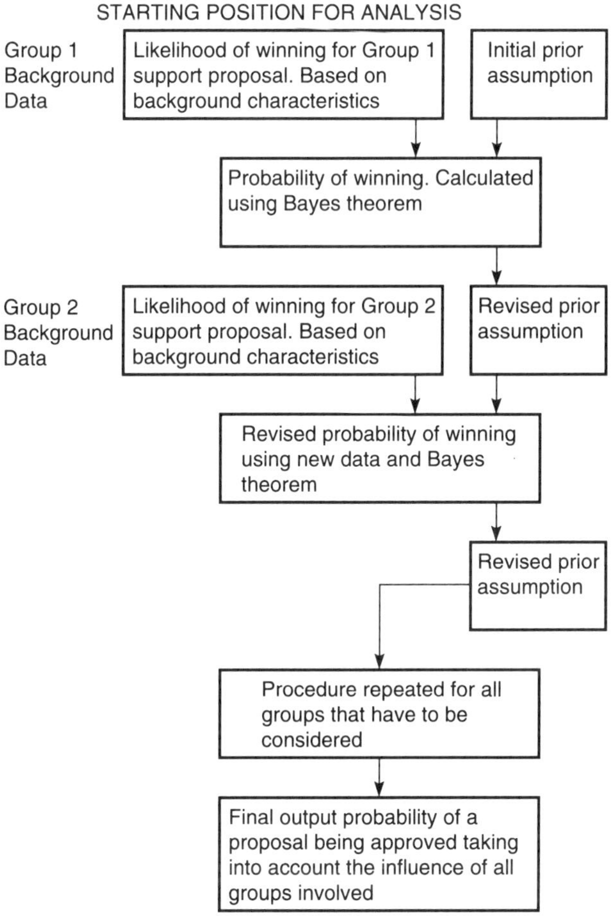
STARTING POSITION FOR ANALYSIS
Group 1 Background Data
Likelihood of winning for Group 1 support proposal. Based on background characteristics
Initial prior assumption
Probability of winning. Calculated using Bayes theorem
Group 2 Background Data
Likelihood of winning for Group 2 support proposal. Based on background characteristics
Revised prior assumption
Revised probability of winning using new data and Bayes theorem
Revised prior assumption
Procedure repeated for all groups that have to be considered
Final output probability of a proposal being approved taking into account the influence of all groups involved

Figure A5.1 Application of Bayes theorem to estimating likelihood of a particular proposal winning support in a mixed group of decision makers.

a is a non-negative constant
b is a non-negative constant } β distribution parameters

If there is no prior information it can be argued that a = 0 and b = 0 which gives:

$$f(\pi) = C'\pi^{0-1}(1-\pi)^{0-1}$$
$$= \frac{1}{C'\pi(1-\pi)}$$

which gives a U-shaped distribution curve.

An alternative suggestion is to assume a and b are both equal to 1. Such an assumption gives a rectangular distribution, which implies that every value of π between 0 and 1 is equally likely. In some ways the conclusion that all values of π are equally likely is a fair description of the implications of a state of complete ignorance.

However, a little understanding of the real world would suggest that a uniform distribution is very unlikely and that it would be more reasonable to assume that a and b are both greater than 0 but less than 1.

If the prior distribution is derived simply on the basis of a single analyst's opinion the view that the prior distribution is biased may be justified. Structured consultation with several experts with genuine knowledge of the subject being studied may yield a more helpful indication of the likely pattern of distribution. Although knowledge of prior distribution is conceptually indispensable to Bayesian analysis such knowledge is not always important in determining the exact shape of the posterior distributions.

This can be demonstrated as follows:

If it is assumed the distribution of interest is a β distribution and the posterior distribution mean

$$\mu = \frac{x + \mathrm{a}}{n + \mathrm{a} + \mathrm{b}}$$

where

n = is the sample size

x = is the number of observations with the desired characteristics

a and b are the β distribution constants of the prior distribution and have values between 0 and 1, or at least are small compared to n.

it can be seen that the characteristics of the prior distribution have little influence on the posterior distribution.

Conclusions about Bayesian approach

Although the Bayesian approach provides a way of improving prior predictions of the likely posterior distributions as real evidence becomes available, it does not make prior distributions guessed in ignorance into precise descriptions of the subject being studied.

Fuzzy data analysis

Moving now to consider the help that fuzzy set theory can give to the art of statistical inference, we start from the statement of set theory that the characteristic function of a set defines all the elements that make up the set. It is generalization about the degree of membership of a set that makes up the variant of set theory known as fuzzy set theory. It is stated that the originator of fuzzy set theory has described the aim of the theory as being: 'The development of a methodology for the formulation and solution of problems which are too complex or ill-defined to be susceptible to analysis by conventional techniques.'

In fuzzy analysis for each component of a set it is possible to assign a degree of membership of the set. If for all components the degree of membership is 1 then the problem is not fuzzy. But if the degree of membership is between 0 and 1 then for those components with a membership of less than 1 their membership is fuzzy. This concept of the validity of a particular value belonging to a particular group or set of data has long concerned statisticians. One method of eliminating weak members of a group (outliers) is known as the Dixon test. The method is based on an assessment of the ratio of the difference between the suspect value (outlier) and its nearest value and the difference between the suspect value and the most remote value.

Various methods exist for massaging the fuzzy members of a set. The object is to improve the veracity of the membership as a whole. The main methods are:

1. to concentrate the fuzzy elements of a set by reducing the membership through elimination of all members that are only partly in the set;
2. to dilute the set by increasing its membership via inclusion of those members that are barely in the set;
3. to normalize membership of the set so that at least one member has a degree of membership of 1;
4. the set can be intensified by increasing the degree of membership to greater than 0.5;
5. membership can be fuzzified by increasing the degree of membership of members with a non-zero degree of membership.

Practical application of fuzzy data analysis

Before looking in detail at the application of fuzzy analysis, attention is drawn to the fact that even supporters of fuzzy analysis recognize that what can be explained by fuzzy subsets can also be explained in other ways. One of the important roles seen for fuzzy analysis is the quantitative analysis of qualitative statements such as 'low', 'somewhat low', 'medium' and 'fairly high'. The essential preliminary step in the analysis of systems of comparative statements expressed in natural language is to establish a way of ranking their meaning. Such a step really amounts to giving a qualitative statement a quantitative significance. A simple description of the kind of relationship that can be established is given in Table A5.1. In analysis of real situations the relationship may be more complex and involve several levels of analysis.

Table A5.1 Example of relationship between qualitative expressions and fuzzy statements

Qualitative expression	Fuzziness or uncertainty
Certain	1
Quite probable	0.7–1
Probable	0.4–0.7
Improbable	0.0–0.7
Impossible	0.0

Exploitation of fuzzy analysis for assessment of complex systems does depend on the use of a computer and for this purpose several programs have been developed including FRA and IPIRISK. Even though in the future it may only be necessary to press a few keys on a computer keyboard to complete a fuzzy analysis it is still important to understand the significance of the method. It is appreciated that in the world of consumer products, fuzzy logic has already been put to use in making television sets automatically increase their brightness as the room grows darker and increase the sound volume when the viewer moves further from the set. Also fuzzy logic video cameras have been made to correct for shake in the arm of the operator so that an unblurred picture is produced. At the heavier industrial level fuzzy control systems have been used to control furnaces for making cement, the departure of subway trains and banks of elevators.

Several attempts have been made to apply fuzzy analysis to assessment of the acceptability of risk. Preyssl *et al.* made an assessment of the acceptability of two major plants, which was not quite a complete fuzzy analysis but used a weighting index of distribution and degree of compliance. This underlines the problem that runs through all applications of fuzzy analysis that have to be based on guessed data and patterns. It is only when the data and patterns can be confirmed that confidence can be established in the conclusions derived from the analysis. In decision-making terms this means confidence in the findings of the analysis can only be established post the decision as the project proceeds and real data are generated. This dilemma is, to some extent, always present in decision making.

Later, Preyssl was more specific in his use of 'fuzzy risk' analysis. In his findings he stresses that fuzzy analysis produces a grade of relative compliance with quantitative criteria of acceptability. To illustrate his analysis he presents the results of a study showing how the chance of major release of radioactivity from a Triga nuclear reactor can be assessed. Complete details of the procedures used are not given.

The Cattaneo *et al.* (1987) paper is particularly interesting as it starts from the problems associated with collecting the data to be analysed. In this case the data described abnormal occurrences recorded during the operation of a sample of 43 of the world's major nuclear power plants. The aims of the study were to examine the data both to identify the pattern of abnormal occurrences and to see what indication they gave of designers and operators learning from experience. The reports of occurrences often entailed imprecise knowledge and/or incomplete or ambiguous verbal statements. By assigning a membership function to each piece of information, it was possible to make a fuzzy analysis of the data. The analysis produced a possibility of risky operation for each of the reactors in the sample. In the examination of the data for any indication of abnormal occurrences being reduced by learning from experience, perfect learning was considered to be the situation in which there is no repeat of abnormal occurrences. At the other end of the scale there is zero learning. On this basis each piece of information was allocated a degree of membership of the learning set. From this data, using fuzzy analysis methods a value for the index of learning was calculated. This index of learning showed that designers and operators of several more recent models of reactor had apparently learnt from their experience of earlier models and that there was a reduction in abnormal occurrences.

General conclusion

Both the Bayesian and the fuzzy data approach provide ways of exploring possible outcomes, but unless they are based on sound relevant data the results can be misleading. However, if they are iteratively adjusted to incorporate new relevant data as they become available the accuracy of the predictions the methods make can play a helpful role.

References

Budge, I. (1978) Representations of political argument: applications within meta-planning. *Political Studies*, **XXV1**(4) (December), 439–61.

Cattaneo, F., DeSanctis, S., Garribba, S. F. and Volta, G. (1987) Learning from Abnormal Occurrences: Results of a Fuzzy Analysis. Paper for the Probabalistic Safety Assessment 1987 Conference, Zurich, 30 August–4 September.

Chicken, J. C. (1986) *Risk Assessment for Hazardous Installations*, Pergamon Press, Oxford.

Civil Aviation Authority (1986) Joint Airworthiness Requirements, Large Aeroplanes, JAR-25. Civil Aviation Authority, Cheltenham.

Fisher, Sir R. A. (1953) *The Design of Experiments*, Oliver and Boyd, Edinburgh, p. 4.

Hayns, M. R. and Unwin, S. D. (1984) A method to Incorporate Uncertainty and a Degree of Compliance in Safety Goals. Paper for conference, San Francisco 1984.

Iversen, G. R. (1984) Bayesian Statistical Inference. Sage University Paper 43, Sage Publications, Beverly Hills, Cal.

Lowe, C. W. (1969) *Industrial Statistics,* Vol. 1. 1st edn, Business Books, London.

Norman, P. and Naveed, S. (1990) A comparison of expert system and human operator performance for cement kiln operation. *Journal of the Operational Research Society*, **41**(11) (November), 1007–19.

Preyssl, C., Cullingford, M. C. and Swaton, E. (1985) Evaluation of Compliance of Risk-sources when Uncertainty and Risk-perception Aspects are included. International Atomic Energy Agency, Vienna.

Preyssl, C. (1986) *'Fuzzy Risk' Analysis Theory and Application*, International Atomic Energy Agency, Vienna.

Reid, T. R. (1991) Fuzzy Logic, but Japan puts it to work. *International Herald Tribune*, 5–6 January, pp. 1 and 8.

Schmucker, K. J. (1984) *Fuzzy Sets, Natural Language Computations and Risk Analysis*, Computer Science Press, Rockville, p. 6.

Walpole, R. E. and Myers, R. H. (1989) *Probability and Statistics for Engineers and Scientists*, 4th edn, Macmillan, New York.

APPENDIX 6: RULES FOR DERIVING DATA FROM EXPERT OPINION

Summary

Rules for deriving data from expert opinion are described.

The six rules listed below should help to minimize the errors in interpretation of the opinions of experts:

1. The experts consulted should have expertise in the field being studied.
2. Experts should also be asked to identify evidence that tends to contradict their opinions.
3. The size of the problems on which expert opinion is sought should be kept to an understandable level.
4. Analysis of the views of several experts is better than the view of a single expert.
5. Structured elicitation of opinions is better than unstructured questioning.
6. Mathematical analysis of opinions is better than some subjective view of opinion.

Conclusion

It must be remembered that no matter how carefully expert opinions are collected and analysed they will still remain qualitative opinions. The analysis will not convert them into quantitative data. It is sometimes difficult to decide how far a problem has to be decomposed to be of understandable size. Certainly a problem should be decomposed to the extent that it matches the expertise of the expert. Such decomposition may reveal parts of the problem for which there is no expert opinion.

References

Mosleh, A. *et al.* (1987) The Elicitation and Use of Expert Opinion In Risk Assessment: a Critical Review. A paper presented at the Probabilistic Safety Assessment and Risk Management Conference, PSA 87, Zurich, September.

Vogel, R. C. and Wall, I. B. (1987) Some Observations on NUREG 1150. Paper presented at the Probabilistic Safety Assessment and Risk Management Conference, PSA 87, Zurich, September.

APPENDIX 7: SUMMARY OF THE WORLD BANK'S GUIDELINES ON THE USE AND SELECTION OF CONSULTANTS BY BORROWERS

Summary

A method of assessing experience and capability of consultants is described, which can be used to assess a wide range of suppliers.

Background

The World Bank has issued guidelines to borrowers on what they consider is good practice in the choice of consultants. These guidelines give an insight into the way the Bank considers the technical competence of suppliers should be judged. In the guidelines, the Bank stresses that before any proposals are invited it must approve the evaluation criteria it is proposed to use.

Method of evaluation

For evaluation of qualifications and competence the Bank recommends the evaluation is based on three factors; general experience, work plan and key personnel. Each factor is weighted on a scale of 1 to 100. In Table A7.1 the weighting given to each factor and the fail and normal rating are summarized.

The precise weighting factor used is determined by the assessor on the basis of his judgement of the significance of the factor for each proposal.

Table A7.1 Summary of ratings

Factor	Score (scale 1–100)	Proposed weighting range and typical value	Weighted rating
Firm's general experience	a	0.1–0.2 Typical 0.15	a × 0.15
Work plan	b	0.25–0.4 Typical 0.35	b × 0.35
Key personnel	c	0.4–0.6 Typical 0.5	c × 0.5

Notes: Equation for overall rating r
Overall rating $r = a \times 0.15 + b \times 0.35 + c \times 0.5$
If r is less than 60 the company would not be acceptable
The normal range for r is 60–90.

Price

The extent to which price is used as a selection factor depends on the comparability of the options being considered. All options may not be directly comparable. it is recommended that the price and technical evaluations of a proposal are carried out independently. The Bank does not recommend any specific method or procedure for assessing the acceptability of a price, but cautions that consideration of price should not be allowed to undermine quality.

Conclusion

The method proposed for assessing the acceptability of consultants is suitable for assessing the acceptability of a wide range of suppliers.

Reference

World Bank (1981) Guidelines: 'Use of Consultants by World Bank Borrowers and by the World Bank Executing Agency', World Bank, Washington, D.C.

APPENDIX 8: ASSESSMENT OF COMPUTER SYSTEM RISKS BY THE INSURANCE INDUSTRY

Summary

The range of considerations that should be included in a computer system risk assessment is described.

Introduction

The way proposals for insurance of the risks associated with computer systems are assessed varies from insurance company to insurance company. With companies with only a small portfolio of computer risks the assessment may be quite simple, but the companies that are specialists in computer and electronic equipment insurance have devised quite comprehensive assessment procedures and detailed guidance on good practice that proposers should follow.

Assessment procedure

The assessment procedures used are based on risk analysis procedures that are used for the analysis of many complex systems, such as aeroplanes, weapon systems, nuclear power plants or chemical plants.

The first stage in assessing the acceptability of the computer system is to review the physical arrangements of the system. Such a review assesses the adequacy of the general management of the system, fire protection, protection against water, protection against technical faults, protection against criminal acts, protection against environmental hazards and protection against other external effects. In Table A8.1 the essential questions that would be asked under each heading are outlined. Determining the acceptability of the answers to the questions outlined in the table involves a systematic analysis of the significance of the evidence. There also has to be collaboration with the proposer so that he has an opportunity to modify his installation to make it acceptable. The iterative adjustment of a proposal may also be associated with discussion about the extent of the cover provided and the premium required.

The adequacy of the arrangements for dealing with emergencies (loss of use of computer system) is an important subject in its own right but has special importance in relation to insurance. This importance stems from the fact that effective emergency arrangements can help reduce the losses that arise if an emergency situation occurs.

Practical considerations

After a severe accident to a complex installation it may be important to get the system operating again as soon as possible, to prevent losses building up. If standby arrangements are adequate such losses will be minimized. However, there can still be high replacement costs for the insurer to bear. These costs can be reduced if

Table A8.1 Outline of computer system insurance assessment questions

Feature	Typical questions
General management	Is the management of the system knowledgeable? Is there an adequate supply of spare parts? Have effective maintenance procedures been adopted? Have effective arrangements been made for dealing with any emergency that may arise?
Fire protection	Building provisions – Is the computer centre in a separate building? Is fire resistant construction used; are cable runs smoke proof; can air ducts be shut off automatically; is there provision of emergency lighting?
	Organizational conditions – Have fire regulations been established? Are fire drills carried out regularly? Are there fire-proof safes for data?
	Fire alarms/extinguishers – Does fire alarm system conform with national requirements? Is a fire extinguisher system installed; are there appropriate portable extinguishers provided?
Protection against ingress of water	Are there water pipes in the vicinity of the computer room? Is there a risk of rising water from drains or floods? Is the roof water proof? Is there a water detection system installed?
Protection against technical faults	Can the air conditioning system give rise to problems such as contamination or excessive humidity? Is the main power system reliable? Is an emergency power system provided? Is the installation protected against lightning, over-voltage and discharges of static electricity?
Protection against criminal acts	Are wall, ceilings, windows and doors of an anti-intruder design? Is access controlled? Are there parts of the building which cannot be monitored by television?
Protection against environmental hazard	Are there external vibrations or intense electric fields that can harm the installation? Are there risks of explosions or release of harmful chemicals in the area?
Protection against other external effects	Is the installation resistant to storm damage and earthquakes? Is the installation on a flight path?

the equipment can be restored. One specialist insurer has established a company to provide a computer system restoration service. The company has branches in Germany, the United States, Switzerland, Austria, France, Italy, Spain, Australia and the Netherlands. Experience has shown that restoring rather than replacing damaged equipment can reduce direct losses borne by the insurer by 80%. For the insurance industry to establish a restoration service to reduce the losses associated with a particular activity is unusual, but the benefit in this specific case is clear.

References

Swiss Reinsurance (1987) *Computer Insurance*, Swiss Reinsurance Company, Zurich.

Tela Insurance Company (1985) *Catastrophes in Computer Centres, Guide for Catastrophe Plans,* Tela Insurance Company, Munich.

APPENDIX 9: ANALYSIS OF COSTS AND BENEFITS

Summary

Methods of assessing costs and benefits are examined and an example is given of a special form of cost–benefit analysis.

Introduction

Before any attempt can be made to quantify the costs and benefits of a particular project, the nature of the costs and benefits relevant to that project must be determined. The first step in such analysis is determining the point of view from which profitability has to be judged. Clearly the acceptability of a proposal to build a car factory will be judged in different terms to a proposal to increase welfare payments. No matter what type of project is considered some allowance will have to be made for the life of a project. With a project of an engineering nature determination of the appropriate life may be relatively easy to define as it can be related to the wear-out of the various components, but with social projects determination of the appropriate life, if there is one, may be somewhat difficult.

Basis for calculations

In purely financial terms benefits have to be assessed on the basis of the total of direct and indirect revenues over the life of the project. Sometimes running costs are deducted from revenue to give a figure for total net revenue, and total costs are considered as only capital costs. it makes very little difference to the usefulness of the analysis, provided the calculations are performed in a consistent manner and all the costs and all revenues are included. The detailed definition of the costs and revenues that should be included is returned to later. The economic life as opposed to the wear-out life of a technical project is quite hard to predict. The rapid developments in technology have shortened the useful life of many complex systems. Organizations have to change their equipment frequently just to keep up with the competition. For example, computers, cars, automated systems and communication systems undergo fairly rapid change. Of course the lower the discount rate considered the more sensitive will be the analysis to the length of economic life considered. Discounting is a way of simplifying the analysis of the value of a stream of payments to a common base so that the various options are easier to compare.

Present value

The present value P_0 of a stream of payments is equal to

$$P_1/(1+r)^1 + P_2/(1+r)^2 + \ldots\ldots P_T(1+r)^T$$

or more briefly

$$P_0 = \sum_{t=0}^{t=T} P_t/(1+r)^t$$

where P_0 is the present value of a stream of payments P_1, P_2 . . . . . P_T arising in years 1 to T and r is the discount rate. In the equation r is assumed to be constant over the period considered. In the real world r may vary over time, as the rate used in the private sector is normally the rate at which bank loans are available. In the public sector the discount rate may be set by some central policy body. This variation in the basis for determining discount rates underlines one problem in comparing private sector and public sector projects.

Net present value

For decision-making purposes it is sometimes helpful to consider the net present value (NPV) or net present worth (NPW) as it is sometimes called, as the basis for determining the relative merits of the options available.

NPW or NPV is the sum over the lifetime of a project of the discounted benefits–costs a project may consider acceptable if NPV > 0. If several options have to be considered the most acceptable one will be the one that has an NPV which is more above 0 than the others.

If there is expected to be inflation during the life of the project the discount rate has to be modified to make allowance for the rate of inflation.

Internal rate of return

A variation of the NPV that is sometimes used is the internal rate of return (IRR). The IRR is the discount rate required to make the NPV equal to zero. Using the IRR the criterion for minimum acceptability of a project is that the IRR should be greater than the rate used for determining the cost of the capital required. One advantage claimed for using the IRR is that it eliminates the need for choosing a discount rate. However, in practice to make the analysis some knowledge of the discount rate is required. Provided that the proposers or planners have set the discount rate correctly, so that it properly reflects the need to control the distribution of capital, then the NPV approach is preferred.

Present value/capital ratio

Other criteria for assessing the acceptability of competing proposals are: the payback period, output capital ratio and present value over capital ratio. With the payback period criterion the most acceptable project is the one with the shortest period for capital repayment. One criticism of this method is that it ignores the significance of the benefits that may occur after payback is complete. For the present value (PV) over capital (K) ratio approach, projects that produce a value of PV/K greater than 1 are acceptable.

All projects passed by the NPV > 0 criterion would also be passed by the PV/K criterion.

The figures used in the methods of analysis just mentioned will not be absolute values; there must be some uncertainty associated with them. Provided every cost and every benefit is taken into account, the significance of the uncertainty can be assessed by calculating the parameters using data from the upper and lower ends of the range of uncertainty. If some costs and benefits are omitted from the calculation the range of uncertainty will be greater. The results of such calculation allow two other criteria, which are known as the maxi-min returns and the mini-max-regret to be used to determine the acceptability of a proposal. The maxi-min return criteria requires the option adopted to be the one with the largest minimum return. In other words the proposal that should be accepted is the one that appears to give the highest return even when the most adverse data are used to calculate the return. The mini-max-regret criterion defines the most acceptable project as the one which would involve the greatest loss of gain if it was given up. The assumption implicit in making such assessment is that the data used in making the calculation for each option have equal degrees of uncertainty associated with them.

Social cost–benefit analysis

A more specific method for assessment of public sector investment is known as the social cost–benefit analysis (SCBA), which has been used to assess public sector investment in the Third World. The basis of the comparison of investment options would be to calculate the net benefit (NB) on the basis of the resulting exports X, imports M and domestic inputs D.

Then NB = X – M – D where X, M and D are valued in consistent currency

For a proposal to be acceptable NB would have to be greater than 0. If several options have to be considered the option that would be most acceptable would be the one that showed the greatest NB. The problems associated with assessing the acceptability of investment proposals in Third World countries are:

1. doubts about the stability of the exchange rate;
2. reliable assessment of the impact of protective practices such as tariffs, quota restrictions and subsidies;
3. availability of labour with appropriate skills;
4. availability of all the required support services.

The list of associated problems shows how using X, M and D in the simple way shown above may be misleading unless in their calculation the problem factors are effectively dealt with in a consistent way. Alternatively, but not so accurately, weighting factors may be used to take account of each problem factor. Such weighting factors may introduce more problems, particularly if they are derived subjectively.

Assuming that the weighting factors can be used with confidence the net benefit equation could be written as follows:

$$NB = a(bcd\,X - bM - cdD),$$

where

a = the weighting factor for exchange rate stability;
b = the weighting factor for impact of protective practices;
c = the weighting factor for labour availability;
d = the weighting factor for adequacy of support services.

Economic cost–benefit analysis

The above equation gives a hint of the significance of the efficiency of pricing which has to be considered in economic cost–benefit analysis (ECBA). But that is not the only feature that has to be considered in assessing the economic acceptability of projects in the public sector. It is sometimes convenient to consider projects from three aspects which are:

1. financial profitability – measured at market prices;
2. economic profitability – measured at efficiency prices;
3. social profitability – measured at social prices.

Evaluation of projects based on non-traded goods

To evaluate a particular project for which the final output cannot be measured directly in market price terms, because the output is in the form of some non-traded good, the composition of the costs involved should as far as possible be broken down into its constituent components such as traded goods, services and labour. Even when the components are identified there may be problems in pricing them as some may have no traded price analogue. Components may be traded, but not on international markets. For example, a machine may be made for a very specific local duty that is not found anywhere else and labour may be so unskilled and lacking in education that it cannot be used elsewhere. A method of converting market prices into economic or social prices is sometimes accomplished using 'accounting ratios' (ARs). Various conventions have been proposed for making such conversions: some just consider the conversions for single goods, others adopt an average conversion factor for a group of factors. These variations in conventions together with the variations in exchange rates, prices and taxes all underline the magnitude of uncertainties that have to be allowed for in making an assessment of the acceptability of a project.

Social opportunity cost

Public expenditure can sometimes be measured in terms of social opportunity cost. The rates of return in private industry or weighted average interest rates are used as the basis for comparative evaluation of this cost. Where the discount rate used cannot be taken as an equilibrium rate, that is a rate that would lead to the optimum allocation of resources, an alternative measure like PV/K or NPV/K, may be used to measure the efficiency of resource use (where NPV = net present value, PV = present value and K = capital).

In assessing the implications of social pricing consideration has to be given to the weighting that should be adopted to allow for distribution of benefits that, as a result of the project being considered, would go outside the project country. An egalitarian view that all benefits are equal, no matter where they arise, is not entirely satisfactory when a project is being assessed in terms of the benefit it will give to the country in which it will reside. Weighting of the importance of a project also has to be considered for the time when benefits arise. It is possible more value may be attributed to benefits that arise in the immediate future than to those that will arise a long time into the future. When project options aimed at satisfying the same specification are being compared, the time when the benefits will arise should be essentially the same. However, if different types of projects are all competing for the same block of money then the significance of the time distribution of benefits has to be weighted.

Weighting of factors

The specification of weights has in some way to reflect what is the desired distribution of benefits, which may be quite different to the present distribution and it may be skewed in favour of a particular section of the population. Whatever the distribution that is decided upon it must be defensible both in terms of the evidence it is based on and its appropriateness to the people who will be exposed to the project. For example, if it is expected that consumption is to have an optimum value N, then, following the rules of diminishing marginal utility of extra consumption, if only lower consumption is possible it would have a marginally higher value N_1 and if only a higher consumption was possible it would have a marginally lower value N_2. For a case with such a pattern of values and consumptions a justifiable system of weighting could be: for consumption level N weighting would be 1, for consumption level N_1 weighting would be greater than 1 and for consumption level N_2 weighting would be less than 1. Exactly how much the weightings of N_1 and N_2 would be above and below 1 would depend on the details of each specific case.

If a project is aimed at producing major structural changes in the pattern of a particular country's economy, or a company's structure, then it would be appropriate to weight the various options according to the likelihood that they would produce the required changes. It can be appreciated that proposals that make a positive contribution to achieving the required structural change would be given a weighting that would increase their acceptability. On the other hand, proposals that would make a negative contribution to achieving the required structural change would be given weightings that would reduce their acceptability. Quantifying such weightings would involve a considerable amount of judgement, which would have a large subjective component and involve a considerable amount of policy making.

Example of the use of cost–benefit analysis

An interesting example of the application of cost–benefit analysis that illustrates some of the points made above has been given by Brüser. He applied cost–benefit analysis to the problem of assessing the acceptability of various proposals for road improvements in Africa-Caribbean-Pacific (ACP) countries. The criterion adopted was that if the value of the discounted investment costs for a project is lower than the value of the discounted road user savings (RUS), then the acceptance of the project on economic grounds is justified. This criterion can be expressed mathematically as:

$$\sum_{t}^{0}[I(\mathrm{a})_t][1+i]^{-t} < \sum_{t}^{0}[\mathrm{RUS}(\mathrm{a})_t][1+i]^{-t}$$

where

t	=	period under consideration (typically 15 to 20 years for road projects)
I(a)	=	investment costs for project 'a'
RUS(a)	=	road user savings resulting from project
'a' RUS	=	(the vehicle operating costs on the present road) minus (vehicle operating costs on the road improved by the proposed project)
i	=	discounting (or interest) – a discount rate of 12% has been used on some of the project considered.

Brüser stresses that it is important that all potential projects are assessed according to the same economic criteria ranking of the acceptability of competing options on the basis of profitability in economic terms, the most profitable being the most acceptable. It is accepted that there may be a minimum level of profitability below which it is considered that the profit level is not sufficient to make it worthwhile going ahead with the project.

A similar approach has been developed for evaluating the merit of road maintenance operations as compared with rebuilding the road. The mathematical expression is slightly different to the one just mentioned and is as follows:

$$\sum_{t}^{0} \mathrm{CM}_t[1+i]^{-t} + \sum_{t}^{0}[\mathrm{VOC}_t - \mathrm{VOCM}_t][1+i]^{-t} < \sum_{t}^{0} I_t[1+i]^{-t}$$

where

CM	=	costs of current and periodic maintenance of project
VOC	=	vehicle operating costs on road
VOCM	=	vehicle operating costs on maintained roads
I	=	proposed road rebuilding cost
t	=	period under consideration
i	=	discounting rate.

While the methods Brüser used are simple and consistent it can be argued that they do not give a comprehensive evaluation of benefits. For example, the equations, as written, do not make allowance for increased traffic, improvements in trade, time saved by vehicles being able to complete their journeys faster and extra pollution resulting from increased traffic. These criticisms, in a rather indirect way, indicate the factors that generate the uncertainty that has to be associated with the results of some calculations of cost–benefit analysis. The degree of uncertainty may be very large when potential indirect losses and indirect benefits are left out of the calculation.

General conclusions

The general conclusions about cost–benefit methods that must be accepted are that the method does not give absolute results and the measure of uncertainty that has to be allowed for is the product of both the uncertainty in the data used and of the accuracy with which the methods of calculation used describes the real world variations they purport to model. Despite the reservations about the degree of uncertainty associated with the various forms of cost–benefit analysis discussed, it is accepted the method can still serve a useful purpose in giving an indication of the relative financial merits of competing options.

References

Brüser, A. (1991) Economic aspects of road transport projects. *The Courier*, 125, (January–February) (EEC, Brussels), 64–6.
Irvin, G. (1984) *Modern Cost–Benefit Methods*, Macmillan, London.

APPENDIX 10: MULTIVARIATE TECHNIQUES

Summary

The nature and present status of multivariate techniques are reviewed.

Introduction

It has been suggested by French that the tremendously increased computational capability resulting from the advent of the computer age in the 1960s allowed more complex models involving multidimensional, non-linear relationships to be explored (French, 1992). This was followed in the 1980s by the view developing that simpler models could be more informative, provided the validity of the model was checked, the role envisaged for complex models being part of the process of checking the adequacy of simple models. The complex model showed whether or not there was any benefit to be gained from making the simple model more complex. These views recognize the fact that unless models are based on accurate information about a proposal and the interactions between all the factors involved misleading conclusions are likely to be indicated. An example of a good model is the representation of the behaviour of an aeroplane for the construction of a flight simulator for training pilots. A model of doubtful value, because of the information it would have to be based on, would be a model of the economy of a Third World country with an unstable government.

Present status of multivariate techniques

A survey by Kathawala of quantitative techniques used by large and small organizations in the United States showed that of the 226 organizations contacted 36% were unfamiliar with multidimensional scaling, 31% made no use of the technique, 19% made minor use of the technique, 10% made moderate use, 2% made frequent use and 2% made extensive use (Kathawala, 1988). The five most popular techniques used by the 226 organizations surveyed were: forecasting, breakeven analysis, statistical sampling, computer simulation and regression correlation. With computer simulation being in the top five popular techniques it seems to imply a fairly high interest in multivariate techniques, higher than suggested by just 14% of users making moderate or greater use of multidimensional techniques.

There are several possible approaches to assessing the acceptability of proposals that are made up of several different independent variables. The basic stages of such assessments (Hogarth, 1987, pp. 280–5) are:

1. structure the problem;
2. determine how the various variables are to be rated;
3. determine the significance of the individual variables for the case being considered and the overall significance of the variables considered. Determining the overall significance requires that the rating of each factor is weighted to put its significance in the correct proportion to the other factors. (This is the procedure adopted in the Risk Ranking Technique.)
4. on the basis of rating of significance, determine the acceptability of the proposal.

Structuring the problem is the foundation on which any analysis has to be built. If the structure is not correctly specified, such as by the omission of a variable, the whole validity of the analysis is undermined. In the case of the Risk Ranking Technique the analysis of proposal variables is brought together under the headings: technical, economic and socio-political. The overall view of the acceptability of these three main variables has to be built up from the analysis of the sub-variables from which they are composed.

Determination of how the various variables are to be rated is essentially setting the criteria for judging acceptability. Many of the possible methods of rating variables have been reviewed by Slovic, Lichtenstein and Fischhoff. Some methods they mention such as Edwards' simple multiattribute rating technique (SMART) and the Multiattribute Utility Models are, because of the calculation steps they involve, more complicated to use than the Risk Ranking Technique. An important point that Slovic *et al.* (1988) make in their review that must be commented on is that reference to money aspects of a proposal will focus attention on monetary aspects of acceptability, whereas an ordinal rating of acceptability will focus attention on probability. These really represent two quite different stages in an assessment and this point has been catered for in the Risk Ranking Technique. Evaluation of monetary aspects specified as taking place at the rating of factors stage and at ranking of overall acceptability is made in a non-dimensional ordinal form. This ordinal expression of overall acceptability gives a numerical indication of likely acceptability on a consistent basis. The question of weighting the significance of factors relative to one another is of special importance. In the discussion of the Risk Ranking Technique in the main text it is proposed the three factors, technical, economic and socio-political, should be given equal weight. As a generalization, particularly for project assessment, this is likely to be the best assumption. However, it has to be recognized that there may be special decision-making environments in which one factor has to be considered as having overriding importance and other factors made subsidiary or even disregarded. Examples of such special environments are wartime, a state of national emergency and a time of special financial restriction.

Allowance for uncertainty

In multivariate analysis, as in any other form of analysis, allowance has to be made for the spread of uncertainty in the data used. Also in the case of major decisions, of the type considered in this study, decisions about acceptability have to be kept under review during the life of the project. The decision-making environment may change during the life of a project – the need for a project may disappear, it may be found that technical objectives cannot be satisfied, sources of funding may disappear or the project may become unacceptable to the public.

Conclusions

In his survey of the status of multiple criteria decision making, Stewart (1992) drew several conclusions. Two of these conclusions are particularly apposite to this study:

1. Any aids to decision making based on multiple criteria decision making should

be simple and efficient to use.

2. The problem of how to deal with uncertainty with multiple criteria decision making methods is one that still has to be solved.

The Risk Ranking Technique appears to satisfy both these points. It is simple to use and the presentation of ranking in the three-dimensional matrix form allows it to display the magnitude of uncertainties in the ranking.

Bibliography

French, S. (1992) Editorial. *Journal of Multi-criteria Decision Analysis*, **1**(1)(July), 1–2.

Hogarth, R. (1987) *Judgement and Choice*, 2nd edn, John Wiley, Chichester, pp. 280–5.

Kathawala, Y. (1988) Applications of quantitative techniques in large and small organisations in the United States: an empirical analysis. *Journal of the Operational Research Society*, **39**(11), 981–8.

Slovic, P., Lichtenstein, S. and Fischhoff, B. (1988) Decision making, in *Stevens' Handbook of Experimental Psychology*, Vol. 2, 2nd edn, John Wiley, Chichester, Ch. 10.

Stewart, T. J. (1992) A critical survey on the status of multiple criteria decision making theory and practice. OMEGA *International Journal of Management Science*, **20**(5/6), 569–86.

REFERENCES

Abdul-Fattah, A-R. F. and Abulfaraj, W. H. (1982) Siting of nuclear power plants in Saudi Arabia using fuzzy decision analysis. *Nuclear Technology,* **58** (September) 404–13.

Allen, R. G. D. (1968) *Statistics for Economists,* Hutchinson University Library, London.

Ashby, E. (1978) *Reconciling Man with the Environment*, Oxford University Press, London, pp. 69–72.

Bank of England (1990a) Notice to Institutions Authorised under the Banking Act 1987. Implementation in the United Kingdom of the Directive on own funds of Credit Institutions, BSD/1990/2, Bank of England, Banking Supervision Division, London.

Bank of England (1990b) Notice to Institutions Authorised Under the Banking Act 1987. Implementation in the United Kingdom of the Solvency Ratio Directive, BSD/1990/3, Bank of England, Banking Supervision Division, London.

Barrett, N. and Byrd, T. (1989) Chunnel phoney war risks total breakdown. *The New Civil Engineer,* 2 November, 7.

Berliner, B. (1982) *Limits of Insurability of Risks*, Prentice-Hall, Englewood Cliffs, NJ.

Blackstone, T. and Plowden, W. (1988) *Inside the Think Tank*, William Heinemann, London.

Braybrooke, D. and Lindblom, C. E. (1963) *A Strategy of Decision,* The Free Press, New York.

Brown, R. V., Kahr, S. S. and Peterson, C. (1974) *Decision Analysis for the Manager,* Holt Rinehart and Winston, New York.

Brown, J., Lee, T. and Fielding, J. (1983) Concerns, Worry and Anxiety about Hazard with Special Reference to Nuclear Power – a Secondary Analysis of Data Collected by Social Community Planning Research for the Health and Safety Executive, a report issued by the Psychology Department of the University of Surrey.

Brüser, A. (1991) Economic aspects of road transport projects. *The Courier*, 125, (January–February) (EEC, Brussels), 64–6.

Buckley, J. J. (1986) Stochastic Dominance: an approach to decision making under risk. *Risk Analysis*, **6**(1), 35–41.

Budge, I. (1978) Representations of political argument: applications within meta-planning. *Political Studies*, **XXVI**(4) (December).

Cattaneo, F., DeSanctis, S., Garribba, S. F. and Volta, G. (1987) Learning from Abnormal Occurrences; Results of a Fuzzy Analysis. Paper, presented at the

Probabalistic Safety Assessment Conference, Zurich, 30 August–4 September.
Channon, D. F. (1988) *Global Banking Strategy*, John Wiley, New York, pp. 155–98.
Checkland, P. (1988) *System Thinking, System Practice*, John Wiley, Chichester.
Chicken, J. C. (1975) *Hazard Control Policy in Britain*, Pergamon Press, Oxford, pp. 78–104.
Chicken, J. C. (1982) *Nuclear Power Hazard Control Policy*, Pergamon Press, Oxford, pp. 148–204.
Chicken, J. C. (1986a) Comprehensive Assessment. Paper presented at the first International Conference on Risk Assessment of Chemicals and Nuclear Materials held at the Robens Institute, Surrey Univeristy, September.
Chicken, J. C. (1986b) *Risk Assessment for Hazardous Installations*, Pergamon Press, Oxford.
Chicken, J. C. (1989) A European View on Computer System Insurance. Paper presented to the NCC Information Technology Conference, Blackpool.
Chicken, J. C. and Hayns, M. R. (1989) *The Risk Ranking Technique in Decision Making*, Pergamon Press, Oxford.
Chicken, J. C. and Hayns, M. R. (1987a) Assessing Social Aspects of Risk Acceptability. Paper presented at the SNS/ENS/ANS Conference on Probabilistic Safety Assessment and Risk Management, Zurich, August.
Chicken, J. C. and Hayns, M. R. (1987b) Comprehensive Safety Criteria. Paper presented at an IMechE meeting, December.
Civil Aviation Authority (CAA) (1985) *Joint Airworthiness Requirements: All weather Operations,* JAR-AWO, Civil Aviation Authority, Cheltenham.
Civil Aviation Authority (CAA) (1986) *Joint Airworthiness Requirements: Large Aeroplanes*, JAR-25, Civil Aviation Authority, Cheltenham.
Commission of The European Communities, Public Opinion in the European Community on Energy in 1984, XV11/282/85-EN, a report published by the Commisson of the European Communities Directorate-General for Energy.
Council of Economic Community (1989a) Council Directive of 17 April on the own funds of credit institutions (89/299/EEC), *Official Journal of the European Communities*, 5.5.89.
Council of Economic Community (1989b) Council Directive of 18 December on the solvency ratio for credit institutions (89/647/EEC), *Official Journal of the European Communities*, 30.12.89.
Cox, L. A. and Ricci, P. F. (1990) *New Risk Issues and Management*, Plenum Press, New York.
Donne, M. (1981) *Leader of the Skies, Rolls Royce: the first seventy-five years*, Frederick Muller, London.
Edwards, E. (1985) Human factors in aviation. *Aerospace*, **12**(6) (June/July).
Feltham, C. (1989) Banks urge Eurotunnel to seek Extra Funding from Investors, *The Times*, 2 October 1989, p. 25.
Fisher, R. A. (1953) *The Design of Experiments*, Oliver and Boyd, Edinburgh.
French, S. (1992) Editorial, *Journal of Multi-Criteria Decision Analysis*, **1**, 1–2.
HMSO (1982) Fixed Channel Link Report UK/French Study Group, Cmnd 8561, HMSO, London, June.

HMSO (1985a) Channel Fixed Link Environmental Appraisal of Alternative Proposal, HMSO, London, December.

HMSO (1985b) Hansard, *House of Commons Official Report*, Vol. 88, No. 24, 9 December, Col. 707, HMSO, London.

HMSO (1988) *Improving Management in Government: the Next Steps. Report to the Prime Minister*, HMSO, London.

Hall, P. (1980) *Great Planning Disasters*, Pengiun Books, Harmondsworth, 1980.

Harvey Jones, J. (1988) *Making it Happen*, Fontana, London.

Hayns, M. R. and Unwin, S. D. (1984) A method to incorporate Uncertainty and a Degree of Compliance in Safety Goals. Paper presented at the ANS Conference, San Francisco, USA.

Health and Safety Executive (HSE) (1978) *Canvey: an Investigation of Potential Hazards from Operations in the Canvey Island/Thurrock Area. A Report by the Health and Safety Executive*, HMSO, London.

Health and Safety Executive (HSE) (1981) *Canvey: a Second Report, a Review of Potential Hazards from Operations in the Canvey Island/Thurrock Area Three Years after Publication of the Canvey Report*, HMSO, London.

Health and Safety Executive (HEC) (1988) *The Tolerability of Risk from Nuclear Power Stations*, HMSO, London.

Hicks, A. J. (1982) The Role of Insurance Safety. Paper presented to the OYEZ 1982 Review Seminar on Risk Management and Acceptability, London, April.

Hilton, G. (1976) *Intermediate Politometrics*, Columbia University Press, New York.

Hogarth, R. (1988) *Judgement and Choice*, 2nd edn, John Wiley, Chichester.

Horne, J. C. V. (1989) *Financial Management and Policy*, 8th edn, Prentice-Hall, Englewood Cliffs, NJ.

Ibrekk, H. and Granger Morgan, M. (1987) Graphical communication of uncertain quantities to nontechnical people. *Risk Analysis*, **7**(4) (December), 519–29.

Ilersic, A. R. (1964) *Statistics*, 13th edn, HFL, London.

Illustrated London News (1985) The race to cross the Channel. *Illustrated London News*, **273**(7048), (November), 29–34.

Institution of Civil Engineers (1985) Ridley ignores calls for Channel Inquiry, *New Civil Engineer*, 7 November, 9.

Irvin, G. (1964) *Modern Cost-Benefit Methods*, Macmillan, London.

Iversen, G. R. (1984) *Bayesian Statistical Inference*, Sage Publications, Beverley Hills, Cal.

Jahresbericht, V. W. (1991/92) Institut für Versicherungswirtschaft, St Gallen, Switzerland, p. 12.

Johnson, C. External Debt Assessment. Paper presented to the International Economics Study Group Conference on the 1985 World Development Report, London, November.

Jones-Lee, M. W. (1986) The Political Economy of Physical Risk. Paper presented at the First International Conference on Risk Assessment of Chemicals and Nuclear Materials, Surrey University, September.

Junge, G. (1988) Country Risk Assessment: Swiss Bank Corporation's Approach, *Economic and Financial Prospects Supplement*, 1, (February/March), 1–16.

Junge, G. and Schieler, M. (1993) Credit risks of industrial countries. *Economic and Financial Prospects*, 4, 4–6.

Keller, L. R. and Sarin, R. K. (1988) Equity in social risk: some empirical observations. *Risk Analysis*, **8**(1), 135–46.

Koutsoyiannis, A. (1982) *Non-Price Decisions: the Firm in a Modern Context*, Macmillan, London.

Kunreuther, H. C., Linerooth, J., Lathrop, J., Atz, H., MacGill, S., Manol, C., Schwarz, M. and Thompson, M. (1983) *Risk Analysis and Decision Processes*, Springer Verlag, Berlin.

Layfield, Sir F. (1987) *Report on the Sizewell 'B' Public Inquiry, Summary of Conclusions and Recommendations*, HMSO, London.

Lindblom, C. E. (1968) *The Policy Making Process*, Prentice-Hall, Englewood Cliffs, NJ.

Lindley, D. V. (1985) *Making Decisions*, 2nd edn, John Wiley, London.

Lowe, C. W. (1969) *Industrial Statistics*, Vol. 1, 1st edn, Business Books, London.

Lygo, R. (1987) Picking winners to safeguard competitiveness in manufacturing. Proceedings of the Institution of Mechanical Engineers, Vol. 201, No. B2, London, 123–7.

MacGregor, D. and Slovic, P. (1986) Perceived acceptability of risk. *Risk Analysis*, **6**(2), 245–56.

Marrey, B. (1988) Birth of a landmark. *Swissair Gazette*, June, 36.

May, W. W. (1982) $'s for lives: ethical considerations in the use of cost/benefit analysis for profit terms. *Risk Analysis*, **2**(1), (March), 35–46.

Merkhofer, M. W. (1987) *Decision Science and Social Risk Management*, D. Riedel, Boston, Mass.

Meyrick-Jones, J. (1986) The insurance viewpoint. *Aerospace*, **13**(6) (July/August), 13–15.

Miles, M. B. and Huberman, A. M. (1985) *Qualitative Data Analysis*, 3rd edn, Sage, Beverley Hills, Cal.

Mingers, J. and Adlam, J. (1989) Where are the 'real' expert systems? *OR INSIGHT*, **2**(3) (July–September), 6–9.

Mosleh, A., Bier, V. M. and Apostolakis, G. (1987) The Elicitation and Use of Expert Opinion in Risk Assessment: a Critical Review. A paper presented at the Probabilistic Safety Assessment and Risk Management Conference, PSA 87, September.

Mumpower, J. (1986) An analysis of the de minimus strategy for risk management. *Risk Analysis*, **6**(4) (December), 437–46.

Munford, A. G. and Bailey T. (1989) Statistical methods in operational research. In Shahani, A. and Stainton, R. (eds) *Tutorial Papers in Operational Research*, Operational Research Society, Birmingham.

Nailor, P. (1988) *The Nassau Connection*, HMSO, London.

National Westminster Bank PLC (1987) Project finance – risk management, the Nat West approach. *Trade Finance and Corporate Finance*, June (Euromoney Publications, London).

National Westminster Bank PLC (n.d.) *An Introduction to Limited Recourse Finance*, National Westminster Bank PLC, London.

Norman, P. and Naveed, S. (1990) A comparison of expert system and human operator performance for cement kiln operation. *Journal of the Operational Research Society*, **41**(11), (November) 1007–19.

OECD (1984) Nuclear Power Public Opinion, Nuclear Energy Agency, OECD, Paris.

Pearce, D. W. (1981) Risk assessment use and misuse, *The Assessment and Perception of Risk*, The Royal Society of London, London.

Peston, M. and Coddington, A. (1978) *Statistical Decision Theory*, Civil Service College Occasional Papers 7, 4th edn, HMSO, London.

Philpott, B. (1984) *The English Electrical/BAC Lightning*, Patrick Stephens, Wellingborough.

Preyssl, C. (1986) *'Fuzzy Risk' Analysis Theory and Application*, International Atomic Energy Agency, Vienna.

Preyssl, C., Cullingford, M. C. and Swaton, E. (1985) *Evaluation of compliance of risk-sources when uncertainty and risk-perception aspects are included. Presentation Material*, International Atomic Energy, Vienna.

Reed Stenhouse (1982) *Accident Costing*, Risk Management Unit, Reed Stenhouse UK Ltd, London.

Reid, T. R. (1991) Fuzzy Logic, but Japan puts it to work, *International Herald Tribune*, 5–6 January.

Rich, B. R. (1989) The Skunk Works' Management Style – it's no secret, published in *Aerospace*, **16**(3) (March), 8–14.

Rosenhead, J. (ed.) (1989) *Rational Analysis for a Problematic World*, John Wiley, Chichester.

Saull, J. W. (1987) Objectives of maintenance – airworthiness. *Aerospace*, (July/August), 41–7.

Schmucker, K. J. (1984) *Fuzzy Sets, Natural Language Computations, and Risk Analysis*, Computer Science Press, Rockville, Maryland, USA.

Schwietert, A. (1988) Country risk assessment: Swiss Bank Corporation's approach, *Economic and Financial Prospects* Supplement, 1 (February/March).

Seiler, F. A. (1987) Error Propagation for Large Errors, *Risk Analysis*, **7**(4) (December), 509–18.

Shahani, A. and Stainton, R. (eds) (1989) *Tutorial Papers in Operational Research*, Operational Research Society, Birmingham.

Sheehan, R. Lloyd's versus computer fraud. *Lloyd's Special*.

Shrader-Frechette, K. S. (1985) *Science Policy, Ethics and Economic Methodology*, D. Reidel, Dordrecht, pp. 16 and 193.

Solomon, K. A., Wipple, C. and Okrent, D. (1978) More on Insurance and Catastrophic Events: Can we expect de facto Limits on Liability Recoveries? Paper presented at the American Nuclear Society topical meeting Probabilistic Analysis of Nuclear Reactor Safety, May.

Stallen, P. J. and Coppock, R. (1987) About risk communication and risky communication. *Risk Analysis*, **7**(4) 413–14.

Stallen, P. J. M. and Tomas, A. (1985) Public Concern about Industrial Hazards. Paper presented at the annual meeting of the Society for Risk Analysis, Washington DC, October.

Stevens Handbook of Experimental Psychology (1988) Vol. 1, 2nd edn, John Wiley, New York.

Stewart, T. J. (1992) A critical survey of the status of multiple criteria decision making theory and practice in OMEGA. *International Journal of Management Science*, **20**(5/6), 569–86.

Swiss Bank Corporation (1991) *Swiss Stock Guide*, Swiss Bank Corporation, Zurich.

Swiss Reinsurance (1987) *Computer Insurance*. Swiss Reinsurance Company, Zurich.

Tait, J. (1988) The role of values in quantitative decision making. *Journal of the Operational Research Society*, **39**(7) (July), 669–74.

Tela Insurance (1985) *Catastrophes in Computer Centres, Guide for Catastrophe Plans*, Tela Insurance, Munich.

The Times (1989) Debit Warning by Bank over property loans, 14 October, 17.

Thomas, K., Maurr, D., Fishbein, M., Otway, H. J., Hinkle, R. A. and Simpson, D. (1980) Comparative Study of Public Beliefs about Five Energy Systems. Paper RR-80-15, April, International Institute for Applied Systems Analysis, Laxenburg, Austria.

Thornhill, W. T. (1990) *Risk Management for Financial Institutions*, Bankers Publishing Company, Rolling Meadows, Ill.

Van Horne, J. C. (1989) *Financial Management and Policy*, Prentice-Hall, Englewood Cliffs, NJ, 8th edn.

Vogel, R. C. and Wall, I. B. (1987) Some observations on NUREG 1150. Paper presented at the Probabilistic Safety Assessment and Risk Management Conference, PSA 87, Zurich, September.

Walpole, R. E. and Myers, R. H. (1989) *Probability and Statistics for Engineers and Scientists*, 3rd edn, Macmillan, New York.

Wilson, R. and Crouch, E. A. C. (1982) *Risk Benefit Analysis*, Ballinger, Cambridge, Mass.

World Bank (1981) *Guidelines on use of Consultants by World Bank Borrowers and by the World Bank Executing Agency*, World Bank, Washington.

INDEX